ARMS TRANSFERS
AND
AMERICAN
FOREIGN POLICY

ARMS TRANSFERS
AND
AMERICAN
FOREIGN POLICY

Edited by
ANDREW J. PIERRE

New York University Press · New York · 1979

Library of Congress Cataloging in Publication Data
Main entry under title:

Arms transfers and American foreign policy.

Includes bibliographical references and index.
  1. Munitions—United States—Addresses, essays, lec-
tures. 2. United States—Foreign relations—1974-
—Addresses, essays, lectures. I. Pierre, Andrew J.
HD9743.U6A73   382'.45'62340973   79-2057
ISBN 0-8147-6575-0

Manufactured in the United States of America

The Contributors

EDWARD R. FRIED, Executive Director, International Bank for Reconstruction and Development, was formerly Senior Fellow, Brookings Institution, and Deputy Assistant Secretary of State for Economic Affairs; he is co-author of several annual issues of *Setting National Priorities.*

ROBERT E. HUNTER, Senior Staff Member of the National Security Council, was formerly Foreign Affairs Adviser of Senator Edward Kennedy and Senior Fellow, Overseas Development Council; author of *Security in Europe* and *The Soviet Dilemma in the Middle East: Oil and the Persian Gulf,* and other works.

GEOFFREY KEMP is Professor of International Politics, The Fletcher School of Law and Diplomacy, Tufts University. His recent publications include (as co-author) *U.S. Arms Sales to Iran,* a study for the Senate Foreign Relations Committee; and *Arms Transfers to the Third World: The Military Buildup in LDCs* (co-editor).

EDWARD C. LUCK is Deputy Director of Policy Studies at the United Nations Association of the U.S.A., where he was previously Project Director of the Conventional Arms Control Policy Panel.

STEVEN E. MILLER is a doctoral candidate at The Fletcher School of Law and Diplomacy and Graduate Fellow at the Center for Science and International Affairs, Harvard University, and co-author of "East European Integration and European Politics," *International Journal.*

RICHARD M. MOOSE, the Assistant Secretary of State for African Affairs, was formerly Deputy Undersecretary of State for Management and previously Staff Director, Sub-Committee on Foreign Assistance, U.S. Senate Foreign Relations Committee.

ANDREW J. PIERRE is Senior Research Fellow, Council on Foreign Relations; formerly with the Brookings Institution and the Hudson Institute, he has taught at Columbia University and served in the State Department; author of *Nuclear Politics, Nuclear Proliferation: A Strategy for Control,* and other works.

DAVID RONFELDT is Staff Member, The Rand Corporation; co-author of *Arms Transfers to Latin America: Toward a Policy of Mutual Respect,* and other works.

CAESAR SERESERES is Assistant Professor of Politics, University of California, Los Angeles, and co-author of *U.S. Military Aid and Guatemalan Politics* and other works.

DANIEL L. SPIEGEL is a member of the Policy Planning Staff, Department of State. He was formerly Special Assistant to Secretary of State Cyrus Vance, and Legislative Assistant to Senator Hubert H. Humphrey.

PAUL C. WARNKE, a partner of Clifford, Warnke, Glass, McIlwain & Finney, was formerly Director, Arms Control and Disarmament Agency, Assistant Secretary of Defense for International Security Affairs, and General Counsel, Department of Defense.

Contents

CONTENTS

ARMS TRANSFERS
AND
AMERICAN
FOREIGN POLICY

Introduction

Andrew J. Pierre

America's large-scale transfer of conventional arms to the Third World has become a matter of growing controversy in recent years. Arms sales by the United States have grown from less than a billion dollars in 1970 to approximately $11.2 billion in 1977. Along with this numerical growth has emerged a new public debate about the wisdom of America's arms transfer policy, a debate which now transcends the Nixon, Ford and Carter Administrations. Rarely is there a period of time when some prospective arms sale is not being debated in the Congress or questioned in the press. Within the foreign affairs community the President, cabinet officers and members of Congress are spending an increasing proportion of time on arms transfer issues.

This should not be surprising, for arms transfers are an important element of the diffusion of power which is in process around the globe. Elements of this diffusion are well-known; they include the erosion of the postwar bipolarity, the new importance of states which have particular natural re-

[1]

sources and economic significance, and the steady expansion of national military capabilities in the developing world, as well as the potential proliferation of nuclear weapons. Many of the states which are assuming greater regional roles, such as Iran or Brazil, see a heightened military capability as concomitant with such a role. The Third World now accounts for 58% of the world's armed forces. The diffusion of power is giving a new significance to regional balances and systems of security, where levels of arms are often determined by purchases from abroad.

As a consequence of this diffusion, annual conventional arms sales worldwide have grown from $3.8 billion in 1965 to well over $20 billion today. The United States accounts for over half of this, but the French and British export of arms has more than tripled in the past five years and there has been a marked increase in the level of Soviet arms transfers. A second significant trend has been the *qualitative* rise which has accompanied the *quantitative* expansion of arms. Whereas many of the weapons transferred in earlier periods were second-generation or obsolete, today they are often the most advanced and sophisticated in the inventories, or new production runs, of the supplier states. A third new trend is the nature of the recipients. In the 1950s and 1960s, most arms that were transferred went to developed countries, usually NATO and Warsaw Pact allies of the suppliers, or to countries with which there were special military links, as in the case of Vietnam. These were usually in the form of grants, often as part of military assistance programs. Today most arms are going to developing countries, including areas of real or potential instability. The largest expansion of arms exports has been to the Middle East/Persian Gulf where Iran, Saudi Arabia and Israel have been the major recipients. Transfers to Africa, Latin America and elsewhere, although comparatively small in absolute terms, nevertheless represent substantial quantitative and qualitative increases in flows into these areas. Almost always, they are now in the form of sales rather than grants.

Arms transfers are an essential component of contemporary international affairs. They have become increasingly used by supplier states as an instrument of foreign policy. Moreover, it is widely recognized that they are a necessary instrument in today's world; only a minute and relatively unimportant minority argue against the very principle of arms transfers. Yet there is much debate about the nature and scope of America's arms transfers. During his election campaign, President Carter spoke of the "almost completely unrestrained" American arms sales of the previous years as being a policy as "cynical as it is dangerous." In the early phase of his Administration the President announced a detailed new U.S. arms transfer policy, whereby transfers were to be viewed as an "exceptional" foreign policy implement, to be used only where it could be "clearly demonstrated that the transfer contributes to our national security interests." But the debate has not receded; if anything it has increased. Some view the Carter policy as naive and some of its major provisions, such as an annual ceiling, as impracticable or unworkable. Others have criticized the Carter Administration for not following in practice, in its actual arms sales decisions, the policy it has adopted in principle. The Congressional concerns about arms sales, which developed during the Nixon-Ford years, and which led to the enactment of legislation designed to put restraints on transfers, have not been stilled, and the whole subject remains one of executive-legislative contention.

The debate on arms transfers is often in the context of particular weapon sales decisions and the foreign policy considerations which accompany them. Nevertheless, a few fundamental arguments can be distilled.

Among the principal criticisms of arms transfers are the following:

—Arms sent to unstable regions may exacerbate political tensions and lead to armed conflict.
—The introduction of new, more sophisticated military technologies into a region may spur an arms race, and should a war break out, make it more destructive.
—The purchase of arms is, for many countries, a wasteful diversion of scarce economic resources which could be more productively spent on economic development and social welfare needs.
—Arms received by repressive regimes may be used to violate the human rights of their citizens.
—The transfer of arms may involve the supplier country in a political and strategic relationship with the recipient which could lead to unwanted commitments and draw it into a local conflict.

The major justifications cited for arms transfers include the following:

—Arms sent to allies will assist them in maintaining an adequate defense capability and augment their self-reliance.
—Arms transfers may restore a local imbalance that could tempt a stronger state to initiate conflict, and consequently create or enhance a regional balance.
—Arms transfers can be an important source of political influence with, or leverage over, the receiving nation.
—Arms can be exchanged for benefits important to the supplier, such as military bases, oil, or agreements on other commodity prices.

—Arms sales may be an important source of foreign exchange and contribute to a favorable balance of payments; other economic benefits include employment in the defense industry and the creation of economies of scale, thereby reducing per-unit costs of weapons manufactured for the armed forces of the supplier country.

The reader will quickly recognize that there are elements of truth in each of these statements, just as there are reasons to doubt their applicability in many circumstances. The fact is that judgments on arms transfers are not easy ones; they often invoke conflicting aims and values. There are no "simple truths" to serve as guidelines for policy. What is valid in the short run may become conspicuously invalid in the longer term. And the longer term can often only be seen in speculative manner. The average weapons system has a "life" of 10 to 20 years, far longer than the politics or policies of nations can be "predicted."

Moreover, judgments on arms transfers will quite frequently involve competing, if not conflicting, goals. The case of South Korea is illustrative. As part of its aim of withdrawing ground forces from that country, in keeping with a revised concept of U.S. commitments in the Far East following the Vietnam war, the United States is sending substantial arms to South Korea in order to enhance the defensive capabilities of an ally threatened by a hostile neighbor. Yet the United States government is also critical of the extent of human rights in that country and wishes to do nothing through arms transfers which could strengthen undemocratic and repressive tendencies in Seoul, or provide weapons which could be used to surpress internal dissent.

The potential conflict between the classical aims of arms limitation and the search for a political accommodation can be seen in the Middle East. This region ranks only after Central Europe as the most heavily armed in the world, with sophisticated weapons in the hands of hostile neighbors in a climate of confrontation. Yet carefully regulated arms transfers by the United States to Arab states (Egypt, Jordan, Saudi Arabia), as well as to Israel, may provide the sense of security which will promote the process of negotiations toward a political settlement. *

Another example is provided by the so-called "dove's dilemma," between the aim of restraints on conventional arms on the one hand, and the pursuit of nuclear non-proliferation on the other. Turning down requests for arms from a nation which wants them for reasons of security or prestige (Iran or Brazil) may have the effect of strengthening interest in acquiring nuclear weapons to enhance national independence. It can also be plausibly argued that providing advanced arms, some of which can deliver atomic as well as regular warheads, as part of a military buildup or modernization of a proud defense establishment can serve to whet the appetite for possessing nuclear weapons.

Arms transfer decisions are often, therefore, replete with policy dilemmas. Unlike the spread of nuclear weapons, there is no general consensus that conventional arms proliferation is, in each instance, undesirable. Prospective arms transfers may or may not be a stabilizing factor within a region; they may or may not promote the broader foreign policy objectives of the supplier or the recipient; they may or may not have economic or military benefits commensurate with possible political or arms control costs.

* See my "Beyond the 'Plane Package': Arms and Politics in the Middle East," *International Security*, vol. 3, no. 1 (Summer 1978), pp. 148-61.

In order to clarify the issues and attempt to bring some intellectual order to the confused debate on arms transfers, the Council on Foreign Relations held a series of seven meetings in Washington during 1976-77. The seven chapters in this book were originally prepared for the meetings and subsequently revised following discussion. Participants included government officials working directly on arms transfer decisions in various parts of the foreign affairs bureaucracy, members of Congress and congressional committee staffs, plus the usual Council representation of knowledgeable academics, journalists, businessmen, and others with expertise in the subject.

The focus of the discussions was the conventional arms transfer policy of the United States: What was it? (Some contended that there was no coherent policy!) And what should it be? Along with questions of policy, there was much debate about the decision-making *process*. How should the executive branch deal with arms transfer decisions? What is the proper role of the Congress? All the participants felt that policy and process could not be separated, but beyond this the meetings were marked less by agreement than by lively debate in which a wide spectrum of views was expressed.

To an unusual extent many of the participants then in private life subsequently entered government service, including Paul Warnke, the Chairman of the Council's group and later Director of the Arms Control and Disarmament Agency. This is the case with four of the seven principal authors of chapters that follow. In writing his contribution, each author was encouraged to develop his personal views. The reader will not find consensus in this book, nor was it sought. Each chapter stands on its own; if some of the data presented from chapter to chapter appear somewhat inconsistent that is in the nature of the available statistics on arms transfers, which are

neither consistent nor comprehensive. The volume is organized so as to deal systematically with the major issues affecting U.S. arms transfer policy; but we have intentionally not
sought to integrate the chapters closely with each other, so as
to avoid the risk of diluting the whole.

The opening chapter, principally written by Geoffrey
Kemp, an early student of this question, is a remarkably comprehensive "map" of the arms transfer phenomenon. In addition to showing some of the historical antecedents of the
present debate, and providing the reader with valuable data on
the magnitude of the international arms trade, it uses a matrix
approach so as to illustrate the competing claims made for and
against arms transfers. Kemp then goes on to provide his
personal assessment of each claim.

The largest increase in recent years has been in arms sales
to the Persian Gulf. Robert Hunter seeks to develop an arms
control framework for transfers to the Gulf, one which would
be based on a three-part combination of restraints: restraints
by the sellers, a regionally based security arrangement, and
bilateral discussions between suppliers and recipients. It was,
of course, not practicable to discuss arms transfers to every
region of the world; Latin America was selected because of the
sharp contrast it offers to the Persian Gulf. It is a region where
organized restraints have been attempted, both in the case of
U.S. arms sales during the Alliance for Progress period of the
1960s and regionally inspired restraints through the Declaration of Ayacucho. Moreover, the region provides a laboratory
for analyzing arms transfer issues which may be typical of the
future global pattern of the arms trade, such as the role of arms
in providing political influence; the interplay between current
human rights policies and arms sales; the interest in arms, both
imported and indigenously manufactured, on the part of a state
of growing regional importance such as Brazil or Argentina;

[8]

and the competition for sales among the principal suppliers. David Ronfeldt and Caesar Sereseres consider arms transfers to be the most important instrument for conducting U.S. foreign policy on a bilateral basis; yet in contrast to Hunter they are deeply skeptical of an arms control approach and critical of past restrictive approaches to arms transfers because of the political costs they have incurred in U.S.-Latin American relations. Accordingly, they question many of the assumptions which are built into the Carter Administration's approach toward arms transfers.

The next two chapters on the U.S. government's policy and policy-process, and on the role of the Congress, were written before President Carter's inauguration by forceful critics of the arms transfer practices of the Nixon-Ford-Kissinger years. Richard Moose at the time of writing was Staff Director of the Sub-Committee on Foreign Assistance of the Senate Foreign Relations Committee, and Daniel Spiegel was legislative assistant to Senator Hubert Humphrey, one of the members of the Senate most concerned with this question. They write from intimate, personal knowledge about the frustrations of the Congress in dealing with arms sales and recount with authority the history of the legislation which led to Congress's major attempt at reform: the International Security Assistance and Arms Export Control Act of 1976. Most of the problems, difficulties, and frustrations which then existed on the Hill are still to be found today. Paul Warnke was certainly one of the most eloquent critics of past policy and, with the assistance of Edward Luck, he draws up a series of recommendations for a new approach. Subsequently, as director of ACDA, Warnke was one of the principal officials responsible for arms sales policy, while Moose has become Assistant Secretary of State for African Affairs, following a period as Deputy Undersecretary of State for Management, and Spiegel is a member of the

Department's Policy Planning Staff. Apart from the sheer impracticality of asking these officials to revise their contributions, it appeared to the editor that there was considerable value in having these chapters remain as initially written. They stand both as evidence of how the problem was seen at the time and, more importantly, as a means by which to measure the Carter Administration's present approach against the proposals of the critics in the past.

Most analyses of arms sales depend upon vague and generalized assumptions about their economic importance for the weapons-supplier states in matters such as the contributions they bring to the balance of payments, the significance of exports for defense industries, their role in lowering unit costs for arms produced and in maintaining levels of employment. Similarly unstructured assumptions exist regarding the social and economic "costs" of arms purchases for recipients in terms of alternative ways in which the money could be spent. Edward Fried moves beyond such assumptions to the facts, disaggregating and systematically examining the available economic data, and comes to some surprising conclusions. In trade with OPEC countries, arms sales have had a smaller role in offsetting the rise in the price of oil than non-military goods. Should the United States reduce its arms exports, even fairly drastically, the overall domestic economic impact would be limited, Fried suggests, and over the medium and longer term there need not be lasting adverse economic consequences.

This volume is focused on American policy on arms transfers. The United States is the world's largest supplier and it is in this country that the debate on conventional arms has been the most acute. Yet the United States can only do so much unilaterally in dealing with the global conventional arms transfer problem. Although the cliché—"if we don't sell, someone else will"—has been overused, and too often has been an excuse for not imposing restraints, it must be recognized that it does have considerable validity. Without an international approach, even the most judicious and far-sighted American policy on arms transfers can only be of limited effectiveness in dealing with the growing proliferation of conventional arms. In the closing chapter Andrew J. Pierre examines the politics and economics of arms transfers, as well as their role in the respective foreign policies, of the three other principal suppliers—the Soviet Union, France and Britain—who, together with the United States, account for 90% of the major weapons transferred to the Third World. The chapter presents ideas for various forms of qualitative and quantitative restraints which might be adopted by suppliers and by recipients, discusses the national perspectives which will influence the outcome of an international initiative, and suggests a strategy for seeking multinational restraints.

In concluding this introduction it may be appropriate to make a comment on President Carter's arms transfer policy. Four months after the presidential transition, the Administration established a concrete set of guidelines designed to impose a new set of restraints on U.S. transfers. The dollar volume of sales was to be reduced from that of fiscal year 1977. The United States would not be the first to introduce advanced weapons into a region. Within the decision-making process, the burden of persuasion would be on those who favor a particular sale rather than on those who oppose it, etc.

Yet no swift or dramatic change has come about in the practice of arms transfers as of this writing. The total volume of U.S. sales for 1977 reached $11.2 billion, an all-time high, underscoring the difficulties of imposing an annual ceiling. The Administration did decide against a number of proposed sales: Iran has not received the F-18L fighter, a decision consistent with a prohibition on the development of advanced

[11]

weapons systems solely for export; Pakistan was denied permission to purchase 110 A-7 fighter-bombers on the grounds that it would have meant the introduction of a new, sophisticated weapons system into South Asia; and Israel was blocked from exporting the Kfir fighter to Ecuador on the basis that as it contained a General Electric engine it was subject to restrictions on transfers to third countries. In Latin America the decision to restrict, on human rights grounds, military assistance credits to Brazil, Argentina and Uruguay had the effect, in part because of angry reactions, of curtailing arms transfers to these countries. On the other hand, the Administration has made a number of notable transfers. It pushed through the sale to Iran of seven AWACs for $1.2 billion despite Congressional skepticism, and it pieced together a controversial $4.8 billion "plane package" deal for Saudi Arabia, Egypt, and Israel under which the Saudis are to receive the F-15, the most advanced fighter-aircraft in the American inventory.

It is not our intention to develop a lengthy analysis of the Carter Administration's policies, for it is still too early to make a mature evaluation. This is especially true with regard to arms transfers because of the time-lead factor. Most U.S. weapons delivered abroad during 1976-80 will have been sold by the *previous* Administration. Indeed, when the new Administration began, it inherited a $32 billion backlog of signed orders which would be in the pipeline for a number of years. Suffice it to say that the arms transfer debate shows no signs of quieting. Critics of the Administration perceive a large discrepancy between declared policy and the reality of its implementation. The President's personal identification with this issue, and its prominent place in the 1976 foreign policy debate, suggests that it will receive attention in the 1980 election, should he be a candidate. The Administration's response will seek to explain the complexity of issues and judgments in dealing with arms transfers and the reasons why they are, at times, desirable or necessary. Meanwhile, legislation has been introduced in both houses of Congress designed to impose greater legislative restraints on future arms transfers. If this book helps to clarify some of the dilemmas surrounding the arms transfer question, it will have succeeded in the authors' expectations.

In closing, I would like to thank my fellow contributors; the members of the Council on Foreign Relations study group and especially its Chairman, Paul Warnke; and the editor of the volume, Robert Valkenier. Research on European policies on arms transfers, discussed in the concluding chapter, was made possible by a NATO Research Fellowship. To reiterate, because a majority of the principal authors entered senior governmental positions shortly after the completion of their writing, we have not sought to bring the chapters up to date. Accordingly, it should be clear that nothing in this volume is intended to reflect in any way the views of the U.S. government or the Carter Administration. Indeed, this work can best be viewed as a statement of the debate which preceded and led to the Carter Administration's new policy on arms transfers. This volume is to be followed by a companion work that I am writing, which will deal with American policy since 1977, and which will examine more comprehensively the policies and perspectives of the other supplier countries, as well as the major recipient nations, as part of the global politics of arms transfers.

February 1978

ONE

The Arms Transfer Phenomenon

Geoffrey Kemp
with Steven Miller

Historical Perspectives

The international transfer of arms and munitions as an instrument of diplomatic, military and economic policy is not a new phenomenon. As long as war and military preparedness have been normal aspects of international relations, the supply of and demand for arms have been an inevitable by-product. Indeed, it is possible to trace the origins of the arms transfer phenomenon to ancient times. The importance of military assistance, for example, is clearly illustrated in Thucydides' *History of the Peleponnesian War,* written in the fifth century BC. Similarly, the playwright Aristophanes argued, in a work entitled *Peace,* that it was the armament makers who were blocking peace in ancient Greece; essentially the same argument was still to be heard in the twentieth century. In short, far from being a dramtically new factor in international politics, arms transfers have been a significant feature in the international environment throughout recorded history.

That arms transfers have played a crucial role in history prior to the post-World War II period is shown by examples drawn from the American past. In fact, the American experience through the sweep of its history demonstrates several different dimensions of the arms transfer phenomenon: from major dependence on imported arms to the problems of being the world's largest arms exporter.

From the outset, the fate of the American Revolution was largely determined by the transfer of arms. The colonies were poorly prepared for war and required the importation of arms to keep the Revolutionary Army supplied. The French were the major supplier of arms and military assistance to the incipient American state because it suited their consistently anti-British policy to play such a role. The importance of French arms to the American cause was such that one major diplomatic historian has concluded that "without the munitions sent [by France] to America in 1776 and 1777 the revolt would have collapsed." [1]

During the American Civil War the Northern blockade of Southern ports was inspired in large part by the South's need for arms from abroad if it was to keep its troops fully supplied. Because the South lacked the industrial capacity to supply its armies, the North pursued a strategy of preventing Southern access to foreign arms. Thus, for example, Anglo-American diplomacy during 1863 was dominated by the affair of the Laird rams, as the North sought to prevent delivery of two new and potentially revolutionary British-produced naval vessels to the South. The Laird rams were iron-clad, steam-powered ships, precursors of the next generation in naval technology. Since it was thought that these ships might enable the South to break the blockade, they were seen to be potentially decisive to the outcome of the war. As a consequence, the North expended enormous diplomatic energy to successfully prevent the transfer of these ships, which ended up in the British navy.[2] This is a strikingly modern example of how the transfer of "frontier technologies" to combatants in "local" wars can have a major impact on the outcome of conflict.

In the twentieth century the American role has generally been that of an arms exporter. It would not be an exaggeration to say that some of the most important decisions determining U.S. involvement in foreign commitments over the past 65 years have been directly related to the transfer of arms and munitions to foreign governments, and arms transfer policy thus played a large role in American foreign policy long before the debates in the mid-1970s.

With the onset of World War I the United States rapidly emerged as the leading participant in the international trade in munitions. During the period of its neutrality—that is, from August 1914 to March 1917—the United States exported approximately $2.2 billion in war supplies to Europe. By 1916 the United States shipped more than a billion dollars of arms in a single year.[3] The enormity of the American presence on the international munitions market is suggested by the fact that as early as 1920 the United States accounted for more than 52% of global arms exports.[4]

Though in theory the United States, as a neutral, could trade in arms with both sides in the conflict, in practice the British blockade guaranteed that American arms went almost exclusively to the Allied powers. This led to a controversy within the United States—particularly heated in 1914-15—over whether this pattern of arms exports constituted a de facto breach of American neutraility and thus jeopardized America's non-involvement in the European war. In January of 1916, for

[17]

example, the prominent international lawyer Charles Hyde sent a note to Secretary of State Lansing, warning of the dangers of America's role in the munitions trade. Hyde noted that the United States was becoming "a base of supplies of such magnitude that unless retarded, the success of armies, possibly the fate of empires, may ultimately rest upon the output of American factories." [5] Hyde urged, as did many others, a re-examination of U.S. arms export policy because of its implications for drawing the United States into conflict. Thus, even prior to the period when Wilson proclaimed the United States to be "the arsenal of democracy," it was one of the world's leading arms exporters and its arms export policy was the subject of considerable attention and acrimony.

This domestic debate in the early years of World War I forms the background to the even greater controversy over the arms trade that developed during the 1920s and 1930s. During these years, the relationship between U.S. arms transfers and foreign policy was one of the most widely debated issues of the time, climaxing in the establishment, in 1934, of a special Senate Munitions Investigating Committee, commonly known as the Nye Committee.

United States arms transfers to the Allied powers were certainly a contributing factor toward American involvement in World War I. But in the interwar period there developed a conspiratorial "devil theory of war" which attributed to the international munitions industry the central role as a cause of war.[6]

Most of the arms trade literature at the time generally advocated the thesis that munitions producers stimulated international conflict to bolster arms sales, engaged in bribery of public officials, and conspired with other arms makers as part of the "international" arms industry.[7] Supplementing this conspiratorial theory were more reasonable arguments which suggested that, once functioning in a wartime environment, the machinery of finance and credit was likely to influence the involvement of the creditor nation (arms supplier) on the side of its major debtors (arms recipients).

The belief that the United States had been drawn into World War I to protect the interests of American and European arms producers and financiers persisted throughout the 1920s and was reinforced by the prevailing mood of isolationism and the increasingly hostile disclosures about the behavior of European and American munitions manufacturerers in the postwar environment. The growing incidents of international violence in the early 1930s aroused fears that the United States would once more be drawn into foreign entanglements as a result of the behavior of those individuals who were believed to profit most from war, namely, the banking-munitions fraternity. The widespread popularity of these beliefs led to the establishment of the Nye Committee.

Thus, the resolution establishing the Nye Committee to investigate the international arms trade declared that "the influence of the commercial motive is one of the inevitable factors often believed to stimulate and sustain wars." The Committee's tasks, pursued between 1934 and 1936, were to decide whether existing law and treaties were adequate to regulate traffic in arms, to review the findings of the War Policies Commission, and to inquire into the desirability of creating a government monopoly in arms production. Senator Nye was convinced from the outset that the way to end war was to remove private gain from its conduct, and the course of the investigation was directed by this conviction. A majority of the Committee recommended nationalization of the arms industry; the minority recommended "rigid and conclusive munitions control" rather than nationalization "except in a few isolated instances." [8]

The Committee finally agreed upon close regulation of private arms manufacture and proposed a number of ways by which abuses resulting from uncontrolled distribution and sale of arms might be prevented. These included increasing penalties for mislabeling of exports, false manifests and destinations, establishing a Munitions Control Board to examine all correspondence as well as records with respect to munitions orders when arms embargoes were in effect, and confining the sale of arms to recognized governments. The Nye Committee also recommended that the American government try to secure more effective international control of the munitions traffic and urged early consideration of its draft proposal submitted to the League of Nations in 1934.[9] The aim of these recommendations was to forestall the private sale of munitions abroad, *even in peacetime.* The neutrality legislation which was passed in 1935 and 1936, largely owing to the work of the Nye Committee, already prohibited sales during time of war.

The impact of the Nye Committee on public opinion was considerable. It received widespread publicity both domestically and internationally and stimulated similar inquiries in other countries. But the Committee's impact on public policy and on the international munitions trade was neither profound nor lasting. The Committee failed to persuade world leaders to restrict the international munitions trade. League of Nations statistics on the arms trade show that global arms exports increased steadily after 1932, indicating how little effect the Nye hearings had on the volume of the arms trade (see Table 1). Similarly, American arms exports were not greatly reduced as a consequence of the Nye Committee efforts; rather, they remained at approximately the same percentage level from 1932 to 1935, and thereafter began to increase rather than decrease. The Committee also focused attention on such issues as bribery, munitions industry lobbying, collusion in the

TABLE 1

World and American Arms Exports, 1920-1937 ($1,000.)

Year	World	U.S.	U.S. as % of Global Trade
1920	$119,836.4	$62,392.2	52.1
1921	42,811.3	6,928.2	16.2
1922	43,033.5	8,454.9	19.6
1923	47,521.5	9,267.6	19.5
1924	45,609.6	9,893.6	21.7
1925	48,102.3	10,676.0	22.2
1926	51,105.2	10,507.1	20.6
1927	58,060.3	9,476.7	19.7
1928	59,408.5	10,724.9	18.1
1929	64,855.3	10,734.5	16.6
1930	55,870.9	6,462.3	11.6
1931	35,365.5	3,897.1	11.0
1932	34,848.1	2,949.6	8.5
1933	37,526.9	3,246.4	8.6
1934	41,353.4	3,722.6	9.0
1935	42,976.3	3,337.0	7.8
1936	49,771.7	4,284.0	8.6
1937	60,434.1	5,634.0	9.3

Source: League of Nations, *Statistical Yearbooks,* 1920-1938.

arms industry, and profiteering by the munitions-makers during World War I, but corrective legislation was not secured.

Perhaps the most important effect of the Committee was that it reinforced the prevailing mood of isolationism in the country. For the Nye Committee, and the popular ideas it reflected, did not cause an American withdrawal from the international arms trade. Throughout the interwar period the United States remained one of a handful of major arms suppliers, generally ranking only behind France and Great Britain.

It was not until World War II and its aftermath that the

United States assumed its current role as the world's major provider of defense articles and services. At the beginning of World War II, as was the case in the early years of World War I, arms transfers were one of the major instruments of foreign policy employed by American policy-makers. The first signal of the direction of U.S. foreign policy after the outbreak of war in Europe was the revision, in November of 1939, of the Neutrality Act which guided its arms transfer policy.[10] The revised legislation ended the legal prohibition of the sale of arms to belligerents, and allowed the "cash and carry" principle to obtain even during wartime. The "cash and carry" principle was thus transformed from a means of limiting American involvement in time of peace to a symbol of American commitment to the Allied powers during the opening years of World War II, for in effect it enabled the British to buy American arms.

As World War II unfolded in Europe, arms transfers increasingly became the vehicle whereby the United States intervened in European affairs. The first great step after the German invasion of France in May 1940 was the famous September 1940 destroyers-for-bases deal with Great Britain. According to this arrangement, the United States exchanged fifty aged destroyers for 99-year leases on a number of British bases in the Western hemisphere, which, President Roosevelt would argue, were vital to American defense.[11] Churchill regarded this action to be such a gross violation of American neutrality as to place the United States effectively at war with Germany; American revisionist historians have seized upon this incident as an example of FDR's efforts to maneuver the United States into the war.[12] Clearly the American transfer of arms to Britain in September of 1940 was a foreign policy decision of the highest magnitude.

This was followed, in March 1941, by the Lend-Lease

Program, through which the United States became the arms supplier of the Allied forces.[13] Literally tens of billions of dollars of arms (as well as food and other war materials) were transferred to the Allies between 1941 and 1945 under the lend-lease program.[14] Once again, as during the years 1914 to 1920, the United States became the principal actor in the international shipment of arms.

Every major American foreign policy initiative in the post-war era has had as a component a program of arms transfers. In the immediate postwar era (1945-55) most U.S. arms transfers were provided to participants in the newly created American alliance system "free of charge" under the rubric of what became known as the Military Assistance Program (MAP). Arms transfers were designed to bolster the defenses of Western countries which felt threatened by monolithic communism, and were seen as a fundamental cornerstone of U.S. foreign policy. Vast quantities of arms were transferred to Europe and in terms of constant dollars the totals were not too different from the figures for the mid-1970s.

In areas such as the Middle East, Africa, Latin America, and South Asia, where a direct Soviet involvement at this time was less apparent, the United States showed considerable reluctance to transfer arms, except to Iran and Pakistan. During this period very few American arms were sold or given to Israel. However, the entry of the Soviet Union into the international non-Communist arms market in the mid-1950s widened the arena for competition between the Western supplier and Communist countries, and, as a result, the diffusion of arms to conflict areas not directly involved in the front-line east-west confrontation increased.

The Vietnam war was the high-water mark of direct U.S. involvement in overseas defense commitments in the postwar period. During the period 1965-73 great quantities of U.S.

arms were transferred to Vietnam in an effort to defeat the North Vietnamese and the Viet Cong, but to no avail. The Nixon Doctrine, which was announced in 1970, marked the beginnings of an American retrenchment and a decision to rely, in the future, upon more indirect ways of upholding U.S. security interests. In particular, arms transfers came to be increasingly used as a substitute for a high U.S. military presence in a region. In addition, by the mid-1970s arms transfers played a central role in American diplomacy in the Mideast and with the oil-exporting countries. In view of the relative decline of U.S. power and influence in the wake of the Southeast Asia defeat, arms transfers became a more important element in implementing U.S. foreign policy than at any time since the mid-1950s.

The purpose of this brief historical survey has been to demonstrate (1) that arms transfers are not a contemporary phenomenon but rather have a long and important history, and (2) that far from being an issue unique to the 1970s, the problem of arms transfer policy has been a central foreign policy issue in the United States almost continuously since 1914.

There has been, however, all too little dispassionate analysis of the impact and implications of the arms transfer phenomenon. In particular, though there exist many regional and case studies on arms transfers, little work has been done toward the construction of an analytical framework for the objective examination of the arms transfer policy process. The sections that follow consist of, first, a statistical description of the arms transfer phenomenon as it existed in the mid-1970s and, second, an attempt to build a framework in which the costs and benefits of arms transfers can be rationally examined.

Though this framework is meant to be applicable to any arms supplier, it is particularly relevant to the United States because by the later 1970s the basic rationales for U.S. arms transfers had become exceedingly complex and for that reason more confusing and more subject to abuse and misinterpretation than at any period before. For this reason a careful review of the statistics and benefits and costs of world-wide arms transfers is essential if sound judgments about future U.S. policy are to be made.

ARMS TRANSFERS SINCE 1945: STATISTICS AND PROGRAMS

Although arms transfers are not unique to the post-World War II era, a number of features distinguish the contemporary arms transfer phenomenon from past experience. Nearly every important aspect of the arms trade has changed dramatically over the past thirty years. These changes in its volume, pace and direction have made the arms transfer phenomenon an important factor in the changing international environment and have once again raised this issue to prominence on the agenda of public policy. However, this is not simply a question of American foreign policy; the debate over U.S. arms transfer policy often obscures the fact that the American experience is only one dimension of a larger phenomenon that in the 1970s has become an increasingly prominent feature of the international scene, involving more arms and increasing numbers of arms suppliers and recipients. What follows describes the changes that have occurred in the global arms trade since World War II.

How Much of What?

The Quantitative Dimension: The quantity of arms that have been transferred between states since World War II is enormous. One source has estimated that nearly $90 billion (in

[25]

current dollars) in arms were transferred between 1961 and 1975.[15] The United States alone transferred approximately $110 billion in arms (in current dollars) between 1950 and 1976.[16]

More significant than the aggregate cumulative amount is the pace at which the arms transfer phenomenon is occurring. It is this trend that largely accounts for the increasing interest in the subject in recent years. The broad trend over the last twenty years has been toward higher levels of arms transfer activity, and the decade of the 1970s has seen annual arms transfer figures reach unprecedented heights (see Tables 2 and 3). For example, between 1963 and 1972, the average annual world growth rate in arms transferred was $400 million in constant dollars. Over that period total annual world arms exports nearly doubled (in constant 1972 dollars) from $4.42 billion in 1963 to $8.72 billion in 1973.[17] That amounts to nearly a 100% increase in the space of a decade. Moreover, large increases have occurred since 1970. Between 1970 and 1971 alone the annual world level of arms transferred rose from $7.7 billion to $10.1 billion (in constant 1974 dollars), an increase of $2.4 billion in one year.[18] And by 1974, the world arms trade was ten times what it had been fifteen years before.[19] Table 3 indicates these trends (although it should be noted that the values only apply to *major weapons* and do not include training, infrastructure and small arms).

These trends can be seen even more clearly in statistics relating to American arms transfers. Between 1963 and 1973 total annual U.S. arms transferred, measured in constant 1972 dollars, nearly tripled, increasing from $1,633.4 million to $4,751.7 million (nearly a 200% increase in ten years). Between FY 1971 and FY 1973 *orders* for arms under the American Foreign Military Sales (FMS) program more than doubled (increasing by 163%) and more than doubled again

[26]

TABLE 2

Annual Total World Arms Transfers, 1965-1974
(In millions of constant 1973 dollars)

	(000,000)		(000,000)
1965	5,315	1970	6,680
1966	6,310	1971	6,940
1967	6,630	1972	9,210
1968	6,690	1973	9,555
1969	7,040	1974	8,365

Source: U.S. Arms Control and Disarmament Agency, *World Military Expenditures and Arms Transfers, 1965-1974* (Washington: GPO, 1975), p. 54.

TABLE 3

Average Annual Exports of Major Weapons
(In millions of constant 1973 dollars)

	(000,000)
1950-59	685
1960-69	1,420
1970-75	3,915

Source: Stockholm International Peace Research Institute, *World Armaments and Disarmament, SIPRI Yearbook 1976* (Cambridge, Mass., and London: The MIT Press; Stockholm: Almqvist & Wiksell, 1976), pp. 252-53.

between FY 1973 and FY 1974 (increasing 147%); such a large backlog of ordered weaponry insures that arms deliveries will remain high in the near future.

Based on current statistics, the indications are that the pace at which arms are being transferred has been maintained at a high level since the 1973 oil crisis, though there has been some decline from the record high years of 1972 and 1973. This is explained by the enormous purchases made by several oil-

[27]

107847

producing states, especially Iran, as well as by the large number of arms deals consumated. The International Institute of Strategic Studies reported that there were 212 known arms agreements between mid-1973 to mid-1975.[20] Table 3 shows this growth.

The Qualitative Dimension: In addition to the acceleration in the quantitative dimension of the arms trade, there has been a significant change in the qualitative nature of the arms now being diffused throughout the system. In the past, arms transferred to nonindustrial states were often the obsolete or second-generation weapons of a major power. During the 1950s, for example, the United States transferred much of its surplus weapons of World War II vintage, such as the piston-engined F-47 Thunderbolt and F-51 Mustang aircraft and various types of naval vessels, to Latin American states.[21]

Today the arms being purchased by rich countries in the less industrial world are often at the frontiers of modern technology. An example of this is Iran's purchase of the F-14 Tomcat fighter and Phoenix missile. The F-14 is one of the most expensive, sophisticated conventional weapons systems ever sold to another country. Furthermore, Iran's air force needs a modern command and control system and has purchased the expensive and modern U.S. AWACS aircraft. Iran has also purchased several new Spruance class destroyers. Saudi Arabia has ordered the F-15 fighter, the most advanced in the U.S. inventory, and the advanced Maverick missiles. Brazil has purchased new West German submarines, and Israel has received some of the most modern U.S. equipment including the F-16 fighter, ECM devices, and laser-guided bombs. Increasing numbers of nonindustrial states are procuring new generations of tactical cruise missiles (especially for maritime missions) which are cheap but sophisticated and potent. Table 4 shows the rapid growth in the number of less industrial countries which have received supersonic aircraft. It must be noted that this trend does not necessarily mean that the recipients' military *capabilities* have increased at the same rate; however, it is a good barometer of the pace of technology transfer.

From Whom to Whom?

Suppliers: The United States has become the largest arms supplier, having accounted for nearly half of all the arms transferred between 1961 and 1974. The United States and the Soviet Union are the source of 75% of the arms trade and, together with Britain, France, West Germany and China, account for 90% of the world's arms supplies.[22] Indeed, over the period from 1950 to 1974 only four countries—the U.S., U.S.S.R., Britain and France—accounted for 89% of cumulative total exports of major weapons.[23]

TABLE 4

Number of Third World States with Supersonic Aircraft, 1955-75

Year	Number	Year	Number
1955 1956 1957	1	1966	22
		1967	25
		1968	28
1958	3	1969	30
1959 1960 1961	4	1970 1971	31
		1972	33
1962	7	1973	37
1963	9	1974	42
1964	10	1975	43
1965	15		

Source: SIPRI Yearbook 1976, p. 18.

[29]

However, although the aggregate world arms market has been dominated by a few major powers, there has been a major proliferation of potential suppliers. In 1945 only five countries—the U.S., U.S.S.R., Britain, Canada and Sweden— had any significant capacity to develop major weapons; by the mid-1970s, there were nine states which had transferred significant quantities of arms, including France, Czechoslovakia, West Germany and Italy, in addition to those mentioned above. Table 5 indicates the wide range of countries which are now to some extent involved in arms sales either as re-transferers or producers. Although the majority of them transfer small quantities of arms in comparison to the "big four," many of them could expand production if the demand were forthcoming, at least for the large number of middle-range weapons which make up the bulk of military inventories.

Another factor relating to the proliferation of potential suppliers is the increased use of licensing and co-production arrangements whereby a country may purchase not merely arms but the technology to produce foreign-designed arms. Licensed production of major weapons in nonindustrial countries—though still small relative to the overall arms trade —increased six times between 1960 and 1973 (in constant prices). Exports of major weapons from nonindustrial countries more than doubled over the same period.[24] An estimated one-fourth of all developing nations are now assembling or producing major weapons.[25] An example of the growth in potential and/or actual suppliers by this means is the case of India, which supplied spare parts (produced under a licensing agreement) for Egypt's Soviet-built planes. These countries which had negotiated licensed production by 1975 are listed in Table 6.

An increasing number of states are developing and producing arms indigenously (see Table 6). States like Israel and

TABLE 5

States Which Have Transferred Arms, 1965-1974[1]

I. States which transferred arms in at least five of ten years between 1965 and 1974.

Australia	(9)[2]	Federal Republic		Saudi Arabia	(6)
Austria	(7)	of Germany	(10)	Soviet Union	(10)
Belgium	(10)	Hungary	(5)	Spain	(9)
Bulgaria	(5)	Iran	(7)	Sweden	(10)
Canada	(10)	Iraq	(5)	Switzerland	(8)
People's Republic		Israel	(8)	United Kingdom	(10)
of China	(10)	Italy	(10)	United States	(10)
Czechoslovakia	(10)	Japan	(10)	South Vietnam	(5)
Egypt	(8)	Netherlands	(10)	Yugoslavia	(8)
France	(10)	Norway	(9)		
German Democratic		Poland	(10)		
Republic	(10)	Romania	(5)		

II. States which have intermittently transferred arms, 1965-1974 (in less than five of ten years).

Algeria	(4)	Jordan	(3)	Portugal	(3)
Argentina	(4)	North Korea	(1)	Singapore	(2)
Brazil	(1)	South Korea	(4)	Syria	(1)
Chile	(1)	Kuwait	(1)	Thailand	(1)
Denmark	(2)	Libya	(1)	Turkey	(3)
Finland	(1)	Morocco	(1)	Venezuela	(2)
India	(4)	New Zealand	(3)	North Vietnam	(1)
Indonesia	(2)	Pakistan	(2)		

---

1. It should be noted that in some cases this involves re-transfer rather than the production of arms for export.

2. Number in parentheses is years involved in arms transfer activity.

Source: ACDA, *World Military Expenditures and Arms Transfers, 1965-1974.*

South Africa often feel compelled for political reasons to develop their own arms industry. In almost every case the internal market is too small to sustain such an industry, which is thus extremely reliant on the export market for its existence—

[31]

TABLE 6

Arms Production in the Third World, 1975

I. *Indigenous Production*

Argentina	South Korea	Singapore
Brazil	Kuwait	South Africa
Egypt	Malaysia	Taiwan
India	Pakistan	Thailand
Indonesia	Peru	Venezuela
Israel	Philippines	Vietnam
Nepal	Saudi Arabia	

II. *Licensed Production of Major Weapons*

Argentina	South Korea	Singapore
Brazil	North Korea	South Africa
Columbia	Mexico	Taiwan
Egypt	Pakistan	Thailand
India	Peru	Venezuela
Indonesia	Philippines	

Source: SIPRI Yearbook 1976

as is true even for the arms industries of the major West European states. Thus there exists in many states not only the capability but also the need to export arms.

This proliferation of potential arms suppliers will no doubt increase as nonindustrial states develop and as military technologies are transferred through the use of co-production and licensing arrangements. It is unreasonable to assume that newly capable states will forego an activity which others have found economically and politically profitable. This has some significant implications in terms of possibly increasing the competition in the arms export market and of reducing somewhat the dependence of recipients on any single supplier or small group of suppliers.

However, it is important to recognize the limits of the potential impact of this trend. No emerging country or group of countries will have the economic capacity to change more than marginally the overall arms export picture. What the increasing number of potential suppliers portends is more weapons available from more sources, and an increasingly complex arms export pattern.

Recipients: As is the case with arms suppliers, a small number of states dominate the aggregate statistics in the arms recipient category. In the last several years the flow of arms has focused on the Middle East/Persian Gulf region. In FY 1974, for example, only three countries—Iran, Israel and Saudi Arabia—accounted for 82% of all arms ordered through the U.S. Foreign Military Sales program. These three states together agreed to purchase nearly $9 billion of American arms in FY 1974. The statistics for FY 1975 show a similar though somewhat less dramatic pattern. The same three countries accounted for 50% of all FMS orders, contracting to purchase $4.8 billion of arms out of a total $9.5 billion arranged through this (by far the largest) American arms transfer program.[26] In addition to these massive purchases of American arms, countries in the Middle East have been buying arms from European sources as well. For example, in the first nine months of calendar year 1976 Saudi Arabia alone purchased $7.5 billion in weapons (including sources other than the U.S.).[27]

Such large purchases have led some to conclude that the arms transfer phenomenon is really derivative from the problems of the Middle East and the Persian Gulf, and that if those areas are excluded from consideration, there is nothing particularly noteworthy occurring in relation to arms transfers. In fact, however, the quantity of arms transferred to the Middle East has simply overshadowed other dynamic changes over a longer time-frame in the spread of military capabilities throughout the globe.

In the most basic sense, a tremendous proliferation of potential recipients has accompanied the proliferation of potential suppliers. The process of decolonization has doubled the number of state actors operating in the international system. Each new actor has its own foreign policy and security interests to be pursued, and, inevitably, the pursuit of state interests requires arms. To the extent that they are able, the countries of the nonindustrial world have been investing in arms. As the SIPRI *Yearbook of World Armaments and Disarmament* commented in 1974, "Although the under-developed countries account for only a small fraction of total world military expenditures . . . the trend has been consistently upward." [28]

This has resulted in a redistribution, or diffusion, of military capabilities. For example, in 1955 the Third World accounted for 5.2% of total world military expenditures of $126.3 billion (in constant 1970 dollars); by 1973 the Third World accounted for 14.4% of $207.4 billion (again in constant dollars).[29] In other words, the Third World now accounts for a larger share of a larger pie. The shift is also reflected qualitatively, as the spread of supersonic aircraft shows.

In addition, the *pace* at which military expenditures have been growing has been higher in the Third World than in the developed world. Between 1963 and 1973, the annual growth rate of military expenditures in the nonindustrial world was 7.2%; for the developed countries, 2% (both measured in constant dollars.) [30] A subsequent report concluded, "It is in the nations of the developing world that the most pronounced relative increase in military expenditures has occurred. In 15

[34]

years, military spending in developing countries more than doubled, from $15 billion in 1960 to $39 billion in 1974 (in constant 1973 dollars)." [31] The regions in which military expenditures (in constant prices) grew the fastest in the years between 1949 and 1971 were, in order, Africa (a factor increase of 23.0) the Middle East (14.6), and the Far East (7.2.)[32]

The developing world is also committing a larger share of its resources to the acquisition of military capabilities than the developed nations are. ACDA data indicate that over the period from 1963 to 1972 the developed world showed a marked decline in military expenditures as a percent of GNP, while the developing countries showed a gradual rise to the point where the percentage was roughly the same for both (approximately 5-6%).[33]

In short, a larger number of "young" states in the international system are rapidly increasing their levels of military expenditures and commitment of national resources to the acquisition of arms. The military needs of these states have fueled the rapid growth in arms exports.

Over the last thirty years, this trend has been reflected in a shift in the direction of arms transfers. Until 1965, most American arms, for example, went to European allies. Between FY 1950 and FY 1965, approximately 56% of all American arms transferred under the Military Assistance Program and the Foreign Military Sales program went to NATO allies. In FY 1975, these same nations received only 23% of the delivered items transferred under the two programs.[34] The main focus of American arms transfers shifted to Third World areas of major concern, first to Indochina, then to the Middle East/Persian Gulf region.

These shifts in arms transfers point to rather obvious relationship between major conflict and arms shipments. In the

1950s Europe was seen as the central area of contention in world politics, and the bulk of both Soviet and American arms went to European allies. In the 1960s Indochina became the point of conflict, with the Soviet Union arming Hanoi, and the United States shipping more than $16 billion in arms to Indochina over the ten years beginning FY 1966.[35] In the 1970s the Middle East has become the most important area of global geostrategic competition and the flow of arms to the region has been commensurate with that importance.

In other words, the direction of the flow of arms is as volatile as world politics. For example, in 1972 the main recipient region was the Far East, which imported 43.1% of the global total of exports of major weapons; the Middle East was a distant second with a 28.7% share. But in 1973, with the Arab-Israeli war erupting, the Middle East accounted for 61.3% of world imports of major weapons.[36] In the 1980s the main recipient region could be southern Africa, if conflict were to break out in that area. Thus, the fact that the Middle East is now the main recipient region does not mean that the Middle East is the heart of the arms transfer phenomenon. Rather, that fact reflects the changed focus in the global flow of arms. The regional shifts over the past decade are shown in Figure 1.

Moreover, coincident with massive, highly visible transfers of arms to a particular region are arms deals which are small relative to the overall scope of the phenomenon, but which can have important impact on specific regional balances. The quantity of arms provided by the Soviet Union to Angola was relatively small but was a crucial variable in determining the outcome of the conflict in that country. A "small" arms race developed in East Africa, contributing to conflict between Somalia and Ethiopia and to tensions between Uganda and Tanzania.[37] Conflict in the Horn of Africa could have an impact on the balance in the Persian Gulf and on oil transpor-

FIGURE 1

Arms Transfers,* Recipients by Region, 1965-1974
(in million constant 1973 dollars)

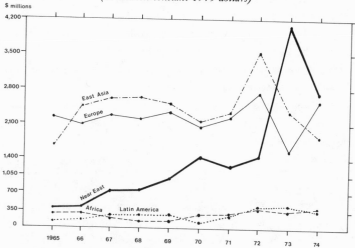

* Actual deliveries (as distinguished from sales) including consummated grants as well as purchases.

Source: U.S. Arms Control and Armament Agency, *World Military Expenditures and Arms Transfers, 1965-1974* (Washington, D.C., 1976), pp. 54-55.

[37]

tation routes. Brazil has quietly been upgrading its Navy so that it is now an important factor in the South Atlantic basin. Over the decade from 1963 to 1973 the states of black Africa imported more than $2.5 billion in constant 1972 dollars, or approximately 40% of the amount imported by the members of OPEC over the same period.[38] This is not an insignificant quantity of arms in a continent rife with conflict and whose littoral states sit astride the West's oil lifeline. In short, the diffusion of arms is occurring throughout the globe, though the level differs from region to region. The fact that large quantities of arms are flowing to the Middle East should not obscure the fact that the same process is occurring at lower levels elsewhere with important regional and even global geopolitical implications.

How Are Arms Transferred?

The number of ways in which arms can be transferred from one nation to another range from grant aid to commercial sales. Here, as with most other aspects of the arms transfer phenomenon, significant changes have occurred over the last ten to fiteen years. However, these changes relate primarily to the arms transfer policy of the largest suppliers, the United States and the Soviet Union.

For most other suppliers, there is a rather narrow range of arms transfer policy options because of economic constraints. Most countries do not have the wealth to provide much military assistance, and out of economic necessity have conducted arms transfers on a commercial basis. This is generally true for the European arms exporters such as Britain and France. The government role in such cases is normally one of expediting commercial sales of arms.

Regarding Soviet arms transfer policy, little is known about the criteria and the means employed in pursuing an arms trade relationship. As a superpower, the Soviet Union has both the incentive and the capability to provide military assistance as part of an influence-building strategy. However, Soviet arms transfers have often involved barter arrangements (as with Egypt) or have been otherwise "tied" in some way so that an economic cost is incurred by the recipient. To the extent that the U.S.S.R. sees arms sales as a means of accumulating hard currency, it may place more emphasis in the future on cash sales.[39] However, because we see only the effects of Soviet arms transfers, with little knowledge of the decision-making process, it is difficult to discern changes in the way the U.S.S.R. transfers weapons and to predict the future direction of Soviet policy.

In the case of the United States, substantial shifts in the way it transfers arms have occurred. There have been four main categories for American arms transactions:

1. Military Assistance Program (MAP)
2. Military Assistance—Service Funded (MASF)
3. Foreign Military Sales (FMS)
4. Commercial sales

Of these four types of arms transfer, the first two are vehicles for military *aid:* MAP is the U.S. government's program of grant military assistance, funded through annual foreign assistance appropriations by Congress. MASF was a military aid program related directly to U.S. involvement in Indochina, whereby equipment provided for allied forces (primarily but not exclusively South Vietnam) was paid for out of the U.S. defense budget.

The other two categories are obviously mechanisms for

selling arms abroad, the difference between the two being the amount of direct government participation. FMS involves government-to-government sales, with the Departments of Defense and State involved throughout the transaction, and with the U.S. government often arranging credit. Commercial sales are simply business transactions between an American arms manufacturer and foreign government, which require government authorization at the time of applying for an export licence after a deal is consummated. Until the end of the 1960s most American arms transfers were in one of the two aid categories. During the decade of the 1950s MAP was by far the largest U.S. arms transfer program; in the 1960s MASF was the largest conduit for U.S. arms sent abroad.

In the 1970s, however, American arms transfers have shifted from the aid to the sales categories. With the end of U.S. involvement in Indochina, the MASF program has virtually disappeared. The MAP program has for many years been gradually declining from its peak in the early 1950s, and since the mid-1960s has been well under $1 billion in annual appropriations (compared with nearly $6 billion in FY 1952). This decline has been caused largely by Congressional opposition to giving grant aid to nations which increasingly seemed able to pay; this was particularly true in connection with America's European allies. By the mid-1970s there was little Congressional support for grant military aid, and the International Security Assistance and Arms Export Control Act of 1976 provided for the eventual elimination of the MAP.

The reduction in American military aid has not meant a reduction in U.S. arms transfers. Rather, the reduction in aid has been more than compensated for by the gradual rise in commercial sales and especially by the large increases in FMS. In FY 1970 FMS orders were about $950 million; by FY 1974 FMS orders totalled nearly $11 billion.[40]

This shift from aid to sales has some important implications. First, it helps to explain the spread of sophisticated weapons throughout the globe. States which were willing to accept obsolete weapons when given them in the form of aid are rarely willing to purchase obsolete weapons. Secondly, it means that the U.S. government has less control over the direction of arms transfers. Who receives American-made weapons is now less a matter of whom the United States chooses to assist than who has the money to buy U.S. weapons (or those of any other suppliers).

A corollary of this is the fact that the old standards for assessing the relationship of arms transfers to foreign policy are less applicable than in the past. While military *aid* was highly susceptible to being fitted into a larger foreign policy framework, arms sales—which often are initiated by the recipient or by a nongovernment member of the supplier country—are not. It is ironic that the public and Congress are increasingly demanding that U.S. arms transfers reflect the interests of U.S. foreign policy at a time when the U.S. government has less control over the scope, direction, and pace of arms sales. This is not to suggest that the United States has *no* control over the arms transfer process, but that sales are less amenable to control than aid.

Another dimension of the problem of how arms are transferred is the importance of the re-transfer of arms. States which have purchased arms or received military assistance can, in turn, transfer some of these arms to another state. As more arms are spread throughout the international system, more states are likely to feel capable of re-transferring arms in the future. By the late 1970s there already were some examples of the phenomenon. During the hostilities in the Middle East in 1973 Libya provided Egypt with Mirage aircraft that had been purchased from France. The crisis in the Horn of Africa in

1977-78 also illustrates this point: Iran was providing American arms to Somalia and Israel was providing American arms to Ethiopia.

There are two significant implications of this trend. First, it means that arms recipients may have more potential influence in regional contests. Second, it again represents a loss of control by the supplier over the ultimate disposition of weapons it has shipped abroad. Arms suppliers have tried to prevent this by including provisions in arms deals which prohibit the re-transfer of arms. However, the fact remains that once the arms are delivered it is possible for the recipient to ship them elsewhere.

In conclusion, then, the two most important changes in the way arms are transferred have been the shift in American policy from aid to sales and the increasing salience of the issue of re-transfer of arms.

How Do We Know Who Sells What To Whom?

As this section has relied on statistics to sketch an overview of the arms transfer phenomenon, it is necessary to add the caveat that these figures should be handled with considerable caution. Aggregate statistics often encompass a broad range of activities, reflect only estimates of costs of various weapons systems, and often are not directly comparable with other sets of data. As a consequence, although the aggregate data can be a useful barometer of trends and overall levels, it is not a precise tool for analysis. The discussion which follows describes the difficulties that arise when considering the statistics of the arms trade.

The basic problem is that most governments provide very little—if any—information about their arms transfer activity. In the absence of official information, statistics often are the product of estimates of quantities transferred and estimates of the cost of the weapon system transferred. This calculation creates a fairly large margin of error.

Moreover, a series of problems arise in using what information is available. First, different sources of information have different definitions of the parameters of their work. Some count only major weapons, others are far more comprehensive. Some rely completely on open information, others are government publications with access to classified information. This result is that statistics are almost never comparable from one source to the next.

A second problem to keep in mind when using arms trade statistics is that dollar figures may be computed in either "current" or "constant" dollars. Current dollar figures are simply the dollar levels as valued at the time of expenditure. Constant dollar figures attempt to adjust for inflation by recalculating past expenditures in terms of the present value of the dollar (or vice versa). Arms transfer statistics look much different depending on whether one is using constant or current dollar figures.

Third, there often is confusion caused by the difference between *orders* and *deliveries*. Statistics on these two stages in the arms transfer process are not comparable because they measure different things. Statistics on deliveries reflect the completion of *past* arms sales activity, whereas *orders* define the scope of future arms export production.

Finally, the aggregate figures that are most often available obscure a wide range of activities. An arms transfer relationship involves more than just shipments of arms. It also requires training, the creation of appropriate infrastructures, and the supply of spare parts. It is usually impossible to obtain a precise breakdown of the level of action in each category. Thus, it is not possible to be certain how much of an arms deal involves strictly combat capabilities and how much relates to support capabilities, though such information is important in assessing the political and military import of arms transfers.

For all of these reasons, comparisons between countries are difficult to make, particularly between the U.S. and the U.S.S.R. The United States publishes more complete data on its own arms transfers than does any other supplier (though the published data, too, are inadequate for many purposes). Data on Soviet transfers are far less complete, owing to the absence of any specific publication by the Soviet Union on its arms transfers. This can lead to over-simplified comparisons of U.S. and Soviet transfers, which are often measured using the index of comparative dollar values. As presently used, this is a clumsy and inaccurate measure and generally tends to underestimate the comparative size of Soviet programs.

In the absence of good comparative data on costs, the best indicator of the magnitude of Soviet transfers is to count the weapons themselves. However, this, too, causes problems because of confusion over Soviet weapons that have been *ordered* or *promised,* those that have been *delivered,* and those that are *operational.* Furthermore, merely counting weapons ignores those defense services and support articles, such as training and infrastructure, which, although not "arms," are essential for the establishment and management of an effective military infrastructure. Since the United States provides a great many support articles and services to its clients, it might be argued that though we may provide fewer weapons to certain regions than the Soviet Union, the overall military impact of our transfers may be greater because of our excellent infrastructure. The point to be made here is that aggregate comparisons of U.S.-Soviet dollar values or unit of weapons transferred are very crude measures and should be treated with great caution.

BENEFITS AND COSTS OF ARMS TRANSFERS

In view of the numerous, often conflicting statements made to justify and condemn arms transfers it is important to examine each of the arguments, using both historical and contemporary examples, and to take into account the trade-offs in supplying or not supplying arms over different time-frames when short-term benefit may be offset by long-term costs and vice versa. The basic approach used in this and the following sections is set out in Figure 2. By using the matrix of the benefits and costs of arms transfers, the merits of the arguments over different time-frames can be systematically considered. The procedure followed here is to examine various interests from a supplier's perspective; but in assessing them, an analysis of recipient interest is included.

FIGURE 2

Matrix For Assessing Impact of Arms Transfers Upon Interests

	BENEFITS		COSTS	
	Short-run	Long-run	Short-run	Long-run
POLITICAL INTERESTS				
MILITARY INTERESTS				
ECONOMIC INTERESTS				

Political Benefits

The political benefits of transferring defense articles and services to friends and allies range from symbolic gestures of friendship, through gaining and exercising influence, to very precisely tied agreements in which the supply or denial of arms is used as a lever by the supplier for obtaining some specific political goal.

1. Symbolism and Friendship: Arms transfers can help to build friendly relations between the supplier and the recipient countries. Here the purpose of arms transfers is to indicate to both parties that a mutually beneficial political relationship is worth pursuing, and the provision of arms is a symbol of that relationship. For example, if the United States were to sell or give small numbers of TOW anti-tank missiles to China, it would be regarded as a symbolic gesture rather than an attempt on the part of either the United States or China to seriously offset Soviet military capabilities along the Sino-Soviet border. Rather, the purpose would be to signal to the Soviet Union that U.S.-Chinese relations were in good standing and that further, more sophisticated arms transfers might become a future component of this relationship.

An historical example would be President Kennedy's decision in December 1962 to offer to supply Britain and France with the Polaris missile system, despite the fact that there were sound military and economic reasons for not offering nuclear weapons to allies. In this case Kennedy felt that good political relations between himself and Macmillan and de Gaulle were more important than strategic concerns.

Assessment: There is no doubt that arms transfers can be an important symbol of friendship and can play a role in cementing overall political relations between political leaders. But it is difficult to calculate in any precise terms just how important these benefits may be. By definition they have nonquantifiable elements; thus assessments fall into the category of the "judgemental" rather than the precise. However, so long as arms remain an important symbol of statehood, decisions to supply or not to supply will often have symbolic meaning out of proportion to their military significance.

2. Influence: The provision of arms and services can provide the supplier with political influence relating to the recipients' overall policies. This influence can generally be broken down into two categories: (1) specific influence tied to specific circumstances; (2) general, or day-to-day influence concerning the recipients long-term political behavior.

Examples of *specific* influence would be the impact of military training programs upon the attitude and behavior of the recipient country's military establishment. In this context U.S. military training programs in Latin America, British training programs in black Africa, and Soviet training programs in Arab countries such as Egypt might be cited to demonstrate various levels of specific influence upon force procurement, tactics and strategy.

Examples of general influence would be United States military sales to NATO, Iran, Saudi Arabia and Israel, and Soviet sales to Warsaw Pact countries and Cuba. In these cases arms are seen as part of a much larger and broader series of relationships which reflect the overall closeness of the political ties between supplier and recipient. The arms relationship provides the supplier with day-to-day access to the recipient's leaders, thus providing the opportunity for numerous policy inputs aside from those specifically relating to arms programs. Thus the U.S. Chief of Mission in Iran was able by virtue of the military sales program to have unique access to the Shah.

The effects or results of this type of day-to-day influence are not easy to document in any hard manner, but most seasoned diplomats would argue that the influence is apparent and does have major benefits for the supplier country.

Assessment: The relationship between arms sales and influence is difficult to demonstrate in any empirically valid manner. For this reason there can be a tendency to exaggerate its importance and to distort the objectivity of decisions relating to arms transfers. It comes very naturally to those bureaucrats working on a day-to-day basis with foreign governments to support measures, such as arms sales, which will ease day-to-day relationships. Thus, requests by foreign governments for U.S. or Soviet or British arms are likely to be approved by country "desk officers." Invariably the costs of turning down major requests are seen in political terms, and support for the sales is often couched in terms of "what we will lose if we don't sell" rather than what are the specific benefits. While this inherent tendency to support sales in the absence of compelling counter-arguments can create future difficulties for both supplier and recipients, there can be no doubt that, at least in the short run, influence is forthcoming which may prove very important in periods of crisis. Thus during the 1973 Arab-Israeli war, Iran refused to join the oil embargo. While there were sound economic reasons for the Shah to continue to sell oil, he did take political risks, in part, it can be argued, because of his close relationship with the United States and the high degree of dependency he had upon American military equipment for his forces.

[48]

3. *Leverage:* The third category of political benefits of arms sales is much more closely tied to specific policy objectives than in the two previous cases. The provision or denial of arms to a friend or ally has often been used by a supplier country to extract a political price from the recipient. Thus in its relationship with Israel, the United States administration has used arms programs in peacetime and in war to change Israeli behavior and, on occasion, to win political support from the Jewish constituency in the United States. For example, the 1975 Sinai agreement which led to a further Israeli withdrawal in the desert was made possible in part because the United States was able both to cajole and at the same time to reward Israel by manipulating arms supplies. As a "reward" for its withdrawal Israel was promised a great many new, sophisticated U.S. arms at very little cost.

There is evidence of similar relationships between the Soviet Union and its arms recipients, especially those in the Middle East. The Soviet Union's leverage over Egypt was considerable despite the ups and downs of the last five years before Egypt expelled Soviet military advisory personnel in 1972.

Examples of leverage through the mechanism of "control by withholding" would be attempts by suppliers to change recipients' behavior in time of war by threatening or implementing arms embargoes. Thus during the 1965 Indo-Pakistan war Britain and the United States successfully put pressure on both countries to stop fighting by instituting an arms embargo. However, in 1974 when the United States attempted to stop Turkey in its war with Greece over Cyprus by imposing an embargo the results were negative.

Assessment: The record suggests that major suppliers do have the capacity to use their arms policies to change the behavior of recipients. However, this is often a short-lived phenomenon. Over time the recipient can often go elsewhere for arms or, in the case of countries like India, Israel and South Africa, develop its arms industries. Generally speaking, a supplier will maximize its leverage when it is the sole source for arms. Thus, over time, the United States probably has greater leverage over Israel, the Republic of Korea and Taiwan than over Iran or Saudi Arabia which have money to buy on the open market. Similarly, over time, the Soviet Union has more leverage with Cuba and North Korea than with Egypt or Syria.

Direct Military Benefits

The military effects of transferring defense articles and services to foreign governments can have both direct and indirect benefits to the suppliers' strategic posture.

1. Support for Military Allies: The provision of arms and services to allies alongside whom the supplier may have to fight in time of war is the most important military benefit of arms transfers. For the United States this would include allies in Europe and countries such as Australia, New Zealand and Japan. As most of them need the type of equipment and infrastructure which the United States can provide, it is certainly in the U.S. interest to see that these countries have strong military capabilities. Training programs are also a critical ingredient of this common defense bond.

Since 1945 the bulk of American arms have been transferred to countries alongside whom we have either been fighting or have been prepared to fight (e.g., Korea, Vietnam, and the NATO allies). The United States gave billions of dollars worth of military assistance to its NATO allies in the 1950s in

[50]

order to counter the Soviet military threat to Europe. The largest recipient of U.S. arms in the 1960s was South Vietnam. On the other side, the Soviet Union supplies large quantities of arms to its Warsaw Pact allies. In short, arms transfers are an important component of military alliance relationships.

Assessment: There is no question that arms transfers can strengthen the military capabilities of one's allies. This can have two direct advantageous consequences from the perspective of the supplier. First, it can lead to relative peace and stability in otherwise potentially explosive, strategically important areas. This has been the case, for example, in Europe and Korea, where American arms (and men) have contributed to relatively stable balances of power that have prevented military or political developments that would adversely affect U.S. geostrategic interests. Second, in the event that war occurs, arms transfers can help to ensure that one's allies are effective military partners. However, the case of Vietnam has shown that simply transferring arms is not enough to guarantee regional stability or militarily capable allies; both depend on other factors besides the mere availability of arms. Yet if arms transfers cannot create stability and competence, they can make major contributions toward the achievement of both objectives.

2. Support for Friends: Arms are provided to allies and friends who, the supplier hopes, will win should war break out, but alongside whom it does not have plans to fight. Into this category would fall most countries to which the United States is not bound by formal defense commitments but in whose survival we have a major interest and whose victory we therefore desire in the event of war. Thus U.S. arms sales to Israel would fall into this category, as indeed might certain U.S.

arms sales to Iran and to Saudi Arabia. Here the argument would be that U.S. military interests were served by having strong friends such as Israel and Iran because we have interests in the region where they may have to fight and their victory or their ability to withstand military pressure reduces the need for direct United States involvement.

Indeed, this line of reasoning was one of the foundations of the Nixon Doctrine, according to which the United States would provide "appropriate" military and economic assistance when necessary to aid a friendly nation against aggression, but would leave the primary responsibility for defense to that nation. Thus the Department of Defense stated in its March 1970 publication "Military Assistance and Foreign Military Sales Facts": "The more rapidly [allied and friendly forces] capabilities can be improved, the sooner it may be possible for the United States to reduce both the monetary and the manpower burden inherent in honoring international obligations." In other words, American interests would be served with less expense and less direct American involvement as a result of arms transfers to friendly nations.

The same general logic applies to Soviet arms transfers. For example, the military relationship with Cuba has enabled the Soviets to reap advantages in Angola, the Middle East and—potentially—Rhodesia, the political and (perhaps) military costs of which would have been too great had the Soviets intervened directly with their own forces. Such activity by the Soviet Union clearly would have been intolerable to the United States, whereas the Cuban actions were not. While this is an unusual example of the benefits to be derived from the transfer of arms to friendly nations, the Soviets also have military relationships of a more typical sort, wherein Soviet regional military interests are served through the transfer of arms to friendly regional states. Syria and North Vietnam are good examples.

Assessment: The military benefits derived from arms transfers to friendly nations are similar to those derived from transfers to military allies. First, they can contribute to regional military stability in important areas, thereby making the need for outside intervention less likely. When, for example, the British withdrew from East of Suez in the late 1960s, the United States decided to rely on Iran and Saudi Arabia to guarantee the stability of the Persian Gulf rather than replace the British presence with an American presence. The magnitude of arms transfers to these two conservative, pro-Western regimes reflects, at least in part, this important role that they perform.

Second, as noted above, strengthening indigenous forces can, in effect, be a surrogate for direct supplier involvement. This benefit, however, suffers from two flaws: (1) Arms alone are not always sufficient to achieve one's politico-military goals, as was the case with U.S. military assistance to Laos. (2) Although arms transfers can sometimes replace supplier involvement, and are sometimes merely the first step toward direct intervention. U.S. arms transfers to pro-Western factions in Angola were opposed in Congress largely on the latter grounds. The example of Vietnam, where what was initially U.S. military assistance led eventually to a long and agonizing war, has made this a politically potent argument in the United States against arms transfers.

Finally, in the event of conflict, arms transfers before or during a war can enable the state or states which embody the suppliers' regional interests to avoid defeat and, hopefully, achieve victory.

[53]

3. Arms for Base Rights: Arms can provide a means of exchange for important base rights for the supplier. There are numerous examples of this type of arrangement whereby the United States and the Soviet Union have procured base rights in exchange for arms. Perhaps the most famous historical example was the U.S. destroyer deal with Britain at the beginning of World War II, when in exchange for fifty American destroyers the British made available important base facilities to the United States in the Caribbean.

In the postwar era there were many occasions when the United States negotiated overseas base rights for its strategic bomber force which, at that time, was dependent upon the medium-range B-47 bomber. As a result, bomber bases agreements were negotiated with countries such as Pakistan, Iran, and Libya, and these bases were crucial to America's capacity to deter the Soviet Union.

While U.S. strategic deterrence no longer depends on medium-range bombers, overseas bases are still important in terms of both tactical airpower and, more importantly, the maritime environment. Modern navies require bases if they are to enable a state to project its power over long distances for long periods of time. The United States thus maintains a network of naval (and air) bases around the world, from Italy and Spain to Japan and the Philippines. The Soviet Union has sought to acquire bases or basing rights in the Indian Ocean (for example, Berbera, in Somalia) and the eastern Mediterranean (formerly at Alexandria, Egypt, now using facilities in Yugoslavia).

However, as many nations, particularly in the Third World, have come to put a higher value on their independence from external influences, overseas basing "opportunities" have diminished—as evidenced by the Soviet expulsion from Alexandria and the American abandonment of bases in Thailand at the request of the Thai government. As with any increasingly scarce resource, the cost of acquiring bases has gone up. Arms are often part of the price. In recent years the United States has had to negotiate with Spain, Greece and Turkey, and is in the process of negotiating with the Philippines, on the price the United States would have to pay for continued use of bases in those countries. Often the result is military and economic aid packages in excess of a billion dollars over five years. In fact, in December of 1976 the Philippine government turned down a billion dollar deal offered by Secretary of State Kissinger in exchange for the continued use of Clark Air Base and Subic Bay Naval Base.

Assessment: Arms transfers are a useful instrument with which to defray the cost of establishing and maintaining overseas bases. However, they are not the only such instruments states have at their command. Cash payments, loans, or other forms of economic assistance can also be used, and American base deals are commonly mixtures of both economic and military transfers. This would suggest that arms transfers could be replaced by economic transfer-payments if the supplier wished to do so, limited, of course, by the extent to which the recipient state demands arms as part of the package. Often, however, they do so, and in such cases arms transfers become an indispensible factor in securing bases abroad which often are considered vital to the security of the United States.

4. Arms in Exchange for Intelligence-Gathering Rights: Some of the most important U.S. facilities overseas have been concerned with intelligence-gathering, such as electronic monitoring or surveillance flights like the U-2 flights over the Soviet

[55]

Union in the late 1950s. The United States has had important intelligence facilities in Turkey and Iran, which are, in part, paid for by U.S. arms sales.

The connection between arms and intelligence-gathering activities was vividly demonstrated by the difficulties that arose between Turkey and the United States after Turkey invaded Cyprus in the summer of 1974. Several months later, Congress put an embargo on further arms transfers to Turkey because it had used American-produced arms in its Cyprus campaign. When it became clear in the summer of 1975 that strenuous effort on the part of the Ford Administration had failed to overturn the Congressional decision, the Turks retaliated by halting operations at 19 of the 20 American bases in Turkey. The most important of these bases were electronic monitoring stations which provided information on Soviet troop movements, air force activities, Black Sea fleet deployments, missile launchings, nuclear tests, and even on possible airlift activity to the Middle East. The closure of these bases thus had serious implications for U.S. strategic operations, for the U.S. 6th Fleet in the Mediterranean, and for NATO activities on the southern flank. A U.S. officer was reported in the *New York Times* to have commented "They've pulled down the blinds on our picture windows." [41]

The Turks explained their decision to take such a serious action by arguing that the July 1969 U.S.-Turkish Defense Cooperation Agreement had lost its "legal validity" because the United States was failing to keep its end of the bargain whereby Turkey provided bases in return for American arms. In short, no arms meant no intelligence. The outcome of this episode was that the United States and Turkey reached a new, four-year agreement in March 1976 that provided for even more American arms ($250 million per year) than had been supplied prior to the embargo.

Assessment: As intelligence-gathering installations are simply one type of overseas base, the conclusions drawn above about the relationship of arms to bases are appropriate here. It might be added that because intelligence-gathering is such a high-priority activity and because the bases are very sensitive to location and are thus harder to replace than other types of bases, the pressures on a supplier government to use whatever instruments necessary, including arms, to maintain its intelligence-gathering facilities will become more intense.

Indirect Military Benefits

1. Conventional Arms Transfers as a Non-Proliferation Strategy: Both the United States and the Soviet Union have felt that it is in their best political and military interests to prevent the spread of nuclear weapons. It has been suggested that conventional arms transfers can be used in such a way as to address the sources of insecurity that might drive an Nth state to pursue the nuclear option, thus making proliferation less likely. The argument is that if a potential nuclear power has a conventional arsenal sufficient in quality and quantity to ensure its military security, that state will have much less incentive to go nuclear. An example of this might be Israel. While there has been some debate over whether Israel already possesses a nuclear capability, there is no question—given the magnitude of Israeli security requirements—that Israel would be forced to go nuclear if it did not have access to large quantities of sophisticated American arms. A hypothetical example would be the case of South Africa. Might not an increasingly isolated white South African government, surrounded by hostile black states and beset with internal difficulties, find the nuclear

[57]

option attractive as it became more and more difficult to purchase conventional arms in the world market?

Assessment: It is clear that in some cases there may be a relationship between conventional arms transfers and nuclear proliferation. It is less clear that conventional arms transfers should be pursued as a general non-proliferation strategy because there are other grounds for going nuclear besides rational calculations of security requirements. In the future, nations may exercise the nuclear option for reasons of prestige, or to further aspirations for regional dominance, or to match capabilities acquired by a regional competitor. In these cases conventional arms transfers would probably have no impact on the prospects for nuclear proliferation. Moreover, a non-proliferation strategy based on arms transfers would almost certainly be subject to the argument that a greater evil was being replaced by a lesser evil, and would therefore be hard to sustain politically, at least in the United States.

2. Testing Combat Equipment: The use of a supplier's military equipment in combat without the use of the supplier's personnel can provide useful information on its basic design characteristics and its applicability to regional theaters. Although this is a minor issue and is never openly used to justify arms sales in the United States, there are some residual benefits to the supplier military establishment in having its weapons tested in foreign wars. For example, the United States, the Soviet Union, Britain and France have all learned a great deal about their *own* weapons systems as a result of their use in local conflicts. A good example of this is the 1973 Mid-East War, in which it was shown that new generations of anti-tank weapons were effective. This "demonstration" prompted debate even in the Soviet Union, which is traditionally tank-oriented, over the future viability of the tank, given the increasing lethality of relatively inexpensive anti-tank weapons and the consequent cost-benefit relationship vis-à-vis extremely expensive tanks.

Assessment: Weapons testing is a marginal military benefit derived from arms transfers. While some useful information on combat capabilities of a supplier's weapons systems may be obtained in this manner, its usefulness is often limited by the fact of different military environments, different strategies and tactics, differing levels of training and technical competence, etc. In addition, such useful information as is obtained is merely an "accidental" benefit of arms transfers in that there is no way of predicting which arms transferred will end up being used in a local conflict (unless, of course, the recipient is involved in an on-going conflict). Finally, it must be remembered that often suppliers will not transfer "frontier" technologies to other states for reasons of their own security, so that the least-tested weapons systems of the supplier are least likely to be tested in a local war.

Economic Benefits

Basically, there are five economic arguments in favor of arms sales.

1. Arms Sales Contribute to a Favorable Balance of Payments: In a time of exchange shortage, arms sales are an important means of offsetting a balance-of-payments deficit in certain regions. During the 1960s it was deliberate United States policy to encourage arms sales to Europe to offset the costs of maintaining American troops. In the 1970s U.S. and European arms sales to Persian Gulf countries are one means of offsetting the

[59]

costs of importing oil from that region. The French, for example, made a concerted effort at economic diplomacy with Arab states after October 1973, which included arms deals with Saudi Arabia, Kuwait, Libya, and the United Arab Emirates.

It is often argued that one of the major reasons why the Nixon Administration began to encourage arms exports in the early 1970s was that the United States faced a severe balance-of-payments problem. For example, in October 1971 the United States showed a net trade deficit for the first time since 1893. By 1973—even before the enormous rise in the price of oil in 1974—U.S. arms exports (in terms of orders) had tripled over the 1970 level. While it is not realistic, given all the other factors involved with arms transfers, to posit a causal linkage between balance-of-payments problems and increased U.S. arms transfer activity, it is reasonable to assume that there was some connection.

Assessment: The world arms market is a potentially lucrative foreign exchange earner for any supplier which is able to penetrate a large portion of that market: Many countries such as France and Britain pursue a conscious strategy of generating export earnings by exporting arms. The important determinant here is the world demand for arms. Even in the best of economic circumstances it is unlikely that a multi-billion dollar market is going to be ignored. In economically troubled times such as we have recently experienced, the economic imperative to sate the demand for arms becomes even greater, especially for countries whose economic health is far more dependent on trade than is the United States. France and Britain simply cannot afford to forego $1 billion to $2 billion a year in export earnings. In the future the Soviet Union may come to see its arms transfers in more explicitly economic terms.

In short, earning foreign exchange is an important benefit to be derived from the transfer of conventional arms.

2. *Arms Sales Help Relieve Unemployment:* The sale of arms abroad in times of economic recession helps unemployment in regions which are highly dependent upon defense industries. Just how many people are affected by arms sales or, alternatively, who would be put out of work if arms sales were not to be approved is a matter of some debate. Nevertheless, on a regional basis the benefits are considerable, especially in terms of local politics. Thus there is abundant evidence that even the most "dovish" U.S. congressmen become somewhat "hardline" when their local constituents seem likely to suffer as a result of a defense cut, such as the cancellation of a defense order, or the closure of a military base.

According to an estimate reported in *Business Week*,[42] every $1 billion in arms exports supports 47,000 jobs in U.S. industry. In FY 1974 and FY 1975, U.S. arms sales in excess of $20 billion were agreed upon. It is evident that exports of this magnitude represent hundreds of thousands of jobs for American citizens. For the smaller and more trade-dependent economies of Western Europe, the employment effect of arms transfers may be proportionally even greater, though lack of data makes it difficult to verify empirically such hypotheses.

Assessment: Arms transfers, particularly on a large scale, can have a large impact on employment within a supplier state. From an economic standpoint, arms exports have the same effect as any other export in the national economy: they generate foreign currency earnings and increase both output and employment. Arms sales are thus not only significant as political and military instruments of policy but can also be an important economic tool as well. In a period of rising raw materials and energy costs and of widespread recession, the economic dimension of arms transfers assumes heightened significance. This factor is certainly responsible in part for the large increase in arms trade activity over recent years. This is particularly true for non-superpower suppliers for whom the political and military benefits of arms transfers have less meaning than the economic benefits.

3. Arms Sales Reduce Unit Costs: The argument here is that longer production runs which result from arms sales to foreign governments reduce both the unit procurement and the unit R & D costs of increasingly sophisticated and expensive equipment. This argument is especially persuasive for countries such as Britain, France and Israel which cannot count on long production runs for their domestic consumers (e.g., their own arms services), yet for national reasons want to retain an indigenous arms production capability. Furthermore, if, in the future, an increasing proportion of total U.S. military procurement is designated for foreign sales, this argument will become more compelling in terms of U.S. costs.

This factor has already shown its effect on the U.S. defense establishment. It explains, for example, why the Air Force and the Navy competed so vigorously over the sale of aircraft (the F-15 and F-14, respectively) to Iran. Each wanted to reap the advantage of lower unit costs. Another example of this phenomenon relates to the Air Force's new F-16 fighter. It has been sold to Belgium, Denmark, Norway, the Netherlands and Iran, with potential orders from Israel, South Korea and Spain. The result is a potential production run of 1,500 aircraft (worth approximately $25 billion); each additional aircraft built lowers the unit cost of all the rest because of economies of scale and because development costs are spread over a larger number of units. The Navy has recently urged that Northrop

Corporation be allowed to sell 250 of its new F-18 fighters to Iran, arguing that they will both lower the unit cost of the plane and recoup from Iran $300,000 per plane of the development cost.

Assessment: There is an incentive for groups within potential supplier states to seek the objective of lower unit costs through arms exports. For smaller countries this process may be necessary if they are to afford new weapons systems. In the case of the United States, lower unit costs make new weapons systems politically more acceptable, and may be an incentive for the armed services to encourage arms sales when there is pressure on the defense budget. We may see incipient competition between the U.S. Air Force and Navy to sell the F-16 and F-18 in foreign markets in an attempt to keep down their own costs.

4. Linkages Between Military Sales and Commercial Sales: There is some evidence that sales of military equipment to well-established Third World countries can lead to further sales in the commercial arena, but this argument is a difficult one to demonstrate in any formal way. Certainly, for Britain and France this linkage is made explicitly, and the role of British and French military attachés in many overseas missions is to help salesmen for their country's industry. In the case of the United States, the relationship between the in-country team and the commercial operators is more obscure, but few would deny that there are some linkages, especially when the U.S. services as well as the industry have a mutual interest in selling a particular piece of equipment.

Assessment: To the extent that arms transfers are thought to further a state's commercial interests in other foreign trade

[63]

sectors, this argument provides a further economic rationale for pursuing arms transfers. But the extent to which this relationship is thought to exist is (as noted above) not demonstrable in any meaningful way. There are, however, several aspects of the arms transfer process which imply a commercial potential in arms transfers. First, large arms transactions commonly entail access to high-level officials in recipient states. Since in many states the government exercises great control over foreign trade, access to high-level officials can influence the recipient state's procurement in nonmilitary sectors. Second, the transfer of sophisticated weapons often requires ancillary deals for the provision of associated infrastructure, such as roads, runways, housing, power grids, etc. Finally, it is possible that a nation's weapons system can act as a sort of "advertisement" for its nonmilitary technologies.

5. *Arms in Exchange for Resources:* Another economic use to which arms transfers are put is that they are sometimes exchanged directly, in barter arrangements, for important resources; oil is the most frequently sought resource in deals of this sort. Although the participating states often object when an arrangement is characterized as "arms for oil," such arrangements are, in fact, not infrequent. Soviet arms transfers to Iraq are thought to be made on this basis. In the aftermath of the oil crisis of 1973-74 the French sought to consummate several long-term barter arrangements with oil-producing states. Recent speculation has suggested that future U.S. arms transfers to Iran will have to be on a barter basis because of that state's declining revenues. The fact is that "arms for oil" barter is a convenient payment method when either the supplier or the recipient has foreign-exchange difficulties.

Short of barter trade, arms transfers can be used in an effort to ensure access to important raw materials. Certainly access has been a factor behind the massive transfer of U.S. arms to Iran and Saudi Arabia, the two largest oil-producing states in the Persian Gulf. The argument here is that a raw material producer would be less likely to interrupt commodity trade with a state on which it is in some degree dependent for arms, spare parts, training, etc., and that on-going arms transfer relationships help to create a political atmosphere in which commodity supply restrictions are unlikely.

Assessment: As the world market for resources grows more competitive, arms are likely to become an increasingly useful tool with which to acquire or to ensure access to raw materials.

Costs of Arms Transfers

As with the benefits, so with the costs: arms transfers must also be examined in their political, military and economic contexts.

Political Costs—Direct and Indirect

In addition to the political costs, both direct and indirect, resulting from arms sales, there are other costs that arise from sociological change and are long term and political in their effect. These further costs concern a supplier's identification with a repressive recipient regime, prestige, and hostages.

1. Reverse Leverage: An arms supplier can become tied to a recipient in such a way that the recipient can apply reverse or negative leverage against the supplier in time of crisis. By establishing a close arms sales relationship, the supplier, in

[65]

effect, enters into a political bond with the recipient in which the trust between governments becomes an important issue. For example, in time of crisis, a decision by the United States to slow down or stop arms sales to an important client could have a precipitous effect upon political relationships. At various times India, Israel, Turkey, the United Kingdom, and France have all threatened the United States with sanctions if certain arms commitments were not met.

In short, lines of influence run both ways in an arms transfer relationship. This is especially evident if arms are, in effect, being used to "procure" important resources or base rights or even influence in a geostrategically important area. In such cases what is being offered by the recipient—for example, Turkish bases or Iranian oil—is sometimes more important to the arms supplier than the weapons are to the recipient. When this occurs, patterns of influence are significantly skewed from the conventional view of supplier-dominated arms relationships, and the recipient may actually have the upper hand. A recent example is the Philippines, now demanding a much better deal in return for continued American access to bases in that country.

Assessment: There are many cases, such as the U.S. arms relationships with South Korea and South Vietnam, where the supplier is clearly the dominant partner. Even in these cases, however, the relationship is never totally one-sided, as evidenced by Thieu's rejection of the 1972 peace agreement and by revelations of serious—and not always legal—efforts by the South Korean government to influence American politicians. Moreover, it is not uncommon that the recipient has "instruments" of leverage which enable it to deal with arms suppliers from a strong negotiating position. It should be recognized that entering an arms transfer relationship involves some constraints for both sides and that, from the supplier's perspective, such constraints are a cost which should be factored into the decision-making process.

2. *Cost of a Supplier's Attempts to Exert Leverage:* While it is clear that arms transfer relationships can give supplier states a large measure of *potential* influence or leverage, actual attempts to utilize that leverage can have quite negative consequences. An attempt to exert pressure on a recipient by manipulating the supply of arms can severely disrupt a political relationship in which the supplier has often made a significant political and economic investment, and can destroy the atmosphere of trust and friendship to which arms transfers contributed. Such an attempt may drive a recipient to seek other suppliers in order to reduce its dependence on the dominant supplier; and, in the worst case, the recipient may even turn to one's adversaries in an attempt to neutralize the initial supplier. There may thus be both a political and an economic cost to attempts to exert leverage, in terms of lost influence and lost sales.

For example, when Congress attempted to influence Turkey's policy toward Cyprus by cutting off U.S. arms shipments to Turkey, the Turks responded by depriving the United States of the use of its bases and proceeded to buy arms from several West European states, all the while pursuing a rapprochement with the Soviet Union. The consequence of the U.S. attempt to exert leverage was, therefore, a serious deterioration of relations with an important ally, lost base rights, and improved Soviet relations with Turkey; in sum, clearly a net loss for the United States, particularly since no progress was made on the Cyprus issue. Another example is the Soviet-Egyptian relationship. Though Egypt was extremely dependent on Soviet arms, Sadat was still able to deprive the Soviets of base rights at Alexandria when Soviet efforts to influence Egyptian policy became too obtrusive.

Assessment: The issue of leverage is one of the great uncertainties about the arms transfer phenomenon. The extent and duration of the leverage thus acquired is unknown and largely determined by the particular circumstances of each arms transfer relationship. What is suggested by the above is that leverage may be both short-term and costly to employ. Unless a state is totally dependent on a single supplier (e.g., unless there is extremely limited reverse leverage), it is more likely that a recipient can attempt to exert rather painful leverage on the supplier. Therefore, while influence and leverage are by-products of arms transfers, they may be limited in practice.

3. An Indirect Political Cost—The Promotion of Regional Arms Races: Although the precise ingredients of an arms race vary on each occasion, the infusion of large quantities of arms into a conflict region can stimulate reciprocal purchases by fearful neighbors. Thus many of the arms transfers to the Middle East and South Asia over the past twenty-five years conform to what might be termed the "arms race" syndrome.

The transfer of various types and quantities of arms into a region increases the risks of conflict and the probability of war, and the effect may well be adverse. Since war in any region of the world is rarely in the interest of major suppliers, especially the United States and Western Europe, overall trends toward arms races can be regarded as a major long-term cost.

Two basic types of arms races can be distinguished. First, there are *competitive* acquisitions whereby one recipient attempts to match in kind the weapons supplied to another in order to maintain a military balance (e.g., the Israeli-Arab arms race). The other type might be called imitative acquisitions whereby a recipient, although not sizing its military forces on a neighbor's inventory, may want to buy or receive similar equipment for reasons of prestige. For example, there is some evidence that although Saudi Arabia does not want to match in quantity Iran's arms purchases, it certainly wants to feel that it can, if necessary, buy the same types of arms from the United States. This, in turn, can contribute to the overall Middle East arms build-up, since Saudi purchases of U.S. arms will be taken into account by Israel in determining its own requests for U.S. arms.

The "arms race" dynamic occurs in areas of the world less visible and less heavily armed than the Middle East. In East Africa a small arms race has been provoked by Uganda's President Amin, whose threats to destroy Tanzania have been accompanied by a flow of arms from the Soviet Union which has included not only small arms but also tanks and aircraft. Tanzania and, to a lesser extent, Kenya have had to respond to the Ugandan build-up by improving their own capabilities. In South America, Brazil and Argentina have long shown a propensity to react to the arms purchases of the other with similar procurements on their own part. Thus, the major program for upgrading the Brazilian navy has resulted in an effort by the Argentines to improve their own naval capability.

Assessment: Arms transfers can make the world a more dangerous place. While they do not necessarily create conflict, they provide the means whereby political disagreements can escalate into armed conflicts. The Rhodesian situation, for example, would be far less explosive if Mozambique and the Rhodesian guerrillas were not being armed by the Soviet Union.

Arms transfers can provide irrational or irresponsible leaders—such as General Amin—with military capabilities which

[69]

make them far more serious threats to peace and which require responses from neighboring states. Arms transfers to regional powers can create an upward spiral of interacting procurements between competitive powers, whether for reasons of prestige or security.

In sum, it is apparent that the "arms race" syndrome often results in the spread of more arms around the globe, an increase in the latent potential violence in the international system and/or regional subsystems, without increased (and sometimes even with diminished) security. However, it is important not to generalize too broadly from these conclusions, for every state does have its legitimate security interests which must be dealt with to its own satisfaction. Moreover, arms transfers can contribute to military balances or make war so costly that stability is enhanced and the prospects for war decreased. Thus, while conventional arms races can be expensive economically and politically, there is no direct correlation between arms and conflict.

Sociological Costs

The provision of arms and infrastructure to developing countries can have long-term sociological implications which may not be in the long-term interest of the supplier. Although this remains a fertile area for more research, there is increasing speculation that the large infusion of arms and infrastructure into relatively backward countries such as Saudi Arabia and Iran may contribute to overall political instability by promoting sociological change. Given the dependency of the West on Saudi and Iranian oil, any trends toward instability on the part of the political elite has worrying implications for the future.

The fear here is twofold. First, it is conceivable that the

sociological change engendered by the introduction of modern technology in less developed societies may be revolutionary in nature. Thus, the rationale that the United States should support and arm a conservative regime in the Third World because it is a stabilizing force may, over a longer time-frame, be self-defeating. Second, large quantities of arms in a less developed society may provide revolutionary forces with the means to engage in disruptive activities, for theft or capture of arms by anti-regime forces is certainly within the realm of possibility.

A final point about the sociological costs of arms transfers is that they generally enhance the role of the military in the domestic politics of the recipient society. One implication of this fact for Western suppliers is that their arms transfers may in the long run diminish the likelihood of the emergence of democracy in Third World states where the more heavily armed military forces have come to play important political and control functions. Similarly, for the Soviet Union the reinforcement of the military's role, which is generally conservative, may make the emergence of a socialist regime less likely.

Assessment: The possible sociological costs of arms transfers are speculative. Because they are both unpredictable and long-term, they do not often enter into the decision-making process. However it should be recognised that short- or medium-term policies may cause long-term problems.

1. Arms Sales Can Identify the Supplier with Repressive Regimes: Since most of the countries in the world have authoritarian governments and many of these are composed of military leaders, the sale of U.S. or European arms can identify the supplier governments with the main organ of repression in many countries. Thus, U.S. arms sales to Chile have been seen as support for the organs of repression rather than for the forces of democracy. This gives the United States a bad image and works against its broader interest in the region.

The problem is a difficult one for states which are concerned about human rights because it is hard to develop a consistent policy. For example, many states observe the embargo against shipping arms to South Africa yet may, like the United States, supply arms to regimes with worse records on human rights. For the United States the dilemma is posed most starkly when military allies are repressive internally, South Korea and the Colonel's Greece being examples. The inconsistent application of moral criteria for arms transfers suggests that, in fact, there are no real moral criteria. Rather, a decision to observe sanctions against a repressive regime will be made on other grounds. For example, sanctions against South Africa are observed because the states of Black Africa have made the political cost of association with South Africa so high. In a generally authoritarian world, it is not easy to make foreign policy decision on moral grounds.

Two dimensions of this problem are of concern to arms suppliers. First, there is the matter of a state's interntaional reputation. It is difficult for the United States (and other Western democracies) to be a "beacon of liberty" when it arms ruthlessly repressive regimes in South Korea, the Philippines, and elsewhere. Similarly, it is damaging to the Soviet Union's reputation as leader of the world Communist movement and "vanguard of the world revolutionary forces" when it arms and aids such conservative and anti-Communist regimes as Sadat's Egypt; the Chinese Communists have attacked Soviet leadership of the Communist world on just these grounds.

Second, should a revolution or change of regime take place

[72]

in a recipient state, the supplier may be discredited by its association with, and support of, the previous, repressive regime. This occurred, for example, when the Colonels were overthrown in Greece; Greeks expressed great bitterness against the United States because it had dealt with the Colonels.

Assessment: The costs of transferring arms to repressive regimes are troublesome, especially for democratic states, but they may be unavoidable except for certain symbolic cases like South Africa and Chile. If a supplier state is to have an active foreign policy and a meaningful arms transfer policy the chances are that it will have to deal with repressive regimes.

2. *Loss of Prestige:* When a supplier state is closely associated with a recipient in a major and sustained arms transfer and training relationship, the performance of the recipient reflects upon the prestige of the supplier. When that recipient, such as Egypt in 1967 or Vietnam in 1975, performs ineptly and/or is defeated decisively, the supplier suffers a loss of prestige; the effectiveness of its arms and support is drawn into question. While intangible and unquantifiable, a loss of prestige can have implications for relationships with other states. For example, Secretary of State Kissinger was greatly concerned that the dénouement in Vietnam would reflect on U.S. commitments elsewhere. U.S. behavior during the Angolan crisis left an impression of indecisiveness and inefficacy, which was bound to have an impact on others' perceptions of U.S. power.

Assessment: This cost is limited in scope in that it will occur only when a recipient state is closely associated with a single supplier and only when that recipient performs badly on the field of battle. As there are few cases and few circumstances when this may occur, the potential loss of prestige is not likely to have a major impact on a supplier state's calculations of the costs and benefits of transferring arms. However, the very fact that this is a relatively rare phenomenon may magnify its importance and impact when it does occur.

3. Hostages: The transfer of sophisticated arms to Third World states commonly required rather large and lengthy programs of training and technical assistance. Often a large number of citizens from the supplier state may be dispatched to the recipient for those purposes. The possibility cannot be overlooked that in the event of revolution, war, a radical shift in the recipient's policy, or even friction between supplier and recipient, these people might become political hostages who could be used to pressure the supplier state. And this hazard can involve sizable numbers. For example, it has been estimated that there are 25,000-30,000 Americans in Iran in capacities related to the U.S. arms transfer program with that country. A severe problem could arise if that many U.S. citizens were caught in the middle of, say, an Irani-Iraqi war or an internal revolution.

This raises some interesting questions whose implications need to be faced. How much leverage would these hostages give a recipient over a supplier state? Could, for example, an American president sacrifice thousands of American citizens? Would the United States resort to force to protect its citizens? Could the United States be drawn into a local war as a result of the presence of thousands of its citizens in the region?

Such contingencies need to be thought about. The potency of hostages as a political weapon is suggested by the continuing issue in American politics of the missing-in-action in Vietnam. Imagine if those were not merely 2,000 soldiers who are

[74]

assumed dead but ten times as many Americans—including wives and children—who are alive and in jeopardy. The severity of such a predicament is clear. The suddenness with which events can change in Third World recipient states is evidenced by the assassination of Saudi Arabia's King Faisal. There are enough Quadaffis and Amins in the world to suggest that American lives could be placed in jeopardy by the accession to power of a radical, anti-Western ruler.

Assessment: There is a clear long-term danger that persons associated with arms transfer programs may at some point be caught in circumstances in which they may become hostages to be used against the supplier state. How great the risk of such a situation occurring is, of course, unknown. But the implications of this potential cost are so great that it deserves greater attention than it has received.

Military Costs

1. Arms Transfers May Lead to Involvement in War: A common argument against arms transfers is that they may be the first step toward supplier involvement in war. Of course, the standard example used to substantiate this argument is Vietnam. What began in the late 1950s as a small U.S. military assistance program to that country became a long and agonizing war. Another example is the policy of President Roosevelt at the outset of World War II to arm the allied powers. This policy would have eventually led to American involvement in the war against the Axis powers even had the Japanese not attacked Pearl Harbor.

This argument is especially powerful in the United States because of its historical precedents. Thus when the Angolan crisis arose, many in Congress sensed that it was a situation analogous to Vietnam in the initial stages of our involvement there. It was largely the believability of this analogy which led Congress to end U.S. arms shipments to pro-Western forces in the Angolan civil war; the result of this action was the defeat of these forces by the Soviet-armed MPLA.

The fear is that the United States (or any supplier) will have so much invested, politically and economically, in a particular regime or faction that it cannot afford to allow its partner to be defeated. This dynamic can lead to deeper and deeper involvement by the supplier, and ultimately to direct intervention as with the United States in Vietnam.

Assessment: It is possible that arms transfers can increase the chances of supplier involvement in a local war. But decisions to wage war are political decisions of the highest order. Except perhaps in the scenario for hostages (as described above), in which war may be forced upon a supplier, the arms transfer process is unlikely to cause that political decision. Rather, arms transfers, and especially military assistance, are symptoms of supplier involvement, not the cause of that involvement.

2. *Arms Sales Can Affect Military Readiness:* The effect of large-scale arms transfers (and particularly those which occur in times of crisis) on the military capability of the supplier has been a cause of major concern in both the United States and the Soviet Union. There are two dimensions to this problem. First, arms recipients draw upon the military stocks of the supplier. In a crisis, such as the 1973 Middle East war, weapons may even be drawn from the active inventories of the supplier, as happened then in both the United States and the Soviet Union. In the United States there was serious objection by the military to the magnitude of the U.S. arms airlift to Israel because it was felt that readiness in the event of war was

reduced. This was evidenced, for example, by a shortage of tanks in the U.S. Army as a result of the arms shipments to Israel.

Even in peacetime, however, arms sales can cause problems in keeping both the U.S. military establishement and arms recipients supplied. For example, customers of the United States, such as Iran, can "buy in" to the U.S. logistics system. The American military must then compete with a foreign government for spare parts and other military wares. On occasion, because of the political importance of the recipient, the foreign government may even have priority access to U.S. military supplies. As a result, U.S. inventories may be reduced to a dangerously low level or even depleted. This could be crippling if a war were to erupt.

The second dimension of this problem is that arms recipients are increasingly buying the most modern weaponry available. In order to accommodate delivery schedules to foreign buyers, domestic producers sometimes delay deliveries to their own government. This occurred, for example, when Iran purchased the F-14. Deliveries to the U.S. Navy were stretched out so that the Shah could receive his F-14s sooner. In other words, U.S. arms deployments may be less than planned because of deliveries to foreign customers, and American readiness is again reduced as a result of arms sales.

Assessment: Arms transfers can have a substantial impact on the military readiness of a supplier state. This is clearly a serious cost and one that is likely, as it has in the past, to generate internal opposition to further arms transfers if the impact becomes too great.

3. *Arms May Be Used Against the Supplier in a Conflict:* There is always the chance, when a state transfers large quantities of

weapons abroad, that through political change in a recipient state or through the capture of weapons by enemy forces the supplier's arms may come to be in hostile hands. The classic case of both these situations was Vietnam. During the war American arms worth billions of dollars fell into enemy hands and many of these weapons were subsequently used against American fighting men in the field. As early as 1964 the noted expert on Vietnam, Bernard Fall, stated in an interview with the *U.S. News and World Report* [43] that 90% of the weapons used by the Vietcong were captured American weapons. Obviously the opportunities would increase as the United States began to pour massive quantities of military material into South Vietnam later in the 1960s.

And when the North Vietnamese succeeded in defeating and overruning South Vietnam, they inherited a substantial arsenal of American weapons which had been supplied to the South Vietnamese government. The arsenal which South Vietnam was reported by the *Military Balance, 1974-1975* to possess in the last year of its existence as a state represented more than a decade of major U.S. military assistance efforts. It included 600 tanks, 1,000 armored personnel carriers, 1,500 artillery field pieces, and unspecified numbers of TOW anti-tank weapons, mortars and anti-aircraft weapons. The South Vietnamese Navy possessed more than 1,000 vessels (most of them small patrol craft suitable for operations in the Mekong River). The South Vietnamese Air Force consisted of more than 500 combat aircraft, including more than 100 F-5As. While not all of this equipment could have been captured in operating condition, it is clear that a sizable store of military goods remained for the North Vietnamese. Thus, some significant portion of the approximately $15 billion in arms which the United States transferred to South Vietnam is in the hands of a hostile state whose regional interests are inimical to those of the United States.

Assessment: There is always some risk involved for the supplier as a result of uncertainty about the eventual destination and/or use of its weapons, which may be lost to an enemy in combat, inherited by a new and hostile regime, or retransferred to hostile states. However, despite the example of Vietnam, the direct military threat to the supplier state is not large. This is true for several reasons.

First, captured or retransferred arms—especially, sophisticated weapons systems—are most likely to fall into the hands of forces which have not been trained to use them. Since the effectiveness of most weapons depends in large part on the competence of the operator, in practice the capability of a force armed with captured weapons may not be nearly as great as the quality of the weapons would suggest.

Second, weapons are dependent upon supplies of spare parts, ammunition, and sustained maintenance for continued effectiveness. In most circumstances these are not likely to be available, certainly not from the supplier whose arms have fallen into hostile hands. This would suggest that the threat posed by captured weapons would be limited in duration because of attrition caused by mechanical failures that cannot be fixed without parts, etc.

Finally, and most important, a supplier state is unlikely to find itself in a situation in which arms it has transferred are being used against it militarily. The United States has sent arms to at least 80 countries in the last two decades, and only in Indochina were these arms used against the United States in a significant way.

In sum, the possibility does exist that a supplier's arms will be used against it in a conflict. But this is more likely to be a rare than a frequent occurrence and consequently is probably not a large factor in arms transfer decisions. More important is the concern (discussed above) that arms may be used in ways which harm the political interests of the supplier.

[79]

4. Weapons May Be Designed for External Markets: The performance of many weapons systems is sensitive to the environment in which they operate. Tanks were not a major asset in the swamps of Vietnam and are limited in mobility by the soft sands of the desert in the Middle East. The effectiveness of close air-support aircraft is reduced in jungle warfare. In short, weapons are most effective in the environment for which they are designed.

The problem here is that arms manufacturers may design weapons whose characteristics are determined more by what is generally desirable in the arms export market than by the security requirements of their own government. As a consequence, a supplier may have in its own arsenal weapons which are not as appropriate for its defense posture as would be weapons designed specifically for its own needs. The implication here is that a state's military potential can be affected by the need of its arms industry to accommodate the expectations of the world arms market.

Assessment: This is another of those intangible and unquantifiable costs that are as a result unlikely to have a major impact on the arms transfer decision-making process. It should be noted, however, that though this cost is largely a hidden one, over time it could have a significant impact on a supplier state's force structure.

5. Technology Transfer: Arms captured in local conflicts (or examined as a consequence of lax security by a recipient) can provide important information about a supplier's weapons systems to its own adversaries. Such information can allow an adversary to assess accurately a supplier's military capabilities, to prepare countermeasures to captured weapons, and even to

[80]

produce similar weapons based on the original supplier's technology.

An example of the intelligence-gathering implications of arms transfers is provided by the Soviet arms relationship with Egypt. In both the 1967 and 1973 Middle East wars Soviet weapons captured by the Israelis proved to be a valuable source of information for the U.S. defense establishment. An illustration of the usefulness of getting one's hands on the weapons of an adversary is the case of the Mig 25 flown to Japan by a defecting Soviet pilot. While this was thus not the result of an arms transfer, it exemplifies how close examination of an adversary's weapons can allow guesses and estimates of capabilities to be greatly refined and can provide detailed technological knowlege of an adversary's weapons.

Assessment: It will be very difficult for a supplier to guarantee the secrecy of any weapon transferred abroad. However, in most cases a concern for the security of transferred weapons technology is irrelevant. Often the general characteristics and capabilities of exported weapons can be found in advertisements and articles in such trade journals as *International Defense Review, Interavia*, and *Aviation Week and Space Technology*. Tremendous amounts of information about American weapons can be found in Congressional hearings. The British and French governments compile catalogues of the arms produced in their countries in order to encourage export sales. In addition to the fact that information about many weapons is generally available, there is the consideration that most weapons transferred are familiar types whose capabilities are widely known. In short, there are few secrets to be kept, and those weapons for which secrecy is a major concern are not likely to be exported.

Thus, the technological cost of transferring arms is probably the source of much more concern to a country which desires and is able to achieve a high level of secrecy about its weapons programs (such as the Soviet Union) than to a country whose arms industry relies upon exports (like Britain or France). For example, the Soviet Union often withholds its most advanced weaponry even from its allies in the Warsaw Pact. From an American perspective the major source of concern would be that the Soviet Union could upgrade its own weapons technology as a result of exposure to technologically superior American weapons.

Economic Costs

1. Arms Industry May Become Dependent on External Markets: The arms industry in every supplier country, except for the two superpowers, must export to survive because internal markets are not large enough to sustain them. This basic economic fact has two important implications. First, it means that the arms export market is extremely competitive. Medium powers such as Britain, France, West Germany and Italy—as well as smaller countries such as Israel—pursue aggressive government-supported campaigns to export arms. Their campaigns are related in part, of course, to the economic benefits of arms exports, but also to the necessity to be aggressive if their arms industries are to survive in an intensely competitive world market. With some twenty states plus the superpowers now significant in the world arms trade, this factor has undoubtedly contributed impetus to the diffusion of conventional arms throughout the globe.

A second implication of this situation is that it bodes ill for attempts to control conventional arms transfers. Unilateral gestures of restraint have little meaning because alternative suppliers exist; thus from an economic viewpoint, self-restraint in arms transfer policy is really self-sacrifice. On the other hand, the scope for multilateral arms control measures is severely constrained by the circumstance that so many of the suppliers transfer arms not so much as a consequence of policy choice but out of economic necessity. Attempts to control the supply of arms available on the world market must inevitably run up against the fact that most suppliers cannot reduce their arms exports without significant economic, and hence political, costs.

Assessment: From the perspective of an individual supplier, this dimension of the arms transfer process represents a cost in two ways. First, to the extent that a supplier state simply must sell arms, regardless of circumstances, arms transfers cease to be an instrument of foreign policy. It is for this reason that the economic benefits of arms transfers are more important than the polical and military benefits to non-superpower suppliers. Israel, for example, feels the need—for obvious reasons—to maintain an indigenous arms industry whose economic viability depends upon exports. Israel must thus sell to all who are willing to buy, including such outcasts in the international community as South Africa and Chile. In sum, the greater the economic compulsion to sell arms, the less utility arms have as a tool of foreign policy because there is little room for political choice based upon calculations of political self-interest.

Even the United States has not remained immune from this syndrome. The health of the U.S. arms industry is also, to a certain extent, dependent on exports. For example, the *Business Week* [44] survey of prospects for the U.S. aerospace industry in 1976 concluded: "The one bright spot in the 1976 outlook, aerospace companies state, is military sales overseas." Major production lines in large American firms rely largely on exports. This is true, for example, of the McDonnell Douglas

[83]

F-4 production line and of what has been called the "once doomed" Rockwell International CV-10 counterinsurgency aircraft. The economic compulsion to export arms exists even for the United States, despite its large domestic market for arms.

The second aspect of the cost to the supplier typifies the phenomenon of economic interdependence. When a state's arms industry is dependent on exports, it means that a major sector of the economy—often one of the largest foreign exchange earners and an important source of employment—is, in a sense, indirectly "controlled" by external forces. This dependency, of course, reduces both the autonomy of the supplier and the control it is able to exercise over its own economy. To the extent that economic interdependence is considered a problem, it may be reckoned a cost to suppliers, resulting from arms transfers.

Finally, from a global—rather than a national—perspective, the most serious cost deriving from the dependence of many states on arms exports is that it seriously reduces the possibility of effective arms control.

2. Arms Transfers Can Interfere with Economic Development: A common criticism of arms sales to Third World countries is that they sap the limited financial resources of the recipient that could better be spent furthering the economic development of that society. This was the rationale that President Kennedy used in limiting U.S. arms transfers to Latin America.

The economic cost to the recipient is clear; the cost to the supplier is more indirect. The argument is that because arms sales contribute to continued underdevelopment in the Third World, they contribute also to the antagonism between the industrialized states and the Third World, which causes political strife, higher commodities prices, etc.

Assessment: This argument is not a very persuasive one. Although there is no doubt that for the recipient, arms purchases may involve deferred economic development, most Third World states spend relatively small amounts on arms. Eliminating arms transfers will not have a sizable impact on the development process in the Third World, especially since most arms are imported by industrialized countries (such as NATO members) or the wealthier states located in the Third World (such as the oil-producing states, South Africa, Australia, etc.).

3. Clients May "Sell" the Arms: There is the possibility of economic loss deriving from arms transfers if the recipient enters the arms trade market offering a supplier's arms. The economic cost is thus a more competitive market and perhaps a reduced market share.

There are two aspects of this problem. First is the re-transfer of arms, whereby a recipient will simply resell arms it has bought or received as aid. Though many arms agreements prohibit this, in practice it is difficult to stop. Second, the more enterprising recipients may enter the market with weapons of their own which are essentially imitations of weapons they have bought elsewhere. The Israeli Kfir fighter aircraft, for example, is based largely on American technology.

Assessment: While this phenomenon contributes further to the complicated supply pattern that currently obtains, it is unlikely to have a major economic impact on the initial supplier.

[85]

4. Arms Transfers May Contribute to Higher Commodity Prices: Most Third World recipients pay for their imports of arms with exports of raw materials or energy. Thus, when reserves of foreign exchange grow low and threaten a weapons import program, the recipient may attempt to compensate by raising the price of its main exports. For example, it has been suggested that one of the reasons that the Shah of Iran was so committed to higher OPEC oil prices was his need to pay for the large quantities of sophisticated weapons he was buying.

Assessment: The impact of this argument is mitigated by two factors. One is that it is difficult to know whether (and what share of) commodity price increases are attributable to the need to pay for arms imports. The other is that for most commodities—with a few notable exceptions such as oil—prices are largely determined by market forces and there is consequently only a narrow range of latitude for action by an arms importer in need of funds.

The exception of oil, however, is not a small one, since the oil-exporting nations (and especially Iran and Saudi Arabia) have accounted for a large share of the arms trade over the last several years. But for most of these countries money is no limitation.

In conclusion, then, it seems that in the current international environment this argument has a limited application; generally it applies only to those oil exporters who have overstepped their financial bounds, i.e., Iran and possibly Iraq. To what extent arms are responsible for price rises is, however, impossible to know.

Conclusion

The foregoing discussion of the matrix of costs and benefits associated with the arms transfer process suggests the complex array of factors which confront the policy-maker. There is no simply way to judge the merit of either arms transfers in general or specific arms deals. Though advocates focus on the benefits of arms sales and opponents emphasize the costs, in fact every arms transaction involves trade-offs between costs and benefits, and the aim of effective policy is to ensure that, on balance, the benefits outweigh the costs. In some cases, such as American arms shipments to NATO allies, this balance is clear, though even here problems exist. But in many instances, particularly in the arms trade with less industrialized countries, the imperative to transfer is much less clear.

Arms transfers are thus a difficult foreign policy issue. To view them simply from an arms control perspective is to miss their enormous potency as an instrument of foreign, military and economic policy. However, it is important to keep in mind several aspects of the cost-benefit matrix which more fully convey the nuances of that calculation and which are only implied in a listing of costs and benefits. It is necessary to (a) differentiate among suppliers; (b) establish the time-frame involved; (c) be aware of the costs of *not* transferring arms; and (d) distinguish between arms control and conflict limitation.

Supplier Subjectivity

No one formula for calculating the cost-benefit trade-offs associated with arms transfer will apply to all the many arms

[87]

suppliers involved in the world arms trade today. Rather, each supplier will determine, from its own, unique perspective, which costs and benefits are relevant to its own policy considerations. These "subjective" definitions of the cost-benefit matrix are enormously varied, shaped by such factors as the size of the supplier, its geographic location, its internal political configuration, its national security requirements, its foreign policy objectives, the size of its arms industry and its economic circumstances. Thus, the costs and benefits discussed above are a composite list of considerations which may be factors in any one arms deal but which are not all uniformly relevant for all suppliers or all arms transfers.

For example, small and medium powers which supply arms are less concerned about the political benefits of arms transfers than the economic; countries like Belgium or Sweden cannot expect to gain a great deal of leverage or influence from their arms sales, though they do earn foreign currency and may gain access to important resources. In terms of the moral costs of arms transfers, repressive regimes are unlikely to be concerned about transferring arms to other repressive regimes, whereas for a democratic supplier this may be a source of genuine concern and domestic opposition to arms transfers.

Occasionally, states will draw precisely opposite conclusions about certain costs and benefits of arms transfers. Thus in the United States the fact that arms transfers may contribute to conflict is counted as a serious drawback, and this fear has contributed to Congressional opposition to growing U.S. arms exports. On the other hand, the Soviet Union has profited handsomely from conflicts in Southeast Asia, the Middle East and Southern Africa in which their arms figured prominently. Since it tends to benefit from conflicts in the Third World, it seems reasonable to conclude that the U.S.S.R. uses its arms to encourage such conflicts, as it is now doing by supplying the Rhodesian guerrillas.

In sum, it is necessary to differentiate among suppliers and to identify those costs and benefits which are of consequence in any particular arms trade relationship.

The Time-Frame Problem

The costs and benefits of arms transfers do not all operate in the same time-frame. This dimension of the arms transfer phenomenon is a crucial determinant of the relative weight of the elements of the cost-benefit matrix. The dynamism of the world arms trade is largely explained by the fact that many of the benefits from this trade—base rights, intelligence-gathering facilities, resources, jobs, foreign exchange, etc.—are immediate (that is, meaningful in the short time-frame that is the purview of the policy-makers), tangible and predictable, whereas many of the costs—sociological change, loss of prestige, loss of weapons, deferred economic development, etc.— are longer-term, more indirect, and rather unpredictable dangers. The policy-making process almost invariably prefers the short term and the predictable to the long term and the more indefinite. The problem is, of course, that over the long run it may be the latter which are of more consequence. For example, the West needs oil and the Saudi Arabians want arms; they are likely to get all the arms they want so long as the West is dependent on imported oil. But in the long run the greatest impact of arms sales on Saudi Arabia may be sociological, the impact of making the transition from camels to Mach 2 aircraft. Will this imposition of extremely sophisticated technology on a very traditional society lead to domestic

[89]

instability, violence, revolution? It could have this effect, but there is no way to know and thus no way to factor such considerations into the policy-making process in a meaningful way.

It is in economic matters that the contrast between the immediacy of the reward and the vagueness of the cost is greatest. Arms exports have four rather compelling short-term benefits: foreign exchange earnings, jobs, reduced unit costs on domestic weapons procurement, and access to scarce resources. The economic costs of such sales are much more nebulous in nature; for most suppliers an unavoidable dependence on external markets, the possibility that economic development may be deferred in the Third World, the chance that a client might re-transfer arms, the fear that arms sales may necessitate increased commodity prices. Three of the four benefits are certainties; the costs are generally only possibilities.

Thus, the time-frame is an important factor in evaluating the cost-benefit matrix, with greater weight being given in the political process to those effects which are short term and less to those which are longer term. Short-sightedness with regard to the latter, however, may lead to serious consequences over the long run.

The Impact of Decisions Not to Transfer Arms

Implicit in the discussion above is the fact that a decision not to transfer arms to a potential recipient is not simply a neutral decision to do nothing. Rather, such a decision is the inverse of a decision that cannot be ignored in evaluating the process. These costs and benefits are often simply the reverse of those which derive from actually transferring arms.

[90]

What is important—though impossible to determine in any quantifiable way—are the relative costs and benefits of transferring as opposed to not transferring arms. Thus, although there are obvious costs associated with being an arms supplier, if the costs of failing to transfer arms are greater, the imperative to transfer arms will be great.

For example, the political costs of a decision not to transfer arms may be very high. Such a decision would seem to be an expression of poor relations between two states or the deterioration of a previously friendly relationship. Failure to transfer arms may deprive a possible supplier of an instrument of influence or even leverage vis-à-vis the recipient state or region, and, conversely, may allow one's political adversary to establish and utilize such an instrument. This latter point, manifest in the U.S.-Soviet context, is especially important because the implementation, or "back end" aspect, of the transfer of sophisticated arms often necessitates a long-term relationship (involving training and infrastructure) that is not easily broken. Similarly, in economic terms, a decision not to transfer arms may simply allow one's competitors to penetrate the potential market and reap the balance-of-payments, employment and other economic advantages. Indeed, if a state's domestic arms industry is dependent on external markets, the economic costs of passing up possible arms deals would be enormous.

Militarily, while decisions to transfer arms often result in local arms races, failure to transfer them may lead to a regional military inbalance that could be more dangerous as a potential source of conflict than mutual arms build-ups. Stability may be related more to a balance than to the absolute level of arms. Thus, Europe has been relatively stable though heavily armed. In the Middle East, the consequences of Israeli military weakness would be dangerous. Another dimension is that decisions not to transfer arms can have enormous military impact on ongoing conflicts. The most famous historical example is the effect of American, British and French neutrality in the Spanish Civil War. Whereas Franco was receiving arms from the European fascist powers, only the Soviet Union made an effort to supply the Loyalist faction, which was soon outmatched by Franco's heavily armed forces. Thus, American neutrality was anything but neutral in effect, for it expedited the fascist victory in Spain. More recently, the decision of the American Congress to prevent American arms shipments to Angola had a decisive impact on the outcome of that Civil War.

In short, an arms transfer decision cannot be made simply on the basis of calculations of the costs and benefits of doing so. The costs and benefits of failing to transfer arms are also important determinants of the decision. From a policy standpoint this means arms transfer decisions are hard ones to make because doing nothing has as many political, military and economic implications as doing something; the policy-maker cannot avoid hard decisions simply by ignoring them.

Arms Control vs. Conflict Limitation

Many who are interested in the arms transfer phenomenon consider efforts to control the spread of conventional arms to be the heart of the matter; great emphasis is placed on the danger of conflict as a consequence of arms transfers and on the need to minimize this danger through conventional arms control. But in fact, the arms transfer process is not amenable to any simple arms control measures for three basic reasons.

First, demand plays an important role in determining the international arms trade. Whether for purposes of prestige, security or aggression, nations want to buy arms. And so long as there exists a market for arms, there will be those who are willing to supply them. The implication of this is that meaningful conventional arms control may have to focus as much— if not more—on the demand side as on the supplier side of the market.

Second, there are compelling reasons—economic, political and military—for a nation to export arms if it has the opportunity to do so. Any attempt to control the arms trade must come to grips with the fact that transfers can be an important and powerful instrument of policy, one which most nations will be unwilling to sacrifice for the sake of arms control.

Finally, there is the fact that the objective of arms control— that is, the limitation of conflict—is on occasion best served by transferring arms. For example, President Bhutto of Pakistan in commenting on the U.S. arms embargo to India and Pakistan said that "the U.S. military embargo has not contributed to stability in South Asia." Bhutto also related his country's attitude toward nuclear weapons to the supply of conventional arms available to it, noting that if the disparity in conventional forces between India and Pakistan became too great, Pakistan "may be forced into a military-nuclear program if its back is to the wall." [45] Thus while the tenets of arms control urge a reduction in global shipments of weapons, in this case withholding arms resulted in both regional instability and the increased likelihood of nuclear proliferation. To take another example, any settlement in the Middle East is bound to include enormous supplies of arms to Israel to compensate it for the much less defensible borders it will have if it withdraws from part or all of the occupied territories. In short, arms may be a necessary ingredient for the political settlement of disputes.

An examination of the cost-benefit matrix has shown that the calculus of arms transfer decision-making is sensitive to a number of variables, including who the supplier and recipient are, the region involved, the economy of the supplier state, etc. Consequently, it is difficult for a general approach to arms transfer policy to encompass the variety of regional settings and local issues which are relevant to each individual arms deal.

Accordingly, overall guidelines for arms transfer policy—such as those announced by President Carter in May of 1977—provide relatively limited guidance to the policy-maker attempting to make a specific arms transfer decision. Ultimately, such decisions are likely to be made on a case-by-case basis in the context of kind of cost-benefit trade-offs discussed above.

NOTES

1. Robert Ferrell, *American Diplomacy* (New York: W.W. Norton and Co., 1969), p. 34.

2. See *ibid,* pp. 272, 283-86.

3. Charles Tansill, *America Goes to War* (Boston: Little, Brown and Co., 1938), pp. 32, 53.

4. League of Nations, *Statistical Yearbook of the Trade in Arms and Munitions, 1926* (Geneva, 1926), p. 90.

5. Tansill, *op. cit.,* pp. 62-63.

6. See Mansford Jonas, *Isolationism in America, 1935-1941* (New York: Cornell University Press, 1966), pp. 136-69, on the "devil theory of war.

7. For representative examples of this literature, see H.C. Engelbrecht and F.C. Hanighen, *Merchants of Death: A Study of-the*

International Armaments Industry (New York: Dodd Mead and Co., 1934); George Seldes, *Iron, Blood and Profits: An Exposure of the World-Wide Munitions Racket* (New York: Harper and Brothers, 1934); Seymour Waldman, *Death and Profits* (New York: Brewer, Warren and Putnam, 1932); Fenner Brockway, *The Bloody Traffic* (London: Victor Gollancz Ltd., 1933); and Otto Lehmann-Russbuldt, *War for Profits* (New York: Alfred King and Co., 1930).

8.   Senate Munitions Investigating Committee, *Report No. 944,* part 3, p. 17.

9.   *Ibid,* part 5, pp. 1-5.

10.   On the Neutrality Act of 1939, see William L. Langer and S. Everett Gleason, *The Challenge to Isolation, 1937-1940* (New York: Harper and Brothers, 1952), pp. 218-35.

11.   See the chapter on the destroyer deal in *ibid.,* pp. 742-76.

12.   See Charles Tansill, *Back Door to War: The Roosevelt Foreign Policy, 1933-1941* (Chicago: Henry Regnery Co., 1952), pp. 595-99.

13.   See Edward R. Stettinius Jr., *Lend-Lease: Weapon for Victory* (New York: The Macmillan Co., 1944).

14.   According to Richard Leopold in *The Growth of American Foreign Policy* (New York: Knopf, 1962), p. 649, the United States spent $50.6 billion on lend-lease aid during World War II.

15.   Ruth Leger Sivard, *World Military and Social Expenditures, 1977* (New York: Institute for World Order, 1977), p. 9. (Hereafter cited as Sivard, *Expenditures.)*

16.   U.S. Depatment of State, Bureau of Public Affairs, *U.S. Conventional Arms Transfer Policy, November 1977.*

17. U.S. Arms Control and Disarmament Agency, *World Military Expenditures and Arms Transfers, 1963-1972*, p. 72.

18. ACDA, *World Military Expenditures and Arms Transfers, 1966-1975*, p. 56.

19. Sivard, *Expenditures 1976*, p. 8.

20. International Institute for Strategic Studies, *The Military Balance 1974-1975* (London, 1974).

21. See Stockholm International Peace Research Institute, *SIPRI Register of the Arms Trade, 1950-1973*. (Hereafter cited as *SIPRI Register.)*

22. See Sivard, *Expenditures 1976*, p. 8.

23. *SIPRI Register*, p. 153.

24. *SIPRI Register*, p. 169.

25. Sivard, *Expenditures 1977*, p. 9.

26. See Department of Defense, *Foreign Military Sales and Military Assistance Facts*, November 1975. (Hereafter cited as DoD, *FMS Facts.*)

27. "Arms Peddling," *National Review*, October 2, 1976, p. 8.

28. Stockholm International Peace Research Institute, *World Armaments and Disarmament, SIPRI Yearbook 1974* (Stockholm: Almqvist & Wiksell, 1974), p. 131.

29. *Ibid*, p. 143.

30. ACDA, *World Military Expenditures 1963-1972*, pp. 2, 14.

31.   Sivard, *Expenditures 1976*, p. 6.

32.   *SIPRI Yearbook 1974*, p. 127.

33.   ACDA, *World Military Expenditures 1963-1972*, p. 1; and *ibid., 1966-1975*, p. 14.

34.   DoD, *FMS Facts*.

35.   *Ibid.*

36.   *SIPRI Yearbook 1974*, p. 147.

37.   See, for example, "East Africa: Arms Race," *Africa No. 48*, August 1975, "Uganda: Arms Build-up", *Africa No. 45*, May 1975.

38.   ACDA, *World Military Expenditures 1963-1972*.

39.   See, for example, "Soviet Foreign Aid in '76 Pushed Sales of Arms, CIA Says," *Wall Street Journal,* October 13, 1977.

40.   DoD, *FMS Facts,* p. 14.

41.   July 27, 1975.

42.   August 11, 1975.

43.   September 28, 1964, p. 60.

44.   January 12, 1976, pp. 27 and 28.

45.   Quoted in Zalmay Khalizad "Pakistan's Nuclear Program," *Asian Survey,* July 1976, p. 591.

[TWO]

Arms Control in the Persian Gulf

Robert E. Hunter

For several years, interest in the growing worldwide traffic in conventional arms has centered on the region of the Persian Gulf, There, orders for American arms have increased radically in recent years.

Raw figures of course tell only part of the story: in themselves they say little about the types and purposes of weaponry, or about their military or political effects. Available data themselves are often imprecise; and order figures reveal little about the pace of arms deliveries. Yet the very shift in the magnitude of the arms trade, however unclear a picture is presented by available figures, indicates a radical departure from the past, and raises a series of issues to be analyzed and resolved.

These concerns are particularly important for the United States. We have a growing direct stake in Persian Gulf oil, and continue to have a vital interest in guaranteed access to oil

TABLE 1

U.S. Foreign Military Sales Act Agreements
(and, in parentheses, Commercial Deliveries)
(In millions of dollars)

Fiscal Years	Iran	Saudi Arabia	Kuwait
1967	144 (2)	124 (34)	— —
1971	386 (27)	16 (8)	(.2)
1972	520 (37)	331 (6)	— —
1973	2,167 (19)	688 (6)	0.05
1974	4,157 (35)	2,017 (18)	31 (.1)
1975	2,495 (49)	1,977 (20)	378 (.2)
1976	1,688 (107)	5,807 (100)	222 (12)
1977	5,803 (122)	1,805 (40)	28 (.2)

Source: Department of Defense, Security Assistance Agency, *Foreign Military Sales and Military Assistance Facts,* December 1977.

supplies for a number of other countries, many of which are almost totally dependent on the Gulf for oil supplies. Increasingly, too, the ability of Western industrial countries to manage the world's market economies is affected by what happens in the Persian Gulf region and by the role that local countries play in the global economy. We are also concerned about the role that one or more Gulf states play in the Arab-Israeli conflict; and we have a continuing need to limit the Soviet position in the area. Each of these objectives is important; and the purpose of this chapter is to analyze the relationship between supplying arms to the Gulf region and the securing of U.S. interests and objectives in the region.

At the same time, the United States is far and away the largest supplier of arms to the Gulf region, with orders in fiscal year 1977 of $7.6 billion, along with several hundred million dollars in commercial sales deliveries. This volume of Foreign

Military Sales and commercial deliveries, far greater than the sales to the Gulf of all other suppliers combined, means that we have the most important influence on the pattern of arms supply, from the standpoint of the sellers, and the major share of the responsibility for understanding and reacting to its implications.

Furthermore, the rapid escalation of our arms sales to the Gulf states reflects a significant shift in U.S. foreign and military policy. At one level, our new role as arms merchant to the Gulf states has been a simple response to market demand and to economic pressures we ourselves are feeling—pressures that appropriately enough emanate in part from some of the same countries that are now providing such a lucrative market for arms. At another level, this escalation in our arms sales has been a direct response to the widely perceived emergence after 1971 of what is termed a "power vacuum" in the region, while direct U.S. dependence on Persian Gulf oil and hence stability went up, although this perception bears careful inspection. And at a third level, our expanded role as arms merchant has been part of a new approach to broader issues of security, deriving from our Vietnam experience, the Nixon Doctrine and its refinements, and concern in some quarters about a perceived shift of military power and influence, in many parts of the world, toward the Soviet Union. As a result, it is important to look at all U.S. objectives in the Persian Gulf region and to balance one against another where they are in conflict. And we will need to judge whether, and where, experience in the Gulf with arms sales could have application elsewhere. In the process, it is important to judge the arms trade in terms of its particular impact on each country and region. From our perspective, that means whether the sale of arms—by level, types and purchaser—will enhance or retard the securing of our interests and objectives.

Gulf Security

For a century and a half, the defense and political stability of
the Persian Gulf region depended largely upon the presence of
Great Britain, which was initially concerned both to balance
Russian influence in Persia and to secure the route to India.
The latter concern was greatly reduced upon India's and
Pakistan's independence in 1947, although the Gulf remained
a staging area for an "East of Suez" policy focused farther
eastward; while the former concern continued through two
world wars, with joint occupation of Persia (with Russia) in
the first, and a shared involvement with the United States in
the second. For a time in the 1950s, Iraq gained an added value
for Britain, as its last major foothold in the Middle East; and
Britain joined with the United States in the abortive Baghdad
Pact, which evolved into the Central Treaty Organization
directed against the Soviet Union. The states along the Gulf
littoral gained direct importance for Britain for the first time
with the sizable build-up in the development of oil resources in
the 1950s, and Britain went so far as to intervene in Kuwait in
1961, to forestall action by Iraq. Yet by 1968 Britain decided
that the economic burden of its presence in the region was not
justified by its value, either locally or in relation to interests
farther East. After seeking to create a Union of Arab Emirates, Britain completed its withdrawal from all of the Gulf but
Oman in 1971.

During the postwar years, the United States had deferred to
British predominance in the Gulf, although it did develop close
ties with Iran (including military support), and Saudi Arabia
(principally in support of ARAMCO, the emerging giant of
the global oil industry). And from 1958 onwards, the United

States maintained a fledgling Middle East Force based at Bahrain, although it was little more than symbolic of some U.S. interest in the region.

With Britain's decision to withdraw its direct military presence from the Gulf and reduce its political role, the United States briefly considered whether to try replacing Britain, but decided against doing so. At the political level, it rapidly became clear that no other outside power could hope to duplicate the web of relations which Britain had built up over a century and a half—relations which were the most important basis of its presence. And at the military level, there was both resistance by all the local states to an outside replacement for Britain, and a U.S. assessment that an augmented military or naval presence was not truly vital for Gulf security, not likely to contribute substantially to it, and not likely to be popular at home in the waning years of the Vietnam War. The United States thus elected to retain the Middle East Force and continue a limited amount of arms aid and sales to selected countries in the region.

In adopting this approach, the United States was implicitly questioning the concept that the withdrawal of British power would inevitably leave a "vacuum" that would have to be "filled" by some other outside power—at least in military terms—to forestall the entry of the Soviet Union. While a rise in Soviet oil imports in the 1980s could bring it into the Gulf in a significant way, it is doubtful that it could or would seek to secure its *economic* objectives through *military* pressure—or that any form of Soviet involvement in Gulf oil could be contained by a military response in the region. To be sure, local states have built up their forces in part, as in Iran, by citing a potential Soviet threat. Yet local forces could not hope to forestall Soviet aggression, even by local build-up; there is a widespread view that direct military entry by the Soviet Union is unlikely.

Following the British decision to withdraw from the Gulf, Iran began increasing its defense program, clearly with an eye to becoming the dominant military and naval power in the region; and it was soon followed in arms build-up by other Gulf states.

TABLE 2

Military Budgets of Persian Gulf States
(In millions of dollars)

Years	Iran	Iraq	Saudi Arabia	Kuwait	United Arab Emirates
1966	436	258	150	40	––
1970	1,160	471	256	88	––
1971	1,620	510	340	107	––
1972	2,140	506	406	115	19
1973	2,700	713	640	134	29
1974	5,970	2,990	1,150	143	41
1975	7,760	1,850	1,750	235	59

Source: Arms Control and Disarmament Agency, *World Military Expenditures and Arms Transfers, 1966-1975.*

In this build-up, a number of factors have been at play, not all of which are limited to the region itself. It is worth looking at each country in turn. The situation in Iran is most complex. In addition to Iran's historic preoccupation with the Soviet Union wherein, however, Iranian military forces could do more than raise the price of Soviet invasion, it has a wide compass of other interests and concerns. These include differences with Iraq, which could reassert themselves despite the 1975 agreement on the Shatt-al-Arab; potential rivalry with other Arab states, and a desire to hedge against events in the

[103]

Arab-Israeli conflict; concern with freedom of passage through the Strait of Hormuz (related to the insurgency in Dhofar Province); wariness about events in West Asia, from Afghanistan through Baluchistan to India; and a view of Iranian interests and concerns extending into the Indian Ocean, itself. The rising price of oil and Iran's economic development goals have also merged in a set of policies that include having sizable military and naval forces.

For Iraq, meanwhile, arms policies reflect a wide variety of concerns, and have an historical dimension in Iraq's once very close association. (alone of the Gulf states) with the Soviet Union, plus its efforts to counter President Nasser's ambitions in the Arab world. Iraq also continues to be concerned with Iran; plays a role in the Arab-Israeli conflict (though not as a "direct confrontation" power); has traditional claims over Kuwait and a concern with guaranteed access to the Gulf; and sustains its rivalries, both with Syria and with "traditionalist" regimes in neighboring Arab states.

Saudi Arabia, which forms the third corner of the basic Gulf triangle, has had more limited political and military ambitions in the region. Indeed, the influx of military purchases has been more concentrated on basic infrastructure—for economic development rather than military purposes—than is true in either Iran or Iraq. Yet Saudi interests, especially in the stability of the region, are not negligible; nor are its differences with its neighbors, large and small, entirely resolved. Indeed, a key element of the Gulf conundrum lies in Saudi reactions to the arms build-up in Iran, in particular; and there is the further question of the role that arms will play in Saudi Arabia's key interest in the Arab-Israeli conflict.

Finally, in the other Arab states of the region military build-up has been related to the rising price of oil, efforts at nation-building, and the growth of Iranian military power—although the first two factors have so far probably predominated over the last in explaining the rise in military budgets.

From the point of view of regional developments, or even our own interests, there is nothing *inherently* wrong with this increase in arms purchases and military build-up. By the same token, there is also little significant military threat to Gulf security from outside the region that could become serious in the foreseeable future, and which thus would require a major military build-up by local states. Indeed, even if the Soviet Union did move forces directly against one or another Gulf state (at high political cost in the rest of the region), such action would surely jeopardize the main Soviet interest in relations with the United States. Nor is it clear that internal conflict in one or another Gulf state—which might lead to more than a temporary cut-off of oil supplies—would derive from causes that could be effectively countered by military build-up; possibly quite the opposite.

The most critical judgments about the value and risks of military build-up in the Persian Gulf therefore derive primarily from the possible course of events within the region itself. From the U.S. standpoint, we must be concerned whether the character and pace of military build-up will contribute to, or retard, the security of individual states and an overall "stability" in the region.

To judge this issue is not easy—and has proved to be difficult even in other parts of the world with a longer tradition of conflict and military deployments. Yet it is still possible to advance some criteria for judgment.

To begin with, there is the classic question about the relationship between arms build-up and either political or military conflict: does the former help produce the latter? Or must the potential for conflict already exist for the situation to be made worse by arms build-up?

Concerning the Persian Gulf, it is probably too early to answer that question with any precision. Yet political rivalries do exist in abundance, some of which have been presented above. How serious these will be in the future is subject to speculation, although since about 1974 there has been a general shift toward better relations among local states. There was the agreement between Iraq and Iran in March 1975; an agreement on the Neutral Zone by Iraq and Saudi Arabia; resolution of some differences between Saudi Arabia and the Gulf Emirates; general support for Iran's military role against the Dhofar rebellion in Oman; and wide-ranging diplomacy among local states. Iran has long since given up its claim to Bahrain; and has offset most of the opprobrium it earned with its Gulf neighbors in 1970 when it seized Abu Musa and the Tumbs. There also continues to be strong concern among all Gulf oil-producers to hold the OPEC cartel together, which has led to a muting of possible points of friction in other areas.

Yet in an area where the potential for suspicion is so high—or even for a degeneration of relations among various states into political conflict—a large-scale influx of arms must inevitably increase wariness, and cannot be discounted as a factor affecting the stability of the region.

Of course, the arms programs of the different Gulf states cannot be lumped together. Iran is far and away the leader in purchasing arms for combat; while the volume of arms sales to Saudi Arabia vastly overstates its capabilities, because of the preponderance of basic infrastructure over weaponry in its purchases. From 1950 to 1975, for example, 86% of arms transfers to Iran were for hardware; the comparable figure for Saudi Arabia was only 20%. Iraq does put more of its purchases into actual hardware; but it trails both of its principal neighbors in quantity of purchases. If anything, therefore, the question of arms sales to the Persian Gulf can be seen more than anything else as a question of Iran—and the potential reactions of its neighbors.

From the U.S. perspective, the ideal arrangement in the Persian Gulf could be Iranian military and naval hegemony as the "chosen instrument." Yet even if this were desirable its occurring is by no means clear. Some observers argue that the Arab neighboring states will acquiesce in a preponderance of Iranian military and naval power. But several factors argue against this optimistic view: these include the traditional rivalries; the lack of any real understanding on a division of regional political influence among the major Gulf states; a growing interest in military power as an aspect of nation-building and entry into international life; and lessons derived from experience in some other parts of the world.

Furthermore, even if unsettled questions of influence within the Persian Gulf did not themselves increase the likelihood of conflict at some time in the future, the nature and quantity of armaments being supplied to Gulf states pose risks that any political disagreements will more easily be militarized, and that incipient conflict will lead to open fighting, if only by accident.

As we have learned elsewhere, several elements must be present for arms and military forces to *increase* stability, rather than to *reduce* it. Where military conflict is possible, there must be an understood relating of the forces on each side to some notion of balance—both political and military, as is true both in Central Europe and even, to a lesser degree, in the Arab-Israeli conflict. More particularly, there must be an adequate assessment of, and response to, the requirements of preventing pre-emptive attack by one party or another, and of prosecuting conflict to a standstill should deterrence fail. And there must be command, control, and communications (C^3) procedures and facilities to reduce risks of accidental war, and to make efforts for deterrence or defense effective.

Alternatively (or in conjunction), there must be a basic understanding among local states of the problems of *mutual* security (and of the sharing of political influence related to it), along with tacit or agreed arrangements among the states within which potential imbalances in weapons and forces can be merged. Indeed, Gulf states like Kuwait and the Union of Arab Emirates cannot hope to gain real military security without some mutual security arrangements—formal or informal—either with several other states or based on dependence on a larger neighbor.

Neither approach—arms balance or mutual security—has yet been pursued in the Persian Gulf to the point of creating much confidence that in the future the level and character of arms and military forces will increase, rather than reduce, the security of local states. Little apparent effort has been made by any Gulf country to relate its military build-up to long-range problems of stability; command and control arrangements are generally poor; high-performance equipment like modern aircraft (which can be employed rapidly over relatively short distances between, say, Kuwait and its neighbors) makes matters more rather than less difficult; and there is limited Gulf interest in pursuing anything that could be called mutual security. Indeed, the Shah's limited attempt to broach this subject at a conference of Moslem leaders in 1975 went nowhere.

ARMS CONTROL IN THE GULF

From the foregoing analysis, it is clear that the United States shares an interest in seeking to relate the level of arms supplied to Persian Gulf states to some framework of "balance" or, preferably, of mutual security. Doing so is important in terms of securing our basic objective in stability in order to promote security of oil supplies and their extraction; and it must be related to other U.S. regional objectives, as well—including the nature of political and other relations with individual governments, and the risks that a *lack* of conventional arms control could impel one nation or another to seek nuclear weapons for its own security.

Furthermore, the United States must be acutely aware of the direct consequences for itself of conflict. With many tens of thousands of Americans in these countries—to service weapons or train local personnel—direct American casualties in conflict are a serious possibility, as well as a period of dilemma for U.S. attitudes toward conflict in which American civilians were being killed. Somewhat less troubling—but not insignificant—is that in the event of internal subversion or conflict these American civilians would become potential targets as the arms agents of established regimes. For the United States, therefore, arms control in the Gulf region is an instrument for reducing the risks to a variety of U.S. (and Western) interests. We must also seek a clear understanding about the relationship between major arms supply and another interest, the price of oil. Does the need for increased oil revenues to pay for arms actually increase the incentives of oil states to raise oil prices? The answer is not clearly "No."

What needs to be done? Any realistic approach to arms control in the Persian Gulf necessarily includes three steps: efforts with local states, attempts to foster regional security, and restraint on the part of arms sellers.

In considering efforts with local states, it is important first to understand that the U.S. interest at this point does *not* lie in a total end to arms sales to the Persian Gulf—even if we had no economic incentive to sell. Perhaps a relatively disarmed Gulf area might be best from the standpoint of our own assessments of threats to security, compared with the risks that an uncontrolled flow of arms would increase the chance of conflict. But it is already too late to gain a prohibition on high levels of arms, or on the introduction of the most modern weapons, at times rivaling the speed with which these weapons are introduced into the inventories of U.S. armed forces, themselves.

Furthermore, the question of national sovereignty cannot be ignored: like it or not, if nations want to buy arms (in the absence of agreement among all suppliers able to produce the desired arms), there will be willing sources of virtually anything short of nuclear weapons. Arms control must be firmly grounded in the Persian Gulf itself if there is to be any real hope that it will succeed. At the same time, it is self-defeating to ignore possibilities for arms control simply by reciting the slogan: "If we don't sell, others will."

Instead of seeking to end arms supply entirely, therefore, the U.S. approach at this point should be to work with each individual country, either directly or through countries like Britain that retain some influence. In the first instance, this effort should be directed toward defining the levels and types of forces and weapons the individual nation needs to attain its *security* objectives, and should proceed from there to consider psychological, sociological, political and economic factors. This is no panacea—especially if one country or another defines its objectives in terms that go far beyond security (e.g., national prestige) or relates arms policies to developments outside the Gulf region itself. The latter factor is particularly important in the case of Iran, with its broader concerns, and potentially in the cases of Saudi Arabia and Iraq, with their particular interests in the Arab-Israeli conflict and wider Arab politics. Nonetheless, this bilateral approach to arms control is a beginning.

The United States can also help each individual country to make assessments relating its objectives to those of other Gulf countries; to point out contradictions in military policies of different states; and to advise on the impact of arms and military forces on relations among them. Of course we should also make our own independent assessment of defense requirements and problems on both a national and a regional basis.

In this regard, the U.S. Senate was undoubtedly wise in 1976 in voting to phase out the Military Assistance Advisory Groups (and to reduce the numbers of military attachés). To be sure, in some cases these military representatives may have acted as a restraining influence (and military expertise will be needed in the diplomatic efforts suggested here). But on balance the presence of American military personnel, as a significant part of the U.S. "presence" in Gulf states, is likely to enhance an interest in military hardware that derives from considerations of prestige.

At the same time, this diplomatic effort with individual Gulf states should be melded into strong support for movement toward regional security by including other arms-selling countries, if possible. This is not a simple matter—especially when the question of the division of political influence among Gulf states has not been answered. Nor can the United States play the decisive role in making determinations of regional security. Yet, at least through 1978 we had not made a real attempt to foster cooperative action by local states, or even committed ourselves to the long process of gaining some real form of arms control in the Gulf. (There is no public evidence, for example, that we supported the Shah's fledgling initiative on this subject in 1975.) The search for regional understanding of the relationship between arms and factors of security and other interests may take many years. It may include many setbacks, even in defining relative levels of arms and types of weaponry for each country; arms control may fail despite our best efforts and those of the Gulf countries; and in the meantime there may even be open military conflict. But none of these doubts is a real or valid excuse for not making a sustained effort to increase understanding in the Gulf area about potential problems posed by a wide-open arms trade, and to urge regional diplomacy in this direction. However little chance this approach has of succeeding, the alternative—continuing a high level of sales with virtually no controls and including high-performance modern weapons—still raises the possibility that events in the region will unfold in ways that will seriously jeopardize our interests there.

THE ROLE OF INFLUENCE

U.S. policy toward arms sales that has placed a high value on local decision about purchases, and a low value on arms control diplomacy, has often been justified in terms of a desire to secure "influence" with individual governments. Of course, "influence" is one of the most difficult concepts in foreign relations to understand: the impact of one nation on the attitudes and policies of another. It is rarely easy to define influence in concrete terms, even though almost everyone talks about influence as a "good," to be pursued through a variety of means.

Maintaining or increasing influence with Persian Gulf states is often cited as an objective of U.S. arms sales policies. Yet influence to achieve what goals, or to forestall what attitudes or policies that might work against U.S. interests? And if having this influence is judged to be important, are there no other ways of securing it?

With regard to the Arab states of the region—and particularly Saudi Arabia—there are essentially five goals that could be sought through our maintaining or promoting beneficial relations: a constructive role in the search for Arab-Israeli peace; an assured supply of oil at reasonable prices; a barrier to Soviet involvement (direct or indirect); stable regimes; and a constructive role in the management of the global economy.

On only two of these goals—resolving the Arab-Israeli conflict and the stability of regimes—does the supply of arms logically make a significant difference, even though an individual government may seek to cast its relations with outside states in terms of arms supplies, as part of the granting of "influence." With regard to the Arab-Israeli conflict, Saudi Arabia and Iraq (which is not eligible to buy U.S. arms) may wish to secure arms in order to be seen as able to play some direct role in a future conflict with Israel. Yet even where, in the Saudi case, supplying arms is seen as part of a broader policy of seeking support for peace efforts, it is precisely this factor of playing a role that raises doubts about an open-ended arms supply relationship, for it includes the risk that arms will be transferred to an Arab confrontation power during a crisis. In the heat of the moment, even requirements of State Department approval for third-country transfers are unlikely to be effective. Would the potential threat to the future of the supply relationship suffice to produce restraint? This proposition has yet to be tested; but in view of past U.S. experience with countries like Turkey (or even Soviet experience with Egypt), there is reason to be skeptical about the whole notion that supplying arms confers a measure of control over their use. The weakness of this argument is similar to that in the oft-stated view that an arms-supplier relationship would permit us to cut off spare parts to a recipient nation, and thus bring local conflict to a halt: that, too, is a dubious proposition.

With regard to the stability of regimes, it is also important for the United States to judge the impact that supplying arms would have, not just on immediate concerns with influence, but also on the evolution of societies like those of Saudi Arabia and its neighboring states. Does a strong Saudi Arabian National Guard, for example, help promote the stability of the current regime, with beneficial effects on policies (as in oil)? Or will it help promote those social changes that could hasten a direct threat to the regime—with a successor regime looking unfavorably upon the nations which supplied arms for the old regime? Less important, but not inconsequential, the United States must judge whether diverting resources from economic development to arms purchase will itself increase the threat to the stability of regimes—bearing in mind that, in such cases as Saudi Arabia, a large portion of "arms" purchases go to true economic development purposes by providing infrastructure.

Whatever the relationship of arms to influence in the two areas just discussed, we must be very skeptical in believing that supplying arms would affect the positions of Arab states on the Persian Gulf on the Soviet Union, on oil, or on the global economy. With regard to the first, attitudes toward communism and the Russians are unlikely to be affected by U.S. efforts to limit the flow of arms—especially since there is no question of a total embargo of arms to the Gulf states that could create temptations of an abrupt shift toward the Soviet Union. The case of Iraq helps make the point. It is a nation which buys no U.S. arms, but which since 1975 has moved significantly away from the Soviet Union.

The behavior of Arab states with regard to oil and the global economy can only have an indirect link to American arms sales policy, in terms of the way relations and expectations are permitted to evolve. Here, Saudi Arabia, at least, has far broader interests, including its own stake in the functioning of the global economy and its desire to be seen as a responsible, participating nation in important economic councils. Even Riyadh's desire to work through and with the United States in many areas is not *necessarily* dependent on the quality of the arms-supply relationship, beyond sales for economic development and essential security. Of course, our helping the states in the region to define "essential security" is a key factor.

The main point is that it is hard to believe that U.S. efforts to promote rational decisions with regard to arms purchases—in terms of local-country interests in Persian Gulf stability that have a strong, objective basis—would invalidate a wide sweep of other efforts that would genuinely demonstrate the good intentions of this country toward the Arab nations of the area. A number of Western efforts have already demonstrated the wisdom of this approach: in changing voting power in the International Monetary Fund; in the North-South Conference; and in the general approach of seeking to promote local economic development and greater involvement in the global economy.

With regard to Iran, it is even harder to understand the U.S. search for influence based partly on an arms-sales relationship. After all, Iran's attitudes toward the Soviet Union derive from centuries of experience, not from friendship with the United States. It is most unlikely that Iran would change these attitudes in ways that would damage our interests in the Persian Gulf, simply because we were seeking to promote a measure of arms control that would reduce risks of conflict within that region. Nor (as noted earlier) could Iran expect to defend itself against the Soviet Union, however many arms it buys, without support from the United States, based on our interest in Iran's independence. Thus, arming Iran against the Soviet Union would offer no real escape for the United States from difficult decisions in the unlikely event of Soviet aggression.

With regard to oil, the supposed U.S. influence with Iran has done nothing to benefit us, as Teheran's leadership in pressing for higher prices attests. Nor can we really say that Iran's willingness to supply Israel with oil offsets the role which Iran has played in pulling the OPEC cartel together and promoting price rises. It was Iran, after all, which used the October War in 1973 as the pretext for the massive price rises that took place in that period.

If there is any interest where the United States could benefit from influence with Iran, it is in relations with its neighbors. Yet this is precisely the area where an uncontrolled supply of arms creates problems. A principal means of seeking influence thus itself becomes a further source of difficulty. And, as in the case of Saudi Arabia, Iran's role in the global economy will derive far more from economic factors, and our attitudes on that specific issue than from any arms-supply relationship it has with us.

In sum, it remains difficult to believe that securing influence is a valid reason for our supplying high levels of arms—and without serious efforts at arms control—to the states of the Persian Gulf. Nor is there decisive evidence that vigorous efforts to promote arms control in the region would be incompatible with other efforts to secure political and economic influence with local governments for those purposes where having influence would genuinely be of benefit to us.

THE ROLE OF THE SUPPLIERS

If a policy of seeking arms control (as part of regional security) succeeds in the Persian Gulf, the role of the supplier states, including the Soviet Union, would be relatively insignificant. Where there was common agreement in the region about the level and types of arms that are admissible, then even high-pressure salesmanship would count for little, and the issue would be shifted to competition among outside suppliers for the available market.

Yet in the absence of that ideal solution, no supplier state can ignore the consequences of an open-ended supply of arms that could, indeed, lead to conflict and the stopping of the oil flow. The Soviet Union today clearly has least to lose; yet it is unclear that even it would escape severe consequences if the major center of Western interest were to be torn by conflict. For other arms-supplying states, there is a compelling interest in being involved in efforts to achieve arms control and regional security or, failing that, in assessing whether some limits should be imposed collectively upon at least the type of weapons sold in the Persian Gulf. Short-term considerations like gaining preferential access to oil in exchange for arms is tolerable for any oil-importing nation only as long as these arms do not contribute to regional instability or conflict.

In the interests of Persian Gulf stability, therefore, the supplier states need a set of guidelines which could help promote arms control, while taking into account the complexities of the undertaking. These guidelines could address themselves to limits on highest-performance weaponry (especially advanced aircraft), the newest technology, the range and effectiveness of weaponry; to the aims of crisis management and control; the *pace* of deliveries; and the sheer volume of lethal weaponry itself.

Beyond these strictly military concerns, and possible remedies, the slogan looms: "If we don't sell arms, others will." In part it reflects a failure to analyze those factors that impel other countries to sell arms—in short, the economic benefits of arms sales. Any U.S. effort to work with other Western arms suppliers must therefore address quite directly the issue of economic benefit. For some supplier states (including the United States), selling advanced weapons abroad is seen as important to lengthen production lines and thereby reduce unit costs to the selling nations' military forces. For the United States, the issue is straightforward: we must calculate the benefit to us of reducing unit costs against the potential costs (in money and lives) of possible future conflict in the Persian Gulf. These costs are possible injury to U.S. civilians living locally, the risks of our being drawn in, and the possibility of oil stoppage.

Except for the risk of oil stoppage, these factors do not impinge on calculations by other Western arms-supplier governments with the same force. Yet this fact itself is strong reason for us to relate our objective in Persian Gulf arms control to military-economic problems of countries like Britain, France, Germany, and Sweden. Nor can we limit these concerns solely to Gulf arms sales; it is small wonder, for example, that the "arms deal of the century" (F-16 sales in Europe) increased the incentives of the French government to sell its Mirage F-1 wherever possible. Thus the overall arms-sales problem will find resolution only if we are prepared to join with other arms sellers in a basic assessment of the relationship between domestic defense costs and the broader risks of failing to devise "rules of the game" for foreign arms sales. Similarly, we should consider sharing-arrangements for all arms markets (including those in the industrialized world), while moving forward on NATO production-sharing agreements.

Broader balance-of-payments considerations are also important. To be sure, compared with the size of total trade, foreign investment, and even the flow of petrodollars, arms sales are still a relatively minor element (and the amount of arms sales to Third World countries that should be *limited* in the interests of arms control and regional stability is even smaller). Yet for individual nations to be prepared to sacrifice lucrative arms sales, there must be a clear return in terms of other economic factors. In short, arms sales cannot be considered only on their own in Western discussions, but properly belong on the table along with other Western economic concerns, to be dealt with in common. Fledgling efforts at "economic summits" and at the OECD have not yet evolved to the extent that factors like arms sales can easily be related to the broader economic context; but this is nevertheless the direction in which we should be moving if we hope to gain real control over economic factors that impel major foreign arms sales.

Like the direct approach to Persian Gulf states both on an individual and regional basis, the effort to gain arms-sales restraint on the part of seller nations is also not guaranteed success. Yet here, too, the dramatic change in the level and character of arms sales to the developing world—plus the consequences of a failure to understand and act upon the potential impact of this trade on broader interests—argues strongly for a bold and committed effort. Having never really tried, we must not predict failure in advance; and even in failure, we could begin a process of awareness that could lead to success the next time.

In summary, therefore, gaining arms control in the Persian Gulf is of sufficient importance to the United States to warrant being a major element of policy toward that region. It is a policy with three elements: working with individual countries on questions of their own security, seeking to promote regional understanding of problems of balance and mutual security, and pursuing diplomatic and economic efforts with other arms supplier states. As by far the world's leading arms merchant, we have a special responsibility, but also a special opportunity to shape the flow of arms to the Persian Gulf and elsewhere in the developing world.

[THREE]

U.S. Arms Transfers, Diplomacy and Security In Latin America

David Ronfeldt
with Caesar Sereseres

INTRODUCTION

U.S. arms sales have become the most prominent, and perhaps the most important, instrument for conducting U.S. foreign policy on a bilateral basis. Meanwhile, U.S. officials charged with the management of weapons sales have become concerned about their apparent relation to the rise of war potential, human rights violations, and military dictatorships in the Latin American region. At the same time, military leaders in Latin America have proceeded to buy a new generation of prestigious, sophisticated weapons systems, including supersonic jet fighters from the United States, guided-missile frigates from Great Britain and Italy, submarines from West

Germany, and medium tanks from France and the Soviet Union.

What is the significance of Latin America as part of the overall "arms transfer problem"? There appears to be a significant discrepancy between the political controversy generated by the concern for arms transfers to the region, and the comparatively low level of Latin American arms acquisitions. Latin American countries have participated in the global surge of arms transfers, seeking moderately advanced weapons systems from U.S. and European suppliers. Yet by most quantitative indicators Latin America remains a relatively lightly armed region where military expenditures and acquisitions have grown rather slowly, compared to the developing world at large. The proportion of U.S. security assistance and sales has also remained relatively insignificant compared to other areas. For example, during the 1973-1975 period, Latin America represented 2 percent of the grant military assistance program, 2 percent of foreign military sale orders, 12 percent of foreign military sale credits, 4 percent of commercial sales, and received but 3 percent of grant excess defense articles from the inventories of the U.S. services. No single country seems to be excessively armed and the pace of acquisition does not seem at variance with historical development, obsolescence, and local capacities to absorb advanced technology. Arms races characterized by spiraling expenditures and swelling inventories do not exist between any two countries. Overall probabilities of regional border conflicts and arms races may be rising—but more slowly than in other areas of the world.

Statistics readily become poetry, however. The numbers that have been recited and updated for more than a decade of studies of rising arms transfers mean little by themselves. They provide political symbols, as well as factual bases, for discussing qualitative issues. These issues are represented as broadly in Latin America as in any other region. Thus Latin America, though a minor quantitative constituent of the global "arms transfer problem," holds nonetheless an equivalent place in which to consider possible qualitative explanations and resolutions. The major issues include assertions that the arms acquisitions and military development may increase the prospects for dangerous, costly arms races, for local border conflicts and possibly wars, and for the strengthening of military dictatorships that violate human rights. At the same time, U.S. interests in good working relations and access, and in the acquisition of some influence and leverage, are said to require that the United States engage in some open marketing and preemptive selling, given the likelihood that the clients may buy elsewhere, mainly from Western Europe but possibly from the Soviet Union. One purpose of this chapter is to discuss pros and cons behind such general assertions, and in particular to challenge the supposition that arms transfers lead to political influence and leverage.

Apart from those general considerations, a seemingly entrenched focus on Latin America *as a region* has given it a unique role in discussions about arms transfers. No other region—whether Africa, the Middle East, South Asia, or Southeast Asia—has been so subject to critical U.S. treatment and legislation *as a region*. Historically, the presumed homogeneity of nations and comparatively low threats to U.S. interests in Latin America have made it easy to generalize and skip exceptions and distinctions that are prominent elsewhere, as in Iran, South Korea, and the Philippines. Moreover, Latin America has often been viewed in the United States as the darker side of the New World, into which a little Northern light should shine. Thus anti-liberal developments in Latin America have tended to arouse moral outrage, commonly paternalistic, in ways that have often taken the form of congressional legisla-

[123]

tion. As a result of these processes, one of the special themes of U.S.-Latin American relations, particularly in regard to arms transfer issues, is that Latin America, because of its distinctive regional characteristics, has periodically become a "dumping ground" for restrictive and discriminatory U.S. legislation that expresses principles eroded more seriously elsewhere in the world—but too difficult to apply without compromise because of the Soviet threat or some other compelling U.S. national interest. This was partly the case during the 1960s and early 1970s, when restrictive U.S. policies toward arms transfers cost the United States political goodwill in Latin America without furthering the advance of liberal aspirations or curtailing the acquisition of modern military weapons. A second purpose of this chapter is to discuss this regional theme about the political costs of U.S. restrictions.

U.S. arms transfers to Latin America have been important more for their impact on political relations than for their contribution to U.S. defense. For the remainder of the 1970s, arms transfers will continue to be an important element of U.S.-Latin American relations. The prevalence of military-dominated governments will assure this. One potentially significant consideration for U.S. policy-makers is that within Latin America prestigious weapons have been more significant for their diplomatic symbolism than for their operational military capabilities in affecting relations between neighbors. In other words, arms transfers are diplomacy by other means. A third purpose of this chapter is to formulate this hypothesis.

We have learned to view the impact of arms transfers on U.S.-Latin American relations from an essentially political perspective. However, the tendency prevails to view the impact on intra-Latin American relations from a primarily military perspective. This latter perspective has been reinforced by the new concern for a rising war potential in some parts of

Latin America. Nonetheless, despite the great attention and controversy surrounding arms transfer issues, arms transfers seem to be of incidental importance to the main developmental struggles inside Latin America. Local military geopoliticians, the very thinkers who have most played up frontier-minded nationalism and potential threats from particular neighbors, have mainly emphasized the need for developing economic infrastructure and pursuing diplomatic initiatives in order to protect national security and sovereignty. A final purpose is to put arms transfers in perspective for the Latin American context by discussing these local geopolitical views.

THE TROUBLED HISTORY

The Latin America region has been dependent upon the industrialized world for the supply of military equipment.[1] Indeed, the evolution of Latin American acquisitions reveals considerable sensitivity to changes in the availability of weapons. Until World War II, arms were obtained primarily from European countries, in part because of U.S. limitations on the export of its weapons and munitions. However, World War II led the United States to seek military alliance with Latin America for hemispheric defense. As the U.S. government sought to maintain a predominant strategic position in the hemisphere, it also became the predominant supplier of most types of military equipment. Thus the availability after the war of a wide range of surplus weaponry from the United States (as well as Great Britain) enabled some Latin American countries to purchase their military equipment at relatively low cost, using the substantial foreign exchange reserves that had accumulated during the war. The United States also instituted policies that would gradually evolve into the Military

Assistance Program (MAP) in the early 1950s. Through MAP, U.S. government grants, and easy credit terms facilitated the transfer of numerous items, many reconditioned from U.S. military inventories, while U.S. doctrine, training, and advice gained predominance in the Latin American armed forces. Surplus Korean War stocks later provided a further source of inexpensive but reliable arms and military equipment from the United States.

The founding in 1942 of the Inter-American Defense Board for military consultation, followed by the Rio Pact in 1947, led to an atmosphere of alliance, supported by the U.S. Joint Chiefs of Staff. Hemispheric security "solidarity" was further strengthened by bilateral mutual defense pacts signed with most countries during the early 1950s. These pacts typically granted the United States a military advisory mission monopoly and thus symbolized *de facto* U.S. military predominance in the region. The emergence of the Soviet Union as arms provisioner to Cuba after the Bay of Pigs was the first significant challenge to what critics had by then come to call a new U.S. "imperial" order. In general, however, U.S. military predominance seemed to be securely established, until surprising reversals in the mid-1960s revealed the position to be more subject to challenge than had been believed.

Several elements were involved. From the beginning of MAP, the United States had tried to maintain some parity among neighboring nations and to keep the level of weapon sophistication very low, providing combat aircraft, ships, and tanks that were at best early 1950s, if not World War II vintage. There was in effect, a tacit, low-key U.S. policy of regional arms balancing and limitation. With the initiation of the "Decade of Development" at the beginning of the Kennedy era, U.S. dedication to the primacy of the economic development objective under the Alliance for Progress intro-

[126]

duced a new concern over Latin American "resource diversion" from development to defense. MAP policies were thus generally reoriented toward support for internal security, and further downplayed external defense except for anti-submarine warfare (ASW) exercises. Latin American inventories of World War II weapons were simultaneously becoming increasingly obsolete.

The underlying tension between declining U.S. responsiveness to requests for weapons for hemispheric defense and the growing obsolescence of major weapon systems held by Latin American countries was initially held in check by cost considerations and political uncertainties. While temporarily postponing military modernization programs, Latin American leaders hoped that the United States could ultimately be maneuvered into sharing some of the escalating costs of modern weapons in the name of military alliance, international anticommunism, and the Rio Pact. But by the mid-1960s, Latin American hopes came to an end that either MAP or the Foreign Military Sales (FMS) Program would provide bargain-basement shortcuts to military modernization.

The main issue was military fighter aircraft. Latin America's first-generation subsonic military jets were rapidly becoming more difficult and costly to maintain (as well as accident-prone) while the advanced military powers phased early models out of their own inventories. Several countries favored the F-5 Freedom Fighter as the replacement for their obsolescent tactical fighter squadrons. A light jet fighter that could break the sound barrier only if carrying minimal armament, the F-5 was developed, partially with MAP funds, by the Northrop Corporation especially for the less developed countries. But attempts to purchase the Freedom Fighter revealed that the U.S. capacity to support such acquisitions would be limited by both economic and political considerations.

[127]

More was involved this time than the general tradition of self-imposed restraint and arms limitation toward Latin America. Though the F-5 was but marginally supersonic, U.S. critics saw it as a prime example of wasteful military expenditures for unnecessarily sophisticated equipment at a time when generous U.S. grants and credits were being extended for economic development. In addition, in 1966 it was revealed that foreign countries with severe debt-service problems were receiving large U.S. credits for arms purchases under the "Country-X" revolving loan feature of the Military Assistance Credit Account which was linked to the Export-Import Bank.[2] Although this revelation only marginally involved Latin American countries, it aroused fierce Congressional reaction that contributed ultimately to substantial restrictions on the amount and terms of credit assistance available to Latin America for military imports.

When key Latin American countries turned to Western Europe for purchases of weapons denied them in the United States, U.S. reaction had profound consequences for economic as well as military assistance policies, and almost brought about Congressional rejection of the 1967 Foreign Assistance Act.[3] The train of events was set in motion by the sale of 50 subsonic A-4B Skyhawk light attack bombers to Argentina in 1965. Chile then sought to purchase the F-5 Freedom Fighter. The United States government, however, was determined to delay the crossing of the supersonic threshold, and informed Latin American governments in 1967 that the F-5 would not be available to the region until 1969. The United States offered instead to sell Chile the A-4B Skyhawk or the F-86 Sabre. Venezuela tacitly accepted the limits set in Washington and bought 74 surplus German-built F-86 Sabres. The angered Chileans, instead of purchasing subsonic U.S. fighters, turned to England for the FGA-9 Hawker Hunter. The readiness of a Latin American country under progressive civilian rule to turn to Europe after being refused a U.S. sale was a portent of things to come.

The modernization of Peru's air force brought the clash with U.S. policy into the open. In harmony with enunciated policy on the F-5 but also in the shadow of Peru's economic troubles and of the controversy over the status of the International Petroleum Company, the United States offered to sell Peru additional F-86s, despite repeated Peruvian expressions of interest in the F-5. Peru then turned to Britain for Canberra bombers (the sale of which was initially blocked by the United States, but finally consummated in 1968), and to France for the faster and more expensive supersonic Mirage 5, thus breeching the supersonic barrier in Latin America for the first time.

The U.S. reaction to the snubbing of its arms control efforts went from exhortation and threats, to a reduction of economic assistance to Peru, and finally to a succession of Congressional reductions and restrictions on military assistance and sales to Latin America. But the U.S. capability to control Latin American acquisitions was sharply limited by the presence of alternative suppliers from Western Europe, many of whom were riding a crest of European economic recovery and aggressive governmental support. More interested in fostering economic development than in being the exclusive arms supplier, U.S. policy had simply collided with the aspirations and sensitivities of increasingly independent Latin American governments which had more options available to them than those presented by the United States. Argentina, Brazil, Colombia, and Venezuela soon joined Peru in acquiring Mirages (the III and the 5 models) at a cost, for the five countries, approaching one quarter of a billion dollars.

By the late 1960s, the importance of suppliers other than the

[129]

United States grew in other areas as well. As in the past, Latin American navies turned to order new construction destroyers, submarines, and other vessels from Western European countries, while relying on the United States mainly for rehabilitated stocks. U.S. armored personnel carriers continued to be very popular, but the United States lacked the necessary tank inventories to be competitive in the Latin American market. Thus French AMX-30s and AMX-13s faced little competition and were ordered by Argentina, Ecuador, Peru, and Venezuela. The United States C-130 air transports were ordered by six countries, but most light transports were obtained from Canada and West European sources.

In the early 1970s, F-5E aircraft became available for cash sale, but the Latin American governments wanted FMS credit. Mainly for the purpose of regaining political goodwill among the Latin American militaries and governments, the Nixon administration authorized in 1973 the credit sale of F-5Es to various South American countries, by invoking a special provision of the Foreign Military Sales Act of 1968. This provision allowed the President, acting in the name of national security interests, to override the Congressional restriction against the sale of "sophisticated military systems" in Latin America. This act was combined with the raising of the statutory military credit ceiling from $100 to $150 million for FY 1973, followed by complete removal of the special regional credit ceiling for FY 1975.

These measures enabled the United States to enter part of the jet aircraft market. Brazil soon ordered 42 F-5Es on credit. Chile, whose government had previously ordered Hawker Hunters from Great Britain, in a deal that subsequently ran afoul of British protests against the harsh new Chilean regime, ordered 18 F-5Es in a cash sale. This was accompanied by additional sales of A-4s to Argentina and of A-37 light counterinsurgency aircraft to Chile, Guatemala, Peru, and Ecuador, while Ecuador also opted for Jaguars from Britain/France and Strikemasters from Britain.

By the mid-1970s local air forces were regretting their earlier decisions to procure Mirage fighters from France. The costs of spare parts and engine overhauls, the slow delivery of some spares, the necessity of shipping the engines back to France for overhauling, the seeming indifference of Dassault-Breguet to such logistics-support problems, and unhappiness with the flight performance of the Mirages, meant that the Latins made renewed efforts to purchase U.S. equipment. This renewed interest, however, was mainly for aircraft purchases.

For much new naval and ground equipment, the United States was not cost competitive, lacked surplus production beyond meeting Vietnam requirements, or simply did not manufacture the kind of systems in demand. The Latins continued to turn to Europe. Argentina, Brazil, Chile, Colombia, Ecuador, Peru, and Venezuela variously ordered new destroyers, guided-missile frigates, and submarines, from Great Britain, Italy, and West Germany. While new U.S. missile systems were classed as being too sophisticated for export to Latin America, South American countries in particular proceeded to place orders for a diverse range of anti-air, anti-ship, and anti-tank missiles, including Cobras, Exocets, Gabriels, Ikaras, Matras, Nords, Otomats, Rolands, Sea Cats, and Sea Darts, from Western Europe, Israel and Australia, as well as Sidewinders from the United States.

Peruvian nationalism and the quest for political independence, combined with the relatively low cost of Soviet equipment, led to purchase in 1973 of T-55 medium tanks. This enabled the Soviets, who had earlier donated military helicopters to Peru as part of earthquake relief, to make their first significant arms transfer in South America. The Peruvians also

[131]

bought long-range artillery and radar-controlled anti-aircraft guns. Then in 1976-77, after considering making a new effort to obtain F-5Es, the Peruvians ordered Sukhoi-22 tactical fighter bombers, in a move that introduced a new level of military capability and greatly disturbed the Chilean and Ecuadorian militaries. The Peruvian move undermined U.S. intentions to restrict the introduction of new technology, to prevent arms races and border disputes, and to support local arms control initiatives in the Andean area. Similar intentions were argued again in 1977 when the United States angered Ecuador by blocking an Israeli sale of its Kfir supersonic fighter-bombers (which are powered by U.S.-made General Electric engines).

Beginning in the mid-1970s, the Nixon-Ford Administrations made a strong effort to make U.S. military sales more responsive to foreign requests and to abolish or circumvent the restrictive legislation that had accumulated for the past decade. In the case of Latin America, motivations were primarily political, aimed at restoring goodwill and preserving access. This opening—apparently the most responsive to local demand since 1945—proved very short-lived, however. Congressional, media, and public concerns began to focus on human rights violations and apparently uncontrolled arms sales abroad. Demands were raised for new controls on arms transfers. These concerns found expression in the International Security Assistance and Arms Export Control Act of 1976. In addition to prohibiting security assistance to any country found in systematic violation of human rights, the legislation prescribed a yearly ceiling on worldwide sales, the termination (in but a few countries) of grant assistance and military assistance advisory groups by September 1977, and stricter Congressional review of arms transfers. These restrictions, with some modification, were maintained in 1977 legislation. The act has been viewed by both President Ford and President Carter as containing unprecedented restrictions that inhibit the Executive Branch's capacity to implement foreign policy.

By the time President Carter took office, Congress had suspended sales to Chile and Uruguay because of human rights violations. During 1977, Argentina, Brazil, El Salvador, and Guatemala announced rejection of U.S. assistance or sales that would be tied to human rights provisions—viewing such conditions as an affront to national sovereignty and as interference into their internal affairs. Once again, U.S.-Latin American relations on a government-to-government basis were becoming the first, and main, casualties of new restrictions aimed at arms transfers worldwide.

PROCUREMENT AND PRODUCTION TRENDS IN LATIN AMERICA

Future procurement trends appear uncertain. Arms demands may level off but will probably not decline. Rising political tensions between neighbors, sovereignty over 200-mile territorial waters, expansion of the Soviet naval presence in the South Atlantic and Caribbean, the demonstration of Cuban military assistance in Angola and elsewhere,[4] improved terms of trade for commodities and raw materials other than petroleum, and possibly a decline in the price of oil, are a few factors that might stimulate further arms demands. The emphasis will be more on force modernization than on force build-up. Yet the cycle of replacing obsolescent equipment appears to be slowly coming to an end, at least in the larger countries, with the major exception of tanks in Brazil and Chile. At least one country will probably seek to obtain F-4s before the end of the decade. The demand for precision-guided munitions (PGMs) of all types of likely to grow, since

[133]

these are highly effective but relatively low cost items that are suited to defensive missions. Their impressive utility has been demonstrated in Vietnam, the Arab-Israeli wars, and in Angola. New demands may also develop for attack-type helicopters, ASW aircraft, and medium/heavy transports.[5]

The number of supply sources is likely to become even more diverse in the future. In particular, Israel is making a determined effort to sell its equipment; and additional Soviet sales cannot be discounted. By the end of the decade Brazil may be making great strides toward developing indigenous military industries, based partly on co-production arrangements with the United States, West Germany, France and Italy for the assembly or fabrication of jet aircraft, transport aircraft, helicopters, tanks, and surface-to-surface and surface-to-air missiles. Argentina produces a light aircraft it would like to sell to its neighbors, and has co-assembly arrangements with various European countries for naval and ground equipment. Co-assembly arrangements for destroyers, submarines, and fast patrol boats are spreading throughout South America. Israel is to establish a plant in Mexico for producing and repairing its transport and light aircraft. Moreover, intra-regional arms transfers of used equipment, training exchanges, and joint exercises are likely to grow. The "miscegenation" or "hybridization" of weapon systems will grow, as components from various countries are mixed together and as business firms propose to modify Soviet systems with Western engines or components for some regimes, as is to be done in Egypt.

Thus, while the United States has recovered its position as a major supply source for aircraft by the mid 1970s, the supply picture looks generally complicated and will surely continue to involve a variety of sellers for the remainder of the decade. From a comparative standpoint, the efficiency of U.S. logistics and re-supply systems has proven to be an advantage to many customers, who have found the French and Soviet systems to be quite irregular, costly and disappointing at follow-on support.

Indigenous Production, Co-Production, and Arms "Miscegenation": Brazil

Anti-dependency arguments are spreading to support the development of local military technologies and industries. As a leading Peruvian military strategist has written:

> . . . The technology of modern warfare has caused industrial development to be a preponderant factor in national power. In Latin America, any change in industrial status affects the hierarchy of government power. . . . A lightning war has such destructive power that . . . after two or three weeks of conflict, the supply capacity of the small belligerent nations is exhausted, as is their ability to replace the destroyed material and to maintain it; and as the requirements increase, they become even more limited. The mechanization of armies requires concurrent creation of an efficient logistic system for supply maintenance, and, consequently, the creation of an industry that will make available, as a minimum, an infrastructure suitable for manufacturing spare parts, ammunition, portable weapons, light military vehicles, etc., so as to gradually facilitate the creation of our own technology in the area of military manufactures and the training of skilled personnel. *The most tyrannical kind of dependence is military technological dependence.*[6] [Emphasis added]

By far the most energetic and advanced country in this respect is Brazil. It is the leading Third World country in terms of the home use and export of locally produced military equipment. Brazil's effort is clearly linked to its quest for national independence, and for reducing reliance on the United States in particular. Indeed, Brazilians now consider theirs to be the only Latin American country, Cuba excepted, that would be capable of surviving as an organized military power without support from the United States.

While local military production has a lengthy history in Brazil, the current effort stems from a decision by the new military government in 1965 to initiate an industrial program for achieving the material self-sufficiency of the armed forces, through projects developed with the collaboration of private industry and state enterprises. The decision was motivated in part by a desire to move away from reliance on the United States for the grant or lease of deactivated U.S. equipment, none of it first-line. Brazil made important advances in the production of air and ground equipment during this period, and the effort has been given new stimulus with the signing in 1975 of a new law to create IMBEL, the War Matériel Enterprise.

It will expand the indigenous production and co-production of modern equipment for meeting local requirements and for export markets. The plan is to increase private participation in the development of local defense industries, partly on grounds that the state enterprises were becoming obsolete and needed internal reorganization. IMBEL will reportedly require that foreign factories interested in establishing production lines in Brazil—the list reportedly includes Krause-Maffei of Germany, which manufactures the famed Leopard tanks, and Armalite of the United States which produces M-16 rifles—must bring technology, capital, and foreign customers into the deal.

Brazilian leaders have repeatedly emphasized that their re-equipment programs are geared to the replacement of old World War II equipment that was not only obsolete and inefficient, but also had come to require excessively high operational and maintenance costs. Yet, going beyond mere equipment replacement, their plans reveal high ambitions for national independence that are consistent with their conviction that security and development are closely linked. Brazil is reportedly following a policy of importing only the quantity of war matériel that is necessary in order to acquire patent rights and specialized technology. The future purchase of new weaponry is to be guided by two concerns in particular: internal security and the domestic production of war matériel. A further important factor is said to be the training of technicians in various skills and specialties. The shortage of technicians is regarded as a great constraint on which, in the final analysis, both national development and national security will depend.

IMBEL is intended to serve primarily the army. Various plants have long produced a range of artillery, firearms and quartermaster equipment, and Brazil has held rights to produce Belgian/NATO and Italian firearms for a number of years. Impressive gains have been made by a firm known as EN-GESA in the original design and production of light armored vehicles. These include the Cascavel armored car and wheeled reconnaissance vehicle, the amphibious Urutu armored personnel carrier, and most recently the Sucuri, another amphibious vehicle. The Cascavel and the Urutu are powered by a Mercedes-Benz engine produced in Brazil, but could accommodate a Brazilian-made Perkins or a Detroit Diesel engine. While the Cascavel may carry locally produced armament, export versions have been fitted with guns removed from old U.S. M3A1 light tanks. A gun turret from the British Scorpion light tank has also been experimentally tested on the Cascavel and Urutu, The Sucuri is to carry a French-made turret.[7] While numerous Cascavels and Urutus have been purchased by the Brazilian army and navy, respectively, others have been

[137]

ordered by Kuwait, Libya, Qatar, and reportedly Bolivia and Chile.[8] Sales negotiations have also taken place with Abu Dhabi, Canada, Israel, Peru, Paraguay, and Turkey. In other production areas, Brazil has exported bulletproof tires for British armored cars, military jeeps to Peru, and heavy all-terrain trucks to various African countries. Co-production of French 90-mm cannons is a future possibility.

Some three-fifths of the operating aircraft of the Brazilian Air Force are reportedly manufactured nationally, and many imported aircraft carry weapons and parts produced in Brazil. For example, Brazil's purchase of F-5Es from Northrop was predicated on partial local assembly and co-production. The F-5s are to be sold to Brazil with Brazilian controls and bomb racks, while Northrop agreed to help manufacture and buy vertical tail assemblies in Brazil.

Through a firm known as EMBRAER, Brazil is presently engaged in an energetic effort to master the entire enterprise, from aircraft design and engineering through fabrication and assembly. Since EMBRAER's founding in 1969, it has proceeded with an ambitious program involving the production of aircraft piston engines and parts in association with Brazil's successful automotive industry. The production of gas turbine engines is being developed. By means of a helpful licensing and co-production arrangement with Aermacchi of Italy, Brazil presently assembles a relatively simple jet fighter-trainer, the Xavante. EMBRAER has also designed and developed, mainly on its own, a twin-turboprop light transport called the Bandeirante, which comes in military and commercial versions, and is powered by two Canadian Pratt and Whitney engines. EMBRAER's goal for the future is to produce STOL (short take-off and landing) aircraft. Plans are underway for the production of a medium-sized transport, powered by a turboprop or jet engine, that could carry troops and paratroopers. EMBRAER and Aermacchi are also proposing the joint development and manufacture of a new light attack aircraft, possibly powered by a Rolls Royce or a General Electric turbofan.[9]

All these aircraft are intended for home use and for export. Brazil's Air Force has purchased numerous Xavantes and Bandeirantes. Xavantes have been exported to Togo. Some military, but mainly commercial versions of the Bandeirante have been exported to various Latin American and African countries. EMBRAER is keenly interested in developing these markets, and is negotiating with a French company to have it provide follow-on maintenance and overhaul for sales in Europe, Africa and the Middle East. Brazil's other aircraft manufacturers produce a military trainer used by Bolivia, Chile, and Paraguay.

The navy is considered to be the service that remains most vulnerable to a possible cut-off of U.S. aid or support, since the navy operates a small number of costly, complex units in which it is very difficult to increase the number of nationally produced components. Nonetheless, diversification through resort to West European suppliers is thought to reduce the risks of dependency. Moreover, Brazil increasingly requires local co-production of its purchases of new naval craft. Of the frigates ordered from Britain's Vosper Thornycroft, Ltd., two are being co-produced under license in shipyards in Rio de Janeiro. Brazil plans to assemble submarines in the future. Furthermore, a mixed company has been formed with a British firm to produce mini-computers for the control of naval armaments.

In the area of missile systems, Brazil has acquired rights to assemble the Cobra anti-tank rocket from West Germany, and to produce the Roland ground-to-air missile from a French-West German consortium. French missile-related systems are to be installed on the frigates acquired from Great Britain. Domestically, Brazilian scientists have gained experience by designing and testing rocket vehicles that can carry a payload of 110 pounds to an altitude of 310 miles. The X-40 and X-20 rocket designs have a range of 40 km and 20 km respectively for the potential destruction of ground targets.

Brazil's progress in the indigenous production, co-production, and "miscegenation" of weapon systems is impressive and may raise various issues for U.S. arms and security policies in Latin America. The more obvious points are that U.S. arms transfers to Brazil may increasingly involve sensitive technology transfers, and that U.S. transfers may provide little military or diplomatic leverage. Moreover, Brazil may become an arms supplier competing with the United States in selected areas, thereby complicating possible U.S. efforts to promote arms controls or to restrict weapons flows into Latin America (not to mention Africa). Indeed, as a result of U.S. restrictions recently imposed on arms sales of Chile, the latter turned to Brazil for the purchase of a range of light equipment items for army usage, and is considering the purchase of a wider range of weaponry for the future.

IMPACT ON INTERNAL POLITICO-MILITARY DEVELOPMENT IN LATIN AMERICA

The troubled history and the prospective supply-demand picture serve to raise issues about the impact or consequences of arms transfers. The next several sections consider these issues in regard to (a) domestic politico-military development within Latin America, (b) intraregional relations between countries, and (c) the evolution of the inter-American security system. The discussion questions some generalizations that have suffused the policy debates, and suggests that the impact of arms transfers tends to be ambiguous, ambivalent, and marginal. The discussion elaborates further the point that restrictive U.S. arms policies have carried political costs for U.S.-Latin American relations. The point is introduced that within Latin America arms acquisitions have been more important as symbolic diplomatic instruments than as operational military weapons.

Military Capabilities

Perceptions of the impact of arms transfers on local military development and capabilities seem greatly exaggerated. In the first place, statistical work on the volume and value of arms transfers has told us very little, perhaps nothing, about the development of military preparedness and combat potential in the separate Latin American countries. Statistics on acquisitions do not readily translate into indicators of development or capability. A country that has three destroyers and three submarines does not necessarily have a stronger navy than a country that has two destroyers and one submarine; nor do such numbers mean that arms acquisitions are out of balance. Indeed, the numerically weaker might be militarily the stronger.

The problem is that very little is known about local technological capacities to absorb, operate, and maintain the equipment whose numbers have been continually recited and updated for more than a decade of studies on arms transfers to Latin America. While the numbers have risen fast enough for some observers to fear an "arms race," an important arms-control constraint on local military activities has been the fact that utilization is determined largely by the operational effectiveness and combat readiness of individual weapons, rather

[141]

than by how modern-looking or "sophisticated" they appear. Relatively weak technological bases, inadequate logistic systems, deficient manpower procurement and personnel systems, poor levels of education, lack of high command interest, and the limited financial resources typically available in the region for preparing and maintaining combat-effective forces, are practical factors that have limited military capabilities and the potential for armed conflict. These internal constraints on weapon utilizations seem to change slowly and remain in effect whether a local military buys from one, two, or a diversity of sources, or whether the military budget is growing or decreasing. Indeed, supply diversification may constrain military preparedness. Greater knowledge about this less publicized dimension of military conditions, long ignored by academic researchers, would help clarify, and probably qualify, inferences that growing weapons acquisitions will result in mounting capabilities, threats and risks of actual utilization. In examining the impact of arms transfers we need to recognize the great variations in technological/operational capability among individual countries and services.

The impact of arms transfers on the institutionalization of the armed forces has also been poorly explored. Major items—the prestigous symbols of national power and institutional dignity, tainted according to one Congressional report as the "pursuit of illusory prestige"—have had much less impact on the institutionalization and centralization of the armed forces than have the acquisition of mundane equipment items for communications, transportation, maintenance, logistics, and administration, along with general educational and managerial advances. These latter, generally non-lethal acquisitions have strengthened the local militaries as central institutions and effective political forces more than have ships from Britain, tanks from France, or jets from the United States.

Local militaries and governments have not had to rely on sophisticated hardware or foreign security assistance for military operations against insurgents, terrorists, or other dissidents. Indeed, U.S. military aid and sales programs probably had only marginal impact on the demise of guerrilla movements, for which favorable local conditions did not exist, and whose failure owed more to local political than military factors. Nonetheless, U.S. programs probably did serve to strengthen central institutions and command structures within the armed forces by contributing to the professionalization of the officer corps.[10] Meanwhile the U.S. emphasis on counterinsurgency missions did not serve to diminish Latin American interests in conventional external defense, against regional neighbors.

Local Politics

Are security assistance programs and arms sales antithetical to American political values? It is often claimed that U.S. security assistance programs have led to the unproductive diversion of scarce economic resources, fostered military intervention in politics, and facilitated the establishement of repressive authoritarian regimes that prove inimical to their own citizens and to U.S. interests in human rights. Recent events in the Southern Cone countries—Argentina, Brazil, Chile and Uruguay—have appeared to lend credence to these hypotheses, and thereby have raised doubts that the United States has interests in the continuation of security programs that associate closely with such regimes.

The few available research studies, using statistical reviews of numerous cases, reveal no consistent or significant support for these generalized claims. Higher levels of military spending may be weakly associated with higher levels of military participation in politics, However, "civilian" governments have been about as likely as "military" governments to allocate resources for military development and arms purchases. Increases as well as decreases in military spending have happened before as well as after coups—or the change back to civilian government. Moreover, the size of past MAP programs also appears to be statistically unrelated to military interventionism and arms orders. Propositions about the wastefulness of resource diversion from development to defense are also proving unreliable. In general, higher defense expenditures seem to be unrelated, or not correlated positively, to higher civilian economic growth rates—just the reverse of the original worry. Major defense expenditures for costly advanced weaponry, as opposed to military programs that emphasize civilian skills, may burden growth potential somewhat—but one must take into account the fact that expenditures for advanced weapons by Latin American countries have been fairly low level by world standards. Finally, the more costly and sophisticated items obtained through U.S. military programs, or purchased elsewhere, are of marginal utility for repressing local populations. It is even doubtful, as noted above, that MAP programs of the 1960s contributed much to the defeat or containment of rural guerrillas. Thus, in general terms, statistical studies suggest that foreign military programs alone cannot be used to account for general trends in local development.[11]

Statistics may be delusive, however. The professionalization of the officer corps and unavoidable local involvement in internal security have evidently fostered institutional military roles in politics. Professionalization, by strengthening central command structures and improving administrative and technical skills, strengthened indirectly the capacity of the military as an institution to adopt roles within the government. At the same time, new doctrines gained favor that national development and national security were linked as mutual requirements,

thereby indirectly reinforcing concepts of military responsibilities for development as well as security, and making officers more sensitive about signs of civilian incompetence.
Professionalism reinforced nationalism, and a new concept of
"participatory professionalism" was fashioned, as exemplified
in Peru where French influences prevailed in the 1960s. Thus
professionalism and counterinsurgency brought a new generation of officers to politics.[12] The demise of liberal democratic
forms was the result in several countries, most notably in
South America. Therefore, some MAP and FMS programs,
especially in regard to schooling and training, may have inadvertently contributed to the trend toward dictatorship. That is,
U.S. programs may have affected the institutional form of
military participation in politics but did not lessen the fre-
quency.

Yet if this argument is to be accepted, then perhaps so must
another: that U.S. efforts to export liberal democracy during
the 1960s may have inadvertently contributed to the current
trend toward authoritarian executive rule. Liberal democratic
experiments under civilian leadership in countries like Argentina, Brazil, and Peru may have failed in part because U.S.-
style democracy did not fit with local conditions. Corporatist-
style regimes, coming in more democratic as well as dictatorial
versions, appear to provide a more acceptable and stable basis
for rule through civil-military coalitions. The attribution of
such great influence to U.S. programs and policies, however,
seems to misjudge local factors that eventually overwhelm
foreign intentions.

The renewing emphasis in Latin America on external defense seems unlikely to reduce military interests in political
participation. Recent indigenous geopolitical writings by military officers in Latin America reveal deep concerns about
national development as being the basis for national security,

especially in regard to the development of isolated or frontier regions of the national territory, and the development of communications and transportation infrastructure for linking a country together. One purpose is to resist potential expansive pressures by neighbors or aggressive economic exploitation by foreign businesses or powers. Moreover, the concern for external defense has raised the necessity for military strategy to be geared to wise political policy—thereby making it useful not only for military officers to study politics, but also for politicians to learn military affairs.[13] Thus even if by the 1980s military rule seems less pronounced, in the long run a return to strictly civilian rule seems highly unlikely in Latin America, whatever policies the United States may pursue.[14] It is difficult to see that U.S. arms transfer programs and policies could or will exert guiding influence on such potentialities in local politics, whose course will be determined mainly by domestic factors in individual countries.

The central importance of military leaders and institutions in Latin American politics, and their potential for making positive contributions to national development in collaboration with civilian sectors, suggest that it is important for the U.S. government to maintain constructive relations with them as well as with elites and institutions in civilian sectors. Relations with military rulers need not, and for historical and ideological reasons often cannot, be close. A general antagonism against military participation in politics, however, is unwarranted. In the past, disapproving measures have reflected prejudicial misconceptions of military and civilian roles in Latin American politics and, moreover, have generally proven ineffective or counterproductive.

The Human Rights Issue

A new priority concern has entered the list: human rights. The U.S. government has maintained close military relations and engaged in major arms deals with various governments that have been reported to commit severe violations of human rights, for example, through torture of political dissidents. The new criterion holds that arms transfers programs should be curtailed to governments that are found to be systematically violating human rights domestically. The grounds are that U.S. military programs should not help even indirectly to sustain such governments, that the denial of arms programs might provide some external leverage for inhibiting brutally repressive practices in some countries, and that in any case U.S. ideals and interests are better served by barely associating with security forces that may be blamed for atrocious violations of human rights.

To some extent, human rights has represented a fallback issue for U.S. liberals who have watched the failure of campaigns in the 1960s to spread democracy as the antidote to both dictatorship and revolution. Now that dictatorships appear to have widely overruled the hopes for liberal democracy in the 1970s, protest against violations of human rights has become a core issue.

Human rights are a proper and useful emphasis for U.S. foreign policy. Even in South American countries where specific Congressional measures have been criticized, there is recognition that the new emphasis has restored a vigorous and progressive image to the United States as a superpower and as a traditional champion of freedom. The problem has lain in giving human rights such singular priority at times, while also

[147]

singling out arms transfers as a tool for leverage and punishment.

One Brazilian newspaper has labeled U.S. human rights policy as representing realism for the strong, and idealism for the weak. Indeed, the human rights criterion is proving difficult to apply in an even-handed fashion since so many governments engage in some internal security tactics of "counterviolence." In practice, it appears easiest to affect the smaller, less important governments, or those governments that are "inefficient" at violating human rights. It seems most difficult to apply the provision to the larger, more important countries, such as Iran or South Korea, where violations occur, but where broader security, political, and economic considerations may "protect" relations. Exceptions also seem likely for governments that newly seek U.S. arms sales and related programs after a history of acquiring weapons from the Soviet Union. In the end, therefore, it would not be surprising if once again Latin America ends up bearing the brunt of the "solution," in part because both the Pentagon and the State Department may continue to be willing to defer to Congress on matters pertaining to Latin America.

Historical experience suggests that, as a lever or instrument for changing the behavior of the arms recipient, the potential effectiveness of the human rights provision is doubtful. It extends the tradition of restrictive legislation that has sought in the past to inhibit excessive diversion of resources from economic development, to prevent the arming of oppressive military dictators, and to punish failures to compensate for expropriated U.S. holdings. The provision is also in keeping with U.S. moves in the 1960s to influence local government successions or policies by suspending assistance and/or diplomatic recognition, with the intention of levering outcomes that would be more in keeping with liberal democratic practices.

These earlier paternalistic measures proved relatively ineffective, and their application often cost the United States political goodwill beyond the immediate case at hand.[15]

Such considerations indicate that U.S. curtailment of arms transfer programs as a sanction against indigenous tendencies to violate human rights will not lead to successful results. Leaders of several Latin American governments—notably in the Southern Cone countries—have shown that they prefer to postpone or diminish relations with the United States over the short run rather than to succumb to U.S. influence and relinquish the use of techniques that have unfortunately proven brutally effective for destroying terrorist movements.[16] U.S. human rights policies, these leaders insist, represent intolerable infringements of national sovereignty and an intervention in domestic matters.

Some changes in harsh government policies have been announced in several Southern Cone countries, but these changes have been largely cosmetic and carefully attuned to improving national images abroad. Nonetheless, in considering the long run, most of the governments affected believe that they are in fact laying foundations for future democracy within their traditions.[17]

Reactions to U.S. human rights measures may have inadvertently pacified the course of intra-regional foreign relations. The claim has been made (albeit facetiously) that the U.S. policy has done more to stimulate South American integration than did Simón Bolívar himself, who originated and fought for the dream in the nineteenth century wars for independence from Spain. Some South American governments have in fact sought to rally common cause against the U.S. policy, while also strengthening their mutual cooperation regarding internal security matters. Moreover, Brazil's relations with its neighbors have been smoothed by U.S. criticisms over human rights issues, which have served to disabuse the Brazilian government of its former, unwanted image as sub-imperial agent of the United States in South America during the Nixon-Ford Administrations.

IMPACT ON REGIONAL ARMS CONTROL AND CONFLICT MANAGEMENT

The potential for intra-regional conflicts has increased in Latin America. External defense missions have regained priority over internal security, although the latter remain important. Small-scale war in Latin America is not an unrealistic scenario. Indeed, evolving regional trends are similar in important ways to trends that transpired in the 1930s, when several border engagements and one protracted conflict took place in South America. At present, the trends include a decline of U.S. power and presence (Latin Americans characterize this as the post-Vietnam/Watergate syndrome), the diversification and expansion of Latin American relations with non-hemispheric nations, and locally rising tensions based in part on geopolitical perceptions. Earlier decades of peace, stretching from the end of the Peru-Ecuador conflict in 1942 through the Honduras-El Salvador clash of 1969, may be attributed in part to U.S. hegemony and to the greater priority that Latin American governments gave to relations with foreign powers over relations with their neighbors.

Thus far the data seem to indicate that at present no arms races characterized by spiraling purchases or rapidly swelling inventories exist in Latin America. Individual governments have made recent acquisitions for a variety of reasons, ranging from generational obsolescence of existing inventories to reactions stimulated by assessing the acquisitions made by neighbors. Some country-pairs, such as Peru-Chile and Venezuela-Colombia, are more sensitive than others, for historical and geographic reasons, but this is to be expected. Some balancing and emulation is occurring—but no two countries have yet engaged in a spiraling arms race that has consumed large expenditures and led to swollen arms inventories.

There are no reliable formulas for judging whether arms transfers are likely to alleviate conflict potential or stimulate arms races under various circumstances. Assessment in this area becomes especially complicated when a country such as the United States provides arms to two neighbors—as in the cases of Peru-Chile, Venezuela-Colombia, and Honduras-El Salvador—for defense against a third-party internal or external threat, and when in fact the two neighbors become more interested in using the weapons for defense against each other. However, it is not necessarily true that an influx of weapons raises the risks that political disagreements will more likely turn to armed conflict. Instead, symbolic strength provided by arms acquisitions may facilitate diplomacy to resolve some dispute at least temporarily, as may have been the case with Peru-Chile, and elsewhere with Iran-Iraq. The limited knowledge that we now possess regarding individual cases does not suggest that arms transfers contribute more to an armed conflict than do local political conditions.

Inflammatory nationalistic journalism during a period of high border tension seems more likely to precipitate a military engagement than would the availability of newly purchased weaponry. Although the Latin American press is generally government-controlled, these controls are not designed to deter the arousal of nationalist passions against potential enemies.

In the past, the argument could be made that an exclusive or highly dominant supply relationship represented a form of

[151]

U.S. arms control. Accordingly, such a supply relationship would enable the United States to influence the type and rate of local arms orders, and to curtail supplies in the event of an unwelcome local conflict. During the 1950s and early 1960s, the United States did in fact attempt to follow a policy of regional arms balancing and limitation. In this respect, the Military Assistance Program and the allocation of Foreign Military Sales credit assistance were used to try to establish some parity among neighboring militaries and to keep the level of weapon sophistication reasonably low. Such a policy, as has already been suggested, is no longer viable.

Some Latin American countries accused of arms racing have simultaneously promoted local arms control measures. Leading diplomatic and military officials from eight Andean countries joined in the Declaration of Ayacucho in 1975 to recommend that their governments prohibit further acquisitions of highly sophisticated modern armaments and offensive weapons. Peru, Chile, and Bolivia, which appeared close to conflict over the land-locked status of Bolivia and the disposition of territory gained by Chile from Peru and Bolivia during the War of the Pacific around 1890, have managed to relax border tensions and to consider entering into a nonaggression pact. This is not to say that all tensions are being adequately managed. Several South American countries have reported concern about Brazil's growing capabilities. However, the fact that seems to disturb them most is the formation of a 7,000-man parachute brigade transported by several squadrons of C-130s, replacing a brigade transported by the much smaller and shorter-range C-47s. This sort of instance does not look impressive in typical, quantitative arms race studies.

The Andean Declaration of Ayacucho

Partly as a result of the ever-increasing proliferation of expensive military weapons, the Latin Americans have not ignored the very real need for arms control efforts in the region. One indigenous effort has been initiated in South America. Following a proposal from Peru to freeze arms purchases for ten years, the six Andean countries of Chile, Bolivia, Peru, Colombia, and Venezuela (along with Argentina and Panama) signed in December 1974 the Declaration of Ayacucho. The signatories thereby committed themselves to "create conditions which permit effective limitations of armaments and put an end to their acquisition of offensive warlike purposes in order to dedicate all possible resources to economic and social development." [18]

Several technical meetings have since been held in Lima, Santiago, and La Paz in the attempt to implement the Ayacucho Declaration. As a result of these meetings, agreement was reached on the following: a ban on certain types of advanced weapons not now present in Latin America, further study of limiting the acquisition of other major weapons, and consideration of a treaty to strengthen peace in the region. In addition, the possibilities were also discussed of reducing border forces, establishing demilitarized zones, and monitoring weapons inventories. Despite the fears and concerns expressed in 1974, by mid-1977 these recommendations were still being taken "under consideration" by the governments of the Ayacucho Declaration. Meanwhile, recent purchases of, or attempts to purchase, Soviet SU-22 attack-bombers by Peru, Israeli Shafrir air-to-air missiles by Chile, and Israeli Kfir high-performance jet fighters by Ecuador, suggest that there still

[153]

remains a wide gap between Ayacucho intent and local national security concerns that require the purchase of modern weapons of both a defensive and offensive nature. While the Ayacucho declaration has not slowed local arms demands, U.S. support for it has become a new decision-making factor in favor of restraining some arms transfers to the Andean region.

As an adjunct to the Declaration of Ayacucho, the countries of Bolivia, Chile, and Peru have engaged in their own discussions about arms limitations and conflict management. After a 1975 meeting, high-level military personnel from the three countries issued a comuniqué to state that they had (1) agreed in principle to find ways to consult regularly and exchange information in advance about military activities along the three borders, (2) acknowledged Bolivian concern for an outlet to the sea, and (3) supported the Ayacucho arms limitations talks. Although their Tripartite Conferences have further proposed establishing an early-warning system along the borders and possibly the signing of a nonaggression pact, the outlook for these arms control measures seem dim. The most likely outcome will be the establishment of consultation bodies as instruments to manage border tensions or accidental clashes between the respective armed forces. Meanwhile spokesmen from all three countries have variously blamed foreign/extra-continental powers and arms salesmen for fomenting the widespread rumors of an impending re-fight of the War of the Pacific.[19] Moreover, denials have emanated from each country that it is engaging in an arms race or harbors military ambitions; the dominant rationales for new arms demands have continued to be the modernization of obsolescent equipment and the maintenance of local power balances that discourage warfare and deter lightning attacks.

The Guatemala-Belize Territorial Dispute

Despite the absence of border conflicts within the hemisphere in the post-World War II period (with the exception of the El Salvador-Honduras "Soccer War"), there exist several "hot points" of periodic tension and arms competition. The difficulty of pursuing an arms control program in these areas of potential conflict is clear in Central America where Guatemala has periodically threatened a military solution to enforce its claims to the disputed territory of Belize, to which Great Britain would like to grant full independence. The case serves to illustrate that a small country will purchase arms according to its own national interests even if it means coming into conflict with its patron power.

Historically, the United States has exercised great economic, political and military influence in Central America. Nonetheless, following the decline in MAP grant aid the Central American countries have diversified their inventories with purchases of new equipment from Western Europe and elsewhere—thereby continuing the pattern that began among the larger countries of South America in the mid-1960s. El Salvador, Honduras, Guatemala, and Nicaragua have all purchased Israeli and French jet fighters, helicopters, and air transport craft, thereby laying to rest traditional U.S. expectations of arms monopoly and standardization even in the Central American region.

Since 1975 military relations between the United States and Guatemala have cooled as a result of American unwillingness to support Guatemalan claims to Belize, but more importantly because of U.S. reluctance to deliver military equipment, weapons, and ammunition. On one occasion this cooling extended to

[155]

the placing of U.S. military advisers on travel restrictions. Since the mid-1975s the Guatemalans have indicated at least twice that they were prepared to engage in armed conflict with the British armed forces to order to forestall a declaration of independence for Belize.

The Guatemalan position is that it must receive a portion of Belizian territory in exchange for acquiescing to independence for Belize. Since the early 1960s, a basic strategy of Guatemala has sought to get the United States into a "good offices" position. The United States has resisted this since 1968, on grounds that the problem is primarily a British responsibility and should be resolved by the three immediate parties without deeply involving the United States. Having failed at this, the Guatemalans in the mid-1970s adopted a different strategy to involve the United States. The new strategy was to begin a substantial and credible armaments program as a way to demonstrate Guatemalan resiliency and determination.

The U.S. government's reaction to the buildup in Guatemalan military capabilities was officially termed "Plan Peace Maya." The Plan was an explicit effort by the United States to regulate the flow of arms into Guatemala (partly as a response to the appeals of Great Britain). However, after experiencing difficulties in purchasing vintage C-47s and M-16 rifles from the United States in late 1974, the Guatemalans placed orders for $20-25 million worth of military equipment from European countries. Israel alone has sold Aravas (a STOL transport aircraft), automatic rifles, armored cars, transportation vehicles, and ammunition. From France have come helicopters; and Spain, Taiwan, Yugoslavia, and Portugual have provided assortments of military equipment and ammunition. (In addition, the Guatemalans investigated the possibility of purchasing armored personnel carriers from Brazil.) Thus despite the concerted U.S. (and British) efforts to limit the military capabilities of a presumed client-state, Guatemala turned to purchase most of what it desired from nontraditional suppliers.

In the process, arms transfers have become a tool of military diplomacy and bargaining. The Guatemalans have consistently sought to make the United States an unwilling participant in their attempt to acquire territorial concessions from the British. Despite repeated efforts, the Guatemalans have been unsuccessful in utilizing the military aid relationship as an instrument to influence directly the U.S. role in the dispute. Nonetheless, the Guatemalans have succeeded in getting both the United States and Great Britain to take Guatemalan diplomacy more seriously.

The case illustrates the limits on U.S. capabilities to regulate the flow of weapons into Latin America, even to a small Caribbean Basin country. A U.S. arms control effort can be circumvented by a country willing to buy from nontraditional sources and by suppliers willing to sell for the purposes of economic and political gain. Israel, for example, has not sought a military presence in the distant Central American region. Israeli export of military equipment is linked to specific foreign policy objectives—that is, military sales are an instrument to gain and maintain political friends in international forums and to gain foreign exchange earnings. Like other suppliers, Israel is prepared to take advantage of opportunities to sell, even at the expense of its most important ally, the United States.[20]

Future Prospects for Arms Control and Conflict Management

Formal arms control agreements among suppliers, recipients, or both seem unlikely.[21] Most if not all Latin American governments would surely resent the imposition of a suppliers' agreement, or treatment as an arms control laboratory by the great powers. The United States and Western European countries seem unlikely to agree on arms limitations for Latin America. It is difficult to spot significant direct gains for the Europeans from entering into such an agreement for the distant Western Hemisphere. Indeed, future European purchases of F-16 aircraft and Leopard tanks, for example, may release a new generation of surplus equipment from existing inventories that the European governments will likely want to sell in the Third World.

While European interests in arms sales to Latin America appear to be primarily economic in nature, this is not the case with other important potential suppliers. In particular, the Soviet Union and Israel, and possibly Brazil in the not too distant future, seem to have political interests at stake in their arms export policies. These political interests militate against their potential agreement to arms control constraints. An arms control agreement does not seem to fit into Soviet interests, for the expansion of its politico-military presence as a great power in the developing world is closely linked to its capacity to transfer arms. Recent Soviet sales to Peru, and offers to several other Latin American countries, indicate that the U.S.S.R. is interested in gaining a foothold by penetrating a regional market heretofore, with the exception of Cuba, off-limits to Soviet arms. While Soviet success in penetrating this market has been confined to Peru, favorable terms and Soviet promises of quick delivery of equipment, combined with local interests to assert independence of the United States, may contribute to more Soviet sales in the Latin American market. Soviet re-equipment programs may also release huge quantities of weapons for sale abroad. If some suppliers' agreement should guarantee the Soviets part of the regional market and leave Cuba with strong capabilities for potential local interventions, then the Soviets might agree.

The prospects for supplier arrangements are further diminished by the continuing appearance of talented new suppliers. Israel, in particular, has high quality weapons to offer, is making a major marketing effort, and will not be restrained easily by U.S. pressures to desist.[22] As noted, Israel seems interested in using arms transfers for the purpose of gaining political friends, as well as for earning foreign exchange.[23] Furthermore, neighboring governments would surely not favor a suppliers' agreement if it left Brazil in a strong position as the major local producer of weapons systems in Latin America.

The assumption is made that a suppliers' agreement to curtail arms transfers would be likely to reduce conflict potential in Third World regions. Even if a suppliers' agreement could be fashioned, the consequences might exacerbate regional tensions and raise the potential for local military conflict. How might that be possible? In a number of cases in Latin America, Africa and the Middle East, acquisitions of advanced weapon systems seem more significant for their diplomatic symbolism than for their military capabilities. Depriving these governments of diplomatically useful symbols might increase the difficulties they may have in avoiding local politico-military disputes or negotiating their pacification. Moreover, intermediate and traditional weapon systems would probably remain available through indigenous production and secondary suppliers, both of which might well be boosted in case of a major suppliers' agreement. Local governments and their militaries might become increasingly likely to focus on developing operational preparedness, and to overract militarily when serious diplomatic disputes arise. If such projections seem possible, then peace might not be served by a major suppliers' agreement to curtail arms transfers.

The varied Latin governments would appear to have considerable interests in arriving at local arms control agreements. Local arms acquisitions and rising border tensions have contributed directly to the deterioration of both the Andean Pact and the Central American Common Market, two major efforts at integrated economic development. Yet the experiences involving the Ayacucho Declaration indicate that the outlook for institutionalized arms controls is dim. More likely is the establishment of new institutional mechanisms for conflict management, such as early-warning systems, command-and-control systems, and consultation bodies.

Despite the poor prospects for arms control, the military-diplomatic efforts made in their favor are still worthwhile to aid balancing, lessen chances of arms races, promote instances of self-restraint, and improve communications about intentions and capabilities among rivals (at the risk of confirming suspicions). Discussions and negotiations can be useful; symbolic temporization can help to pacify the current of affairs. Indeed, it is not inconsistent to arm for war and parley for peace at the same time.

Having weapons may in fact be a precondition to having a voice in peace discussions, as has been illustrated in the past. At the inter-American conference convened in 1942 to settle the Peru-Ecuador conflict that cost Ecuador a piece of its territory, Ecuador was sternly criticized for having depended on the principles of international law and Pan Americanism for protection. The Ecuadorian representatives were admonished that these principles "exist to solve problems. You are not a problem for America. You, with your lack of military resistance, have not made your problem an American problem." [24] A recent episode is reminiscent of Ecuador's earlier experience. After learning that the United States had blocked the sale of Israeli Kfir jets to Ecuador, its Minister of Foreign Affairs reportedly accused the United States of criminal action by selling arms to some countries while leaving others defenseless.

In sum, arms transfers are diplomacy by other means. Having arms, especially prestigious arms, appears to be essential for the successful conduct of traditional diplomacy. Indeed, arms have often been more important for their diplomatic symbolism than for their military capabilities. The acquisition and display of advanced weapons have seemed useful not so much to prepare for war, as to gain effective diplomatic instruments for negotiating and resolving conflicts short of war. Thus as a result of Guatemala's independent acquisition of Israeli arms, Guatemala's intentions and capabilities are taken much more seriously by the United States and Great Britain in regard to the Belize issue. Elsewhere, it has been suggested that U.S. arms transfers to Egypt might serve to strengthen its confidence in its military capacity, so as thereby to encourage diplomatic negotiations with Israel. Even the maintenance of the U.S.-Soviet strategic balance, the course of their arms limitation negotiations, and their superpower images abroad have depended in part on the diplomatic symbolism of their weapon systems. The lessening of U.S. influence in Latin America and the expansion of intra-regional relations probably mean that military diplomacy, based in part on the acquisition of prestigious weapons, will be increasingly significant in the conduct of intra-hemispheric relations and in the resolution of potential conflicts. Particularly in South America, a country deprived of arms modernization may well become diplomatically as well as militarily defenseless.

IMPACT ON THE INTER-AMERICAN SECURITY SYSTEM

Following World War II and throughout the cold war era, U.S. arms transfer policies were intended to operate in tandem with broader U.S. policies to fashion an inter-American secu-

[161]

rity system for hemispheric defense and peacekeeping.[25] A multilateral framework and bilateral ties were developed through the establishment of the Inter-American Defense Board (IADB) in 1942, formulation of the Rio Pact in 1947 against extra-hemispheric aggression, and of the Pact of Bogotá in 1948 for peaceful settlement of disputes within the inter-American system. The inclusion of Latin America as a Mutual Security Act grant aid recipient in 1951 led to a series of bilateral Mutual Security Treaties. Through the Military Assistance Program (MAP), U.S. advisory missions and training efforts spread throughout the hemisphere during the 1950s. Significant developments during the 1960s included creation of the Inter-American Defense College, establishment of the Central American Defense Council (CONDECA), an increase in the size and significance of the regional U.S. Southern Command (SOUTHCOM) with headquarters in the Panama Canal Zone, the periodic convening of regional conferences of the chief commanders of each service branch, frequent joint maneuvers and exercises such as the navies' "Operation UNITAS" for anti-submarine warfare, and the creation of inter-American radio nets.

Throughout this time Latin American governments kept the Organization of American States (OAS) essentially free of military organs. The IADB was specifically excluded from the formal OAS structure. A strong reaction by Latin America to the U.S.-dominated Inter-American Peace Force that intervened in the Dominican Republic in 1965 largely prevented permanent institutionalization of that entity. Measures taken successfully through the OAS since 1969 to help resolve the Honduras-El Salvador "soccer war" dispute have been largely diplomatic, though military observers were stationed along the border. A Special Consultative Committee on Security was established to monitor Cuban subversion during the 1960s, but it was disbanded in 1975. Furthermore, the Rockefeller Commission did not receive a favorable response to its proposal in 1969 for establishing a Western Hemisphere Security Council linked to the OAS.

It appears in retrospect that U.S. arms transfer policies were more successful in supporting bilateral security relations with individual countries than in promoting or supporting U.S. goals for complex multilateral collaboration. During the 1940s and 1950s, "hemispheric defense" proved to be a practical rationale for U.S.-Latin American security cooperation and U.S. arms assistance. However, the U.S. goal of weapons standardization, long considered essential to joint military action, could not be realized. The diversity of interests and national characteristics ruled out the possibilities for "standardization" of matériel, doctrine, organization, or activities under U.S. leadership. During the 1960s, when "internal security" became the dominant rationale for U.S. arms assistance, the Latin American governments demonstrated considerable capacity for dealing with local guerrilla threats, without requiring a significant expansion or strengthening of the collective security apparatus. Bilateral U.S. assistance, advisory, and training programs meanwhile helped to secure U.S. access to local decision-makers and to build U.S. contacts with several generations of officer corps in Latin America.

U.S. restrictions on arms transfers that took effect after the mid-1960s were a contributing factor to the subsequent deterioration of U.S.-Latin cooperation in sustaining an inter-American security system. But this deterioration resulted from numerous complex factors involving global as well as regional changes that have made the system anachronistic. It is by no means clear that U.S. arms policies were a decisive factor. Indeed, a more responsive U.S. arms transfer policy in this period might well not have made such difference.

[163]

While most of the institutional apparatus of the inter-American security system has remained intact since its establishment in the 1940s-1960s, events in the past few years reveal a degree of deterioration that requires new attention and fresh ideas. The prior U.S.-sponsored emphases on defense against an extra-hemispheric threat and subsequently against Cuba/ Communist subversion have given way to new, locally-sponsored concepts. In 1975 during the OAS meeting in San José, Costa Rica, members voted to incorporate the principle of "ideological pluralism" into the Rio Pact. A further prominent proposal, essentially referring to certain activities of the United States and multinational corporations, has called for a concept of "collective economic security" and defense against "economic aggression" to be written into the OAS Charter, if not also the Rio Pact. Meanwhile, Cuban military assistance to Angola, the Guatemala-Belize dispute, Peru-Chile border tensions, and Soviet arms sales to Peru have served to stimulate traditional concerns about preventing conventional military conflicts from developing within the region.

For several years, OAS members have been working to draft a new OAS Charter. They aim to respond to the changes in the context of inter-American relations wrought by the emergence of détente and the growing capacity of the Latin governments to influence each other and the foreign powers. In addition, regional meetings of military commanders have continued to consider proposals for revising or reforming the inter-American security system. A proposal to make the IADB into the centerpiece has not met with success. Part of the problem is lack of agreement over the definition of the "threat." Thus at the eleventh regional meeting of army commanders in 1975, there was a sharp split over whether the greater danger came from the Left or the Right, from pro-Communist or pro-capitalist extremists, and over whether military training schools should teach anti-subversive tactics against the Right as well as the Left. The army commanders also discussed the issue of economic aggression by foreign powers and companies. Despite all this activity and searching, redefinition of the inter-American system is far from settled.

U.S. Roles

The revision or reform of the inter-American security system involves so many complex issues that U.S. arms transfer policies will likely have only marginal influence on what emerges. Nonetheless, despite recent efforts by some Latin American countries to form organizations that may diminish, exclude, or oppose U.S. roles in some problem issues, most Latin American governments do not want to exclude the United States from playing a significant role in hemispheric security. The United States is needed not only as one source of weapons technology, but also as a potential mediator and balancer in case of local conflict or war. It has even been pointed out, by a Peruvian military intellectual, that politico-military planners should anticipate U.S. or OAS roles in terminating a military conflict, should one arise.

It will be the responsibility of politics, through diplomatic negotiations both before, during and after the conflict, to obtain and maintain the support of the great powers, especially that of one them, to neutralize the others (or other) in the event that they attempt to intervene on behalf of the adversary, by supplying the latter with arms, or if they try to stop the war before it has succeeded in securing the objectives concerned.

In a local limited war in Latin America, military action

will occur with the likelihood that the United States, or the OAS, through a meeting for consultation of the ministers of foreign affairs, will restrict the progress of the hostilities in time, by curbing or halting them. Therefore, there must be an appropriate correlation between the political objective (the purpose for which the war is being fought), the available facilities and the probable duration of the conflict, a result of the international political situation.[26]

The more the Latin American countries become wary about each other as potential threats, the more some may blame the United States for instigating or exacerbating the potential threats; yet the more most will want the United States to remain in the game as a potential mediator and balancer. U.S. interests will surely be best served by an absence of regional conflicts, and thus U.S. policies should aim in part at supporting peaceful balances. This may prove to be a difficult objective. In the recent decades of low local threat perception and weak intra-Latin American contact, local balancing was easier—in part because the symbolic prestige of weapons was diplomatically more useful, and militarily more important, than were actual military capabilities. In the future, however, capabilities may begin to loom larger than prestige in the assessments made by some Latin American armed forces.

U.S. Security and Regional Powers: Brazil

In the future the two Latin American countries with which the United States seems most likely to share a sense of mutual mission requirements are Brazil, in part because of its interests beyond Latin America, and Venezuela, because of its potential presence in the Caribbean Basin area. Brazil and possibly Venezuela belong to a class of emerging regional powers, along with Indonesia, Iran, and Nigeria among others, whose emergence depends much more on economic growth than on military development, and whose disposition will have increasingly important consequences for U.S. security in the changing international environment. Indeed, by the 1980s U.S. security relations with major regional powers may attain the importance accorded in the past to lesser NATO-West European allies.[27]

Close relations with regional powers in the Third World hold great attraction for the United States. Politically, most have relatively strong, stable government institutions and at present are ruled by nationalist elites that are fairly pro-American and anti-Soviet. Economically, these countries possess and export important energy and other raw materials on which the United States and its traditional allies are increasingly dependent. Militarily, they are developing as the major regional forces, a few as clients of U.S. military programs; and they may play important balancing rather than destabilizing roles in regional security affairs.

Close relations, however, may lead to creeping commitments that entail risks for the United States. Three stand out. First, adventuresome or hegemonial regional powers may draw the United States into local conflicts in which it has no direct interest. Second, close relations may jeopardize relations with neighbors in which the United States also has significant local interests. Third, there is a risk of the internationalization of local conflicts when rival foreign powers become closely associated with local proxies. Overall, there is a risk of loss of leverage over the presumed client, and even of "reverse leverage" in which entanglement leads to manipulation of the generally stronger partner by the presumably weaker client.

[167]

"Superclients" exist as well as superpowers. Clearly, the United States faces a challenge in building professionally close, but correct, military relations with regional powers like Brazil, especially if the regional power should acquire nuclear weapons.

A different set of incentives and risks appear to confront policy-makers within a regional power. Although on balance U.S. security in the evolving world context would probably be served by close cooperation, if not alliance, with selected regional powers, the local security and development of those regional powers will probably require distance, if not disassociation, from close identification with the United States. Local security is a key factor: the regional power seems best served by a clear status of independence and even non-alignment in order to promote diplomatic initiatives that will prevent or manage potential regional conflicts. Local flexibility and sovereignty are perceived to depend upon reducing national dependency and reliance on U.S. goodwill and suppliers. Furthermore, negotiating and bargaining with the United States seem to be advanced by assertions of national independence, and at times by threats to reduce future collaboration and ties.

In light of such considerations, it is unclear how Brazil may and should fit into U.S. security policies. What is clear is that Brazil seems to be growing as a regional power, and its military government has taken steps in recent years to become increasingly independent of the United States.[28] Arms transfers will likely remain a critical policy area having broad impact on overall relations.

COMPLEXITIES FOR U.S. POLICY-MAKING CRITERIA

The preceding material suggests that arms transfers will continue to prove difficult to orchestrate as an instrument for protecting and promoting U.S. policy interests. Arms transfers have constituted an important element for political goodwill. Yet, in general, U.S. arms transfer measures appear to have had ambiguous, if not ambivalent and unexpected, consequences for other U.S. policy concerns. Under these circumstances, there has been no easy solution to the design and application of standardized criteria for incremental arms transfer decisions. Commonly argued truisms do not hold; each case becomes different. And we do not clearly understand the conditions that may make each case different.

In terms of general foreign policy objectives and decision criteria, the U.S. government has traditionally aimed to transfer arms that (1) meet "valid military requirements" and (2) gain "political influence and leverage" for the United States.[29] The criterion of meeting valid military requirements has generally been the preference and responsibility of the Defense Department, while the quest for political influence and leverage has mainly governed State Department decisions. This is a rough generalization, but it helps to characterize the past ten to fifteen years. The practice of (3) pre-emptive selling is more recent, and has owed mainly to the emergence of supply competition.

Valid Military Requirements

It has become increasingly difficult for the U.S. government to assess and set valid requirements for militaries that are determined to fix their own requirements and to emphasize local defense missions against neighbors, especially where these missions do not involve Soviet threats and thus may be of disinterest to the U.S. military. The situation becomes even more difficult where the United States supplies both parties to a potential arms race or regional conflict (as in the cases of Honduras-El Salvador, Peru-Chile, India-Pakistan, and Greece-Turkey), or where the United States aims to maintain close, positive relations with all parties to a dispute (as in the case of Guatemala, Belize, and Britain), or where the equipment being demanded does not appear justifiable in terms of the local threat or absorptive capacity. The criterion of meeting valid military requirements was much clearer in earlier periods when collective defense against Communist external and subversive threats was based on some shared perceptions of threats and enemies. Now the United States is asked more and more to accept the local assessments of specific equipment needs, and to subordinate requirements in regard to the size and timing of orders and the local technical capacity to absorb and operate the deliveries.

For many countries the U.S. military "requirement" has shifted away from simply defending against shared threats, toward just maintaining some U.S. military access, cooperation, and assets in the recipient country. The present environment in Latin America makes it more difficult than in the past to justify arms transfers in terms of valid military requirements that clearly relate to U.S. defense interests. There may exist some sharing of threat perceptions and mission objectives in the South Atlantic with Brazil and Argentina, in the Caribbean Basin with Venezuela, and with Panama regarding the Canal. Latin America in general remains an important source for some strategic raw materials and natural resources, such as petroleum. Brazil's northeastern bulge might represent a strategic location in case of a conflict involving the United States in Africa. Nonetheless, these few points, most of them very traditional, represent a meager basis for roundly justifying significant arms transfer programs in terms of shared threat perceptions and mutual mission requirements.

An acceptable, limited military rationale may be found in simply trying to maintain professional military access and goodwill through correct, respectful relations that may necessarily involve responding favorably to some local arms demands. That at least would provide a basis for limited relations which could be expanded if a future need should arise. Local absorptive capacity may need to be treated as a limiting criterion that could be discussed technically with the purchasing country, in the interest of finding a mutually agreeable, technical basis for limiting some weapons demands. For many years "local absorptive capacity" has been treated rhetorically as a limiting factor—but in fact little empirical analysis has been undertaken. While the capacity of a client to bargain in a buyer's market reduces U.S. capacity to shape and restrain military requirements, it is not necessarily unwise for the United States to provide weapons that may not be used for promoting U.S. military security interests.

These considerations relate to a significant issue that we have never seen discussed in either policy or academic literature: How best to evaluate the impact of arms transfers on intra-Latin American relations? U.S. policy-makers tend to evaluate the impact on U.S.-Latin American relations from a primarily political perspective. But the impact on relations between Latin American countries is normally treated from a primarily military perspective. A point that emerges from the preceding discussion is that, in accordance with the symbolic significance of prestigious weapons, a more political-diplomatic perspective should also be adopted in evaluating the potential impact of U.S. arms transfers on intra-Latin American relations.

Political Influence and Leverage

The U.S. Government has tended to expect arms transfers to return benefits in the form of political influence and leverage. Indeed, arms transfers are an important element within the web of relations, and may serve to create dependencies and interdependencies. Certainly arms transfer programs can contribute to a climate of political goodwill and can provide access to influential military and political elites. In addition, during a moment of crisis the dependence on U.S. logistics and re-supply may be manipulated for short-term gains—though often at some expense to longer-term goodwill and influence, as in the cases of Honduras-El Salvador, India-Pakistan, and Greece-Turkey.

In between the extremes of routine *access-goodwill* and crisis *leverage,* the potential returns for diplomatic *influence* are unclear and appear to be greatly exaggerated. Multiple-case research is needed to analyze the linkages and consequences of arms transfers with respect to related political issues. A distinction among the objectives of access, goodwill, influence, and leverage might serve usefully in constructing an analytical framework. On balance, it would appear easier to use arms transfers for gaining access and goodwill than for acquiring influence and leverage.

A distinction may be useful between cases in which the arms transfer objectives relate to a *specific issue* or activity, such as a recipient's stance toward U.S. basing rights or toward military relations with the Soviet Union, in contrast to U.S. objectives that may be quite general or *systemic in nature,* such as reinforcing the stability of a particular regime and the policy paradigm it espouses. For instance, transfers have proven very important for maintaining U.S. access and support with Latin American militaries in whose potential political future the United States may have some interests, as in the cases of Brazil in 1964 and Chile in 1973. Elsewhere, arms transfer policies have served to keep King Hussein and the Shah in power as moderate rulers of Jordan and Iran, respectively.

At times a direct *quid pro quo* may be the issue: the arms transfers represent currency for negotiating the use of bases and facilities, or some other concrete trade-off or offset. This has generally not been the case in Latin America except in regard to U.S. access to raw materials during World War II, and possibly for negotiations in the 1950s relating to the temporary installation of missile-tracking stations in Brazil and the Dominican Republic.

Where the *quid pro quo* is not clear and is supposed to follow at some future time, then the quest for political influence and leverage through arms transfers often leads to meager investment returns. While a "superclient" like Iran has at times provided an example of this, the United States has also encountered difficulties in exerting control over a small client like Guatemala, which turned to buy Israeli military transports and put the U.S. military mission on restriction after the United States bowed to a British plea to deny the sale of U.S. transports. In another earlier instance, the suspension of military assistance and sales to Ecuador did not halt the seizure of U.S. fishing boats. It appears that, where effective, the presumed leverage requires constant renewal in the form of further arms transfers, whose utility is of short-duration and noncumulative as a form of political investment currency. Furthermore, the presumed leverage depends greatly on *local sensitivities* and priorities regarding the non-arms transfer issues to which it is being linked.

Another distinction might be useful between issues or ob-

[173]

jectives that seem *closely linked* to arms transfers, such as local diplomatic-military negotiations to end a border conflict, and those issues or objectives that may be distantly and quite *indirectly linked* to arms transfers, such as a recipient's commercial policies. A further distinction may be made between influencing a recipient's *foreign policy* behavior, and the often much more sensitive area of its *domestic policy* behavior. In general, arms transfers would appear to have some potential utility for influencing closely related foreign policy issues, and are most likely to arouse counterproductive reactions where the U.S. objectives relate to sensitive domestic issues that are distantly related to arms transfers, as in the area of local human rights practices.

A distinction may be made between *short-term* and *long-term* effects. Expectations, of influence may relate less to present conditions than to future contingencies that may possibly arise. In some cases, however, arms transfers might bring immediate leverage on some particular issues, but at the cost of future goodwill and influence regarding other issues—whereas in another case immediate goodwill might not lead to future leverage. In some cases the U.S. government may treat an incremental arms transfer as an investment for future influence, but the recipient may treat the same transfer as a payoff or reward for some cooperative action already taken. While these distinctions may be useful, there is always the problem of knowing whether a presumed cause-effect relationship is in fact due to arms transfers, or whether it is due to some other factor or consideration, such as domestic policies.

It is rarely true that the more arms the United States transfers to a country, the more leverage the United States obtains. This is especially the case for governments that have become skilled at negotiating with the United States and that have the option of resorting to alternative suppliers. Yet even recipients that are almost totally reliant on U.S. supplies may not lack a capacity to bargain and to manage U.S. attempts at influence. Indeed, U.S. economic and military assistance programs in the 1960s seem to have provided an important training ground for foreign elites to learn how to negotiate with U.S. bureaucracies, to exploit U.S. objectives and programs, and at times to exercise "reverse leverage." Thus, arms transfers may sometimes be more an indicator of local bargaining capacity than of U.S. influence and leverage. Even though it is unclear and uncertain that arms transfers serve to build political influence and leverage, it nonetheless seems true that U.S. restrictions on transfers may well lead to a deterioration of political goodwill and military access. Such restrictions may also open the door to increased presence and roles for extra-hemispheric suppliers.[30]

Pre-emptive Selling

Given the fact that it has been a buyers' market, pre-emptive selling has become a leading criterion for arms transfers. It has evidently become more significant than meeting valid military requirements. Pre-emptive selling has been touted as a means to minimize third-party sales that may jeopardize U.S. military advisory and training relationships, that may lessen potential U.S. leverage through logistics and re-supply functions, that may prove more costly to the recipient and divert greater economic resources than would U.S. sales, and/or that may potentially lead to the disruption of good U.S. access and relations with individual Latin American countries. The measure of U.S. influence becomes the pre-emption or limitation of a rival supplier's potential influence. Accordingly, if the United States will not sell to them, then the clients may buy elsewhere; if they are going to buy something anyway, then the United States might as well sell it to them.

No one has yet made an attractive case to refute the reasonableness of this policy line. Yet there are grounds for being wary. It is clear that various governments have threatened to buy elsewhere, partly in order to gain bargaining leverage for the sale of U.S. weapons on good terms. Moreover, in the evolving international context there may sometimes be advantages to the United States in not being or trying to be an exclusive or highly dominant supplier.

U.S. domination of Latin military relationships during the 1940s through the 1960s served to "control" arms transfers, maintain local military balances, and preserve the regional peace that existed from the end of the Peru-Ecuador conflict in 1942 until the El Salvador-Honduras "soccer war" in 1969. In the current international and regional environment, however, it is no longer feasible for the United States to dominate hemispheric military relations and arms transfers. Most governments, in Central as well as South America, have learned to be wary about both the reliability of U.S. support in the event of local conflict, and the likelihood of U.S. interference with the supply of necessary parts and ammunition. As a result, some governments appear to be diversifying so that their armed forces have both U.S.-equipped and non-U.S.-equipped units. Moreover, some may have begun to stockpile light arms and ammunition, and to seek potential re-supply arrangements with neighboring countries that have similar equipment inventories. The more that Latin American governments endeavor to circumvent potential unilateral U.S. arms control and designs, at conflict management, the more "unstable" Latin America may look to U.S. observers who would prefer to return to the "arms stability" of the years after World War II.

Nonetheless, in the current environment important reasons may be emerging for the United States to prefer not to win virtually every arms sales contract.

Important advantages for U.S. interests may accrue from developing policies that stress the potential politico-military benefits, rather than the presumed costs, from regional arms diversification. Being one among varied suppliers may prove to be a useful position at times. A very close or dominant arms transfer relationship may no longer optimize political influence and leverage—if it ever did. At present, a very close relationship carries the risk that a client or superclient may be able to exercise reverse-leverage. Local supply diversification serves to put distance between the recipient and the United States, thereby possibly making it easier for the United States to minimize association with regional tensions or conflicts and to act as a mediator for their settlement if they occur. In this regard, it seems useful to recall that the era of small-scale Latin American wars in the 1930s was also an era of declining U.S. influence and intervention in regional affairs and of increasing diversification of local military relations with the European countries. Yet this was also the era of the "Good Neighbor" policy, which proved very constructive for U.S.-Latin American relations, while the local military conflicts in themselves had only marginal impact on relations.[31]

A Policy Principle: Unrestricted but Unsubsidized Sales

Fitting the various criteria and considerations into an overall policy design has proved complex and difficult. In retrospect, it seems clear that during the past ten years restrictive U.S. arms policies have incurred serious political costs. Restrictive measures contributed to the deterioration of U.S.-Latin American

[177]

military relations and stimulated the rise of political nationalism and the resentment of U.S. paternalism and indifference.
Restrictive arms measures became a prominent way to offend
local governments. Contradicting the spirit of the 1947 Rio
Pact and the Mutual Defense Treaties of the 1950s, the U.S.
lack of response in selected military matters adversely affected
Latin American judgments about U.S. responsiveness in other
policy areas. These reactions were especially strong where the
judgments were made by governments headed by military
men who had had counterproductive encounters with the
United States over arms sales.

The United States may only create continuing problems in
hemispheric and bilateral relations by continuing to engage in
restrictive or punitive arms sales policies that mainly serve to
discriminate against Latin America governments, often more
so than against governments in other regions. Nonetheless, the
United States would have little to gain, and much to lose, from
adopting large, aggressive, or promotional arms transfer programs. Indeed, the central policy considerations should not be
framed in a manner that leads inexorably to getting a country
to "buy American," regardless of the potential noneconomic
costs.

On balance, the principle of unrestricted but unsubsidized
military sales has appeared to provide an acceptable policy
guideline for arms transfers to Latin America so long as arms
demands remain moderate.[32] Implementation of such a principle would seek to minimize both the restrictive and promotional tendencies that have prevailed in much of the policy
debates. Such a policy approach would facilitate the U.S. capacity to respond to Latin American requirements within a
framework of "correct" regional relations and international
competition, while seeking to avoid the pitfalls of past policies
that have strained relations. Nonetheless, while this principle

rests on central lessons from the past, *by itself* it constitutes only a limited guide to dealing with the complex trends, potentialities, and problems that seem likely to mark the future and that may enter into individual, incremental arms transfer decisions.

A foreign policy dilemma is facing the United States on how to effectively pursue U.S. national politico-military interests in Latin America, without having to depend on restrictive as well as punitive policies that attempt to impose standards of behavior deemed unacceptable by many countries of the hemisphere. While many of the Latin American governments are military-dominated (and most likely will remain so into the 1980s), current attitudes in the United States may be stimulating a quasi-ideological reaction against "military dictatorships," and even against the Latin American region. A return to anti-militarism, and to a paternalistic attitude toward Latin America, could place the United States on the verge of a new era of recrimination and mutual alienation. The way in which U.S. arms transfer policies are managed for the region and for individual nations will have central consequences for the extent and intensity of this potential alienation.

KEEPING ARMS TRANSFERS IN PERSPECTIVE: GEOPOLITICS AND DEPENDENCY

Even though U.S. arms transfers will continue to be central to U.S.-Latin American relations, arms transfers are nonetheless incidental to the central struggles developing within Latin America. While U.S. politico-military analysts have shown concern about the effects that arms transfer policies may have on development and U.S.-Latin American relations, Latin American military intellectuals have been showing greater concern about the effects that economic development policies may have on intra-regional relations and security conditions. Their concerns are embodied in a growing literature on geopolitics, whose leading outlet has become the polished journal *Estrategia,* published in Argentina. This new geopolitical thinking is both similar to, and substantially different from, the voguish "dependency analysis" that has been formulated by civilian intellectuals in Latin America and in U.S. academic circles.

Military leaders in Latin America are presently demonstrating an interest in geopolitical thinking similar to that experienced in Europe and the United States during the late nineteenth and early twentieth centuries. The claim is made that geopolitics is being rescued from foreigners who had originally used it to justify big-power colonialism and to condemn Latin America to perpetual backwardness and vassalage. Thus geopolitical thinking in Latin America is being used to urge the formation of new plans for economic progress, and to create optimistic visions of future national potentials, while at the same time calling attention to sensitive nonmilitary factors at home and abroad that may adversely affect local development and security. While this trend is most prominent in the larger nations comprising the southern cone of South America, armed forces in the smaller nations, such as Panama, also lay claim to having geopolitical doctrines of their own. In addition, different service branches may have different geopolitical perspectives to stress their separate roles and importance. At times somewhat ideological in nature, the new geopolitical thinking comes in association with both pro-socialist and pro-capitalist ideas—but the central thrust is a frontier-minded nationalism.

The geopolitical thinking focuses on the spatial distribution and organization of natural resources, population, and the economic infrastructure within the national territory. The primary objective of all geopolitics is the territorial integration of the nation-state. Countries are analyzed as consisting of regions, "islands," or "peninsulas" that are poorly interconnected and unevenly developed. The keys to development become the creation of new "development poles" so as to fill interior voids and eliminate the economic isolation of potentially rich regions, especially those on the borders. The march into the interior is necessary not only to exploit resources but also to prevent foreign penetration and influence. The main policy instruments are to be dynamic colonization, and the engineering of new infrastructure for transportation, communications, and hydroelectric power, especially highways, canals, railroads, ports and dams.[33] Spatial maladjustment, not class structure, is treated as the central cause of economic stagnation and political instability.

The new geopoliticians generally agree that Brazil has exceptional comparative advantages. The "sub-continental heartland" or the "continental welding area" is seen to fall almost entirely within Brazil's boundaries, and extend partly into Bolivia and Paraguay. Brazil also embraces most of the Amazon, and parts of the Plate and Orinoco river systems. Thus, Brazil is present in all the major geopolitical zones of South America, giving it great advantage over its "Balkanized" neighbors. This suggests that the territorial integration of Brazil will necessarily involve some Brazilian intervention in the spaces beyond its borders—yet it also implies a great Brazilian resonsibility for sub-continental stability.

If Brazil is the strong point, Bolivia is seen to be a critical soft point of fulcrum for South American geopolitics. Bolivia connects the Andean spine to the Amazon and Plate basins, and represents a strategic crossing between the Atlantic and Pacific Oceans. Thus it represents the "continental hinterland," "a nerve center," the "intermediary void between

[181]

Brazil-Chile and Argentina-Peru," a "dangerous focal point for conflict in the southern cone," as well as a "contact zone . . . key stronghold for the development of a universal strategy for Latin America." Bolivia is regarded as a competitive arena for Brazil and Argentina, not only for "marching" to the Pacific by building road, rail, and river transportation infrastructure, but also for gaining access to needed raw materials, including iron, oil, and gas. Furthermore, the need for secure linkage to Bolivia becomes an argument for promoting the development of provinces in Argentina and Brazil that border on Bolivia.

While only Brazil is favored with a geographic structure to "go it alone," its Spanish American neighbors cannot afford to turn inward. They must emerge from their limited national spaces if they expect to defend their sovereignty and have bargaining power. Andean integration and diplomatic cooperation are considered to be necessary among the Spanish American countries, including Argentina because of its weak position as a downstream country on the Plate river system. Yet the Andean countries face difficult geopolitical problems. For example, Ecuador's access to the Amazon and Bolivia's access to the Pacific are prevented by earlier losses of territory, in both cases in wars involving Peru.

Rivers are extremely important to South American geopolitical thinkers. One great goal is the future development and interconnection of the three major river systems: the Plate, Amazon, and Orinoco. This prospect entails great concern about the distribution of potential benefits, and the consequent need to create inter-state commissions for purposes of bargaining and discussing trade-offs and plans that lead to equitable results. In this regard, a very sensitive issue area between Argentina and Brazil is the hydroelectric development through the Corpus-Itaipu projects, and any related diversion of waters in the Plate system. Argentine geopoliticians are profoundly worried that Brazilian interests and plans will prove detrimental to Argentina. It is said that the "essence of the nation's future is at stake," and that geopolitical issues involving the development of the Plate basin will determine the roles Argentina can and will play during the next 30-40 years.

The potential development of neighbors makes it imperative to develop one's own country. Otherwise, security and sovereignty may become meaningless. Brazilian expansionism in particular, its concept of "living frontiers," is viewed as being geopolitically innate and representing a potential threat to Spanish America. Potential foreign threats and the need to maintain a peaceful "equilibrium" in South America are often raised in order to motivate home efforts to undertake great projects that will serve to forge a sense of national unity and will. Thus, even though the potentially threatening nature of a neighbor's development may be stressed, the policy implications of most geopolitical thinking are essentially defensive in nature, amounting to recommendations to put one's own house in order first.

The new geopolitical thinking is not at all status-quo oriented. Indeed, much of it calls for combating "forces of the status quo" that may be said to block great projects in part because of ties to foreign capital. For example, Argentina's inability to develop has been blamed in part on the control wielded by traditional forces of the status quo, and on the absence of national sectors from the centers of state power. According to one leading geopolitical analyst of Argentina's relations with Brazil,

   . . . an understanding will be difficult and a conflict of interests could reach dangerous proportions if the regime

[183]

in either country is controlled by powers alien to the area, or by foreign financial and economic groups whose self-interest prompts them to provoke regional conflicts.[34]

Such thinking leads to criticism of governments that do not give priority to proper domestic engineering and migration projects, and that do not undertake diplomatic initiatives for settling problems with neighbors. Requirements for future progress are often said to include internal reorganization and planning, along with the building of national will, on the basis of new determinations of the kind of country that is desirable.

In sum, geopolitical writings reflect the fact that decisive battles for the defense of national interests are not won or lost in wars only. Indeed, war is to be avoided because it would only compound the economic problems and geopolitical disorganization that already exist. National development is accordingly the most secure approach to defending a nation-state against encroachment and exploitation by immediate neighbors and foreign powers, including the United States. The objective is to build nations through socio-economic projects, and to create appropriate legal-jurisprudence frameworks and use diplomatic initiatives for settling disagreements with neighbors well short of war. Geopoliticians exhibit a pronounced preference for negotiation and diplomacy; the point is repeatedly made that most border and boundary problems in Latin America's history have been resolved through diplomatic negotiations.

Geopolitical thinkers have led the way in analyzing and emphasizing potential threats from neighbors. Yet their analyses reveal that, for them at least, arms transfers are of marginal significance. The major "threats" are nonmilitary and need to be met by nonmilitary means. What happens to economic infrastructure projects seems far more serious to intra-hemispheric relations than whether or not Argentina or Brazil acquires another squadron of jet fighters.

NOTES

1.   A concise history of the evolution of U.S. military aid policies and the purchasing patterns of Latin American countries in the post-World War II period is provided in L. R. Einaudi, H. Heymann, Jr., D. F. Ronfeldt, and C. D. Sereseres, "Arms Transfers to Latin America: Toward a Policy of Mutual Respect," The Rand Corporation, Santa Monica, June 1973. Also see Stephen S. Kaplan, "U.S. Arms Transfers to Latin America, 1945– 1974," *International Studies Quarterly,* December 1975, pp. 399-431; and Michael T. Klare, "How to Trigger an Arms Race," *The Nation,* August 30, 1975, pp. 137-42.

2.   Foreign Relations Committee Study, *Arms Sales and Foreign Policy,* U.S. Senate, 90th Cong., 1st Sess. 1967.

3.   Latin American governments had similarly turned to Europe in the 1950s for combat aircraft and ships when the United States refused to supply them, but with smaller total outlays and less U.S. reaction than in the 1960s.

4.   For a discussion of Cuba's Angola venture and its possible ramifications for the Western Hemisphere, see Edward Gonzalez, "Castro and Cuba's New Orthodoxy," *Problems in Communism,* Vol. XXV (January-February 1976), pp. 1-9. Also see Gonzalez and Ronfeldt, *Post-Revolutionary Cuba in a Changing World,* The Rand Corporation, Santa Monica, R-1844-ISA, December 1975, pp. 71-78. Cuba's military involvement in Angola (with Soviet assistance) and Cuba's increasing presence elsewhere on the African continent has demonstrated to the Latin American nations that a

conventional threat from Cuba may become a contingency. Nonetheless, it seems unlikely that Cuba's intervention in Angola will be duplicated in the Caribbean or Central American area.

5. Nuclear proliferation for military purposes lies in the longer-term future. Meanwhile the demand for conventional weaponry may be rationalized in part as a way to forego resorting to nuclear weaponry. In the long run, the heavy spread of conventional weaponry in an area may then become a rationale for resorting to the acquisition of nuclear weaponry for allegedly defensive purposes.

6. By General Edgardo Mercado Jarrín, "Relations between Policy and Military Strategy," *Oiga* (Lima), March 15, 1974, pp. 18-20, 44-46, and also published in *Estrategia* (Buenos Aires), March-April 1974, pp. 16-29.

7. See R. M. Ogorkiewicz, "Engesa Wheeled Armoured Vehicles," *International Defense Review,* February 1977, pp. 328-30.

8. Sales to OPEC countries are important to Brazil because of its dependence on oil imports.

9. While the discussion above has focused on military aspects of local production, Roberto Pereira de Andrade, "Brazil Stresses Air Capability," *Air International,* September 1976, pp. 111ff., makes the important point (p. 112) that,

> ... the principal role of the FAB is seen in most Brazilian official circles—if not necessarily in the FAB itself—as an instrument of economic development; its missions are predominantly social and, in consequence, the average Brazilian thinks of the FAB not so much as a fighting force but as a state-owned enterprise for the transportation of passengers, mail and freight into and out of places into which commercial operators cannot or will not fly, for mitigating the effects of natural disasters and

for aeromedical tasks, including such hearts-and-mind duties as transporting doctors, vaccines and relief aid into the interior.

10. Such conclusions are elaborated in one case study by Brian Jenkins, Caesar Sereseres, and Luigi Einaudi, *U.S. Military Aid and Guatemalan Politics,* Arms Control and Foreign Policy Seminar, California Institute of Technology, Pasadena, March 1974, and reprinted in *Armed Forces and Society,* Summer 1977, pp. 575-94.

11. For example, see Phillipe C. Schmitter, "Foreign Military Assistance, National Military Spending and Military Rule in Latin America," in Schmitter, ed., *Military Rule in Latin America* (Beverly Hills: Sage Publications, 1973).

12. For an analysis of the links between U.S. military assistance and the evolution of a new military professionalism in Latin America, see Jenkins, Sereseres, and Einaudi, *op. cit.*; Alfred Stepan, "The New Professionalism of Internal Warfare and Military Role Expansion," in Stepan (ed.), *Authoritarian Brazil* (New Haven: Yale University Press, 1976), pp. 47-65; Luigi Einaudi and Alfred Stepan, *Latin American Institutional Development: Changing Military Perspectives in Peru and Brazil* (Santa Monica: The Rand Corporation, 1971); and John S. Fitch, "The Political Consequences of U.S. Military Assistance to Latin America," paper presented to the Military Policy Symposium on Inter-American Security and the United States, U.S. Army War College, Carlisle, Pennsylvania, January 20-22, 1977.

A good general reader on military participation in government is Abraham F. Lowenthal, ed., *Armies and Politics in Latin America* (New York: Holmes and Meier, 1976).

13. See Mercado Jarrín, *op cit.,* which states that "Some of the problems would disappear if, in peacetime, the politician would learn to consider military factors; and the military man, in turn, would learn to consider political concepts."

[187]

14. The melding of corporativist tendencies and technocratic capabilities may lead to new kinds of civil-military systems based largely on the sophisticated concentration and control of information—a kind of "cybernocracy." As the world enters the post-industrial era, "information" may well surpass "capital" as a currency of political power and struggle for change. If so, then "surplus information," mainly concentrated in state bureaucracies, may replace "surplus capital" as a central intellectual concern.

15. The target of some restrictive amendments was not only Latin America but the executive branch of the U.S. government which, from a variety of Congressional views, seemed lax in utilizing military and economic assistance to protect U.S. investments, tuna boats, human rights, democratic government, and discourage Latin American purchase of expensive and sophisticated military hardware. An excellent review of past efforts to dictate behavior via the supposed "leverage" obtained from U.S. assistance programs is provided in Herbert Goldhamer, *The Foreign Powers in Latin America* (Princeton, N.J., Princeton University Press, 1972), pp. 260-302.

16. In Argentina, for example, the release of hundreds of political prisoners by former president Hector Campora in 1973 is one explanation for the subsequent rise of terrorism.

17. On this point, see Mariano Grondona, "South America Looks at Détente (Skeptically)," *Foreign Policy,* Spring 1977, pp. 184-203.

18. For the complete text of the Ayacucho Declaration see "Eight Latin American Governments Sign Declaration Aimed at Limiting Armaments," in *U.N. Monthly Chronicle,* March 1975, pp. 54-57.

19. The U.S. position on the Ayacucho Declaration and the tripartite negotiations has been to keep at a distance because of the sensitivites of these nations. The fear is that a strong U.S. involvement and/or encouragement would be perceived as an effort to keep these countries militarily weak and dependent on the United States. See

the Hearings before the Subcommittee on Foreign Assistance, *International Security Assistance*. U.S. Senate, 94th Cong. 2nd Sess., Washington, D.C., 1976, p. 26.

20.   Israel has apparently been able to utilize its recent military sales to Guatemala as a lever to acquire additional commercial sales. The American company Texas Instruments was said to have "sewn up" a lucrative $2.5 million radar system sale prior to U.S.-Guatemalan arms purchase problems. However, the Israeli sale of Arava transports is reputed to have provided access to the lucrative commercial deal. The Arava which has a selling price of about one million dollars, has also been sold to El Salvador, Mexico and Nicaragua.

21.   The arms control literature on Latin America includes Edward Bernard Glick, "The Feasibility of Arms Control and Disarmament in Latin America," *Orbis,* Fall 1965, pp. 743-59; Geoffrey Kemp, "The Prospects for Arms Control in Latin America: The Strategic Dimensions," in Schmitter, ed., *op. cit.,* pp. 189-243; and John R. Redick, "Prospects for Arms Control in Latin America," *Arms Control Today,* September 1975, pp. 1-3.

22.   The United States was able to prevent the sale of Kfirs to Ecuador in early 1977 because the aircraft contained American-made engines. However, the U.S. government may have indirectly reimbursed the Israeli government for loss of the sale by adding $285 million to the 1978 International Security Assistance Act appropriation for Israel. In most cases, the United States will not possess an ability to prevent the sale of military equipment to Latin America by third countries.

23.   In 1976, Defense Minister Shimon Peres claimed Israel would export $320 million worth of weapons that year, and was aiming to export $1 billion in overseas sales within the next few years.

Israeli sales efforts in Guatemala, discussed above, are not an isolated case in the Latin American region. In 1973, Israel quietly added fuel to the smoking relations between El Salvador and Honduras when it sold old Ouragan jet fighters on easy credit terms to El Salvador. This disturbed the local power balance and spurred the Honduran purchase of Israeli Super Mystere interceptor/ground attack jet fighters.

24. The admonition of Ecuador for its inability to defend itself against Peru is described by Bryce Wood, *The United States and Latin American Wars, 1932-1942* (New York: Columbia University Press, 1966), p. 315.

25. Research papers by Col. Charles D. Corbett, "Inter-American Security and U.S. Military Policy," and by Lt. Col. John Child, "The Inter-American Military System: Historical Development, Current Status and Implications for U.S. Policy," both presented at the U.S. Army War College Military Policy Symposium, January 1977, were useful as background preparation.

26. From Mercado Jarrín, *op. cit.*

27. A future structure for U.S. security might well emphasize three principal braces: NATO/Japan, friendly regional powers in third areas, and trilateral North American interdependence with Canada and Mexico.

28. Brazil's recent cancellation of military assistance agreements with the United States, although timed as a protest against U.S. human rights policies, had actually been under consideration for months and was due to broader considerations.

29. Economic objectives of arms sales to Latin America are not discussed here. They are not as important as are political and military objectives in relations between the U.S. and Latin American governments.

30. Observations that it is difficult to analyze whether Soviet arms

transfers have afforded the Soviet Union with direct political leverage appear in: Roger F. Pajak, "Soviet Arms Aid in the Middle East," Center for Strategic and International Studies, Georgetown University, January 1976; and Uri Ra'anan, "Soviet Arms Transfers and the Problem of Political Leverage," prepared for a conference on Implications of the Military Build-Up in Non-Industrial States, The Fletcher School of Law and Diplomacy, Tufts University, May 6-8, 1976.

Abraham S. Becker, "Arms Transfers, Great Power Intervention, and Settlement of the Arab-Israeli Conflict," The Rand Corporation, July 1977, P-5901, also deals with this issue, and questions assertions that arms transfers necessarily have a destabilizing impact on regional affairs.

31. These considerations, which would militate against pre-emptive selling practices, suggest a possibility for the United States to use its arms transfer policies for bargaining with other potential suppliers. Instead of asking what benefits can be obtained from the recipient by concluding a proposed sale, a more useful question might become: Could a trade-off or offset be obtained from a supply competitor by offering to withhold or adversely affect U.S. competition for a proposed arms transfer, so that the competitor is able to conclude the arms deal. Such offset arrangements have apparently been negotiated in the past outside Latin America. They may be worth discussion in regard to some situations in Latin America.

32. This policy principle was originally presented and elaborated at length in Einaudi, et al., *op. cit.*, and was extended by Ronfeldt, "Future U.S. Security Assistance in the Latin American Context," for A Report of the Commission on United States-Latin American Relations, *The Americas in a Changing World* (Quadrangle/The New York Times Book Co. 1975). The Commission adopted the principle for one of its policy recommendations—except in the case of nations engaging in military hostilities or practicing systematic violations of human rights.

33. See note 9, above.

34. From a translation of an article by General Juan Enrique Gugliamelli, "Argentine Response to Brazil's 'Misiones Offensive,' " appearing in *Estrategia,* November 1972-February 1973, pp. 7-15. General Gugliamelli is Director of *Estrategia.*

FOUR

American Arms Transfers: Policy and Process in the Executive Branch

Paul C. Warnke
with Edward C. Luck

INTRODUCTION

Critics of the U.S. arms sales program charge that it is out of control, moving under its own momentum without defined guidelines or limits. Rather than simply claiming that the policy is faulty, many of these analysts contend that, in fact, there is no coherent U.S. policy regarding arms sales at all. They focus their attention on the inadequacies of the policy-making process, which, in their eyes, is responsible for this lack.

This chapter examines both the policy and the process by which it is made in order to suggest a series of reforms in each. A basic thesis is that, while there are glaring weaknesses in the policy-making process, the fundamental problem lies in the perspectives and priorities of those high-ranking officials who determine what weapons the United States is willing to sell and to what countries.

Recent trends in U.S. arms exports have fostered the impression that there is a lack of control over the program. During the past few years, there have been major shifts in the volume, composition, direction and financing of U.S. arms exports, which have been undertaken without a comprehensive public statement of policy from the White House, State Department, or Defense Department.

Today, the United States retains its position as by far the world's leading arms supplier. During the past decade, the United States has transferred almost as many defense articles and services as all other nations combined.[1] The pace of completed U.S. arms transfers has more than doubled over the past decade, while orders for U.S. arms sales have expanded even more rapidly, promising a higher level of transfers in the future.[2] From an arms control perspective, an even more disturbing trend has been the increasing sophistication of the weapons being transferred to the Third World. No longer content with receiving second-hand or even present inventory arms, some developing countries, especially in the Near East, are demanding and getting some of the most advanced weapon systems in the U.S. arsenal, such as F-14, F-15 and F-16 fighters, Lance missiles, and Spruance class destroyers.

Throughout the cold war years, the great majority of U.S. arms exports were made in the form of grants to nations which we believed to be threatened by the expansion of Communist influence, especially in Western Europe and East Asia. From 1950 to 1965, the leading recipients of U.S. military assistance and sales were France, West Germany, Italy, Turkey, Taiwan, and South Korea.[3] But since the oil embargo and the Yom Kippur War, the Near East has emerged as the primary recipient region, with Iran, Saudi Arabia, and Israel as the principal customers for U.S. arms sales. (Figure 1 compares the flow of U.S. arms to various areas from 1966 to 1974.) Furthermore, during the latter years the shift from grant aid to sales as the major means for U.S. arms exports has been substantially complete. Military sales, which constituted less than one-third of U.S. arms exports from FY 1950 to 1970, exceeded military assistance by more than a nine-to-one margin between FY 1971 to 1975.[4] Table 1 shows U.S. arms sales and military assistance, FY 1966-75. Foreign orders for arms sales through U.S. government and commercial channels, under $1.5 billion in FY 1970, have averaged more than $10 billion over the three years, FY 1974-76.[5] In contrast to the growth of arms sales, the President has signed legislation requiring the phase-out of Military Assistance Programs by September 30, 1977, unless subsequently authorized by Congress on a country-by-country basis.[6]

Recent Policy

The growing emphasis on sales rather than assistance in the U.S. arms export program has been the product of a deliberate policy shift enunciated in the early 1960s. At that time, it was recognized that many more developing countries were making sufficient economic progress to assume a greater share of the financial burden of their defense. There was also increasing appreciation of the potential economic benefits of arms sales for our balance-of-payments position and in support of our domestic arms industry.

[195]

FIGURE 1

U.S. Arms Trade, by Region, FY 1966-1974*
(in billion/million current dollars)

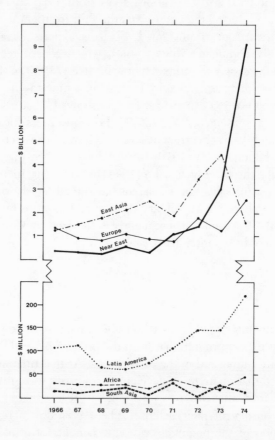

* Foreign Military Sales orders, commercial sales, Military Assistance Program, and Military Assistance—Service Funded.
Source: Department of Defense, Security Assistance Agency, *Foreign Military Sales and Military Assistance Facts, November 1975,* pp. 14-15, 22-23, 24-25, 32.

TABLE 1

U.S. Arms Sales and Military Assistance, FY 1966 through 1975
(In millions of current dollars)

	Sales[1] (000,000)	Assistance[2] (000,000)
1966	1,733	971
1967	1,217	876
1968	1,056	596
1969	1,802	453
1970	1,391	382
1971	2,054	755
1972	3,685	546
1973	4,770	590
1974	11,311	785
1975	9,511	584

1. Foreign military sales orders and commercial sales deliveries (the government does not keep a record of commercial sales orders). Department of Defense, Security Assistance Agency, *Foreign Military Sales and Military Assistance Facts*, November 1975, pp. 14 and 22. FY 1975 commercial deliveries are estimated to be $547 million by the Department of State, Office of Munitions Control.

2. Military Assistance Program. *Ibid.*, p. 24., Military Assistance-Service Funded, which primarily went to South Vietnam, is not included.

In October 1961, an office of International Logistic Negotiations (ILN) was established in the Department of Defense to supervise military sales. ILN successfully engaged in a two-dimensional effort to encourage U.S. arms manufacturers to seek foreign markets and to stimulate foreign countries to purchase U.S. weapons. In FY 1961, military aid had been twice as large as sales. Five years later the proportions were just the reverse.

From the viewpoint of those who wish to see the arms trade

[197]

controlled, the U.S. sales effort has been all too successful. Short-run economic considerations which argue for an open-ended and unrestricted arms sales program may be inconsistent with more important objectives in foreign policy, national security and arms control. Although official statements concerning U.S. arms sales policy generally de-emphasize economic motivations, the stress on sales encourages recipient countries to view arms transfers as no different from international trade in other commodities—and to assume we view them that way too. Accordingly, if they can afford the purchases, the sales should be allowed. In this view, to restrict arms sales is to interfere with free trade. As numerous developing countries have gained large amounts of capital, especially in the oil-rich Persian Gulf area, the demand for U.S. arms has expanded rapidly. Thus far, this growing demand has been matched by the willingness of the United States and other major suppliers to increase the availability of arms.

Yet it would be overly simplistic to claim that there have been no unilateral restrictions on U.S. arms exports in recent years. Obviously, foreign policy and national security considerations have foreclosed the transfer of weapons to many unfriendly nations, even though such transactions might have had economic benefits. The Foreign Military Sales Act, which covers government-to-government (FMS) sales, permits arms sales only if "the President finds that the furnishing of defense articles and defense services to such country or international organization will strengthen the security of the United States and promote world peace." [7] At present, 95 nations and 4 international organizations are eligible to purchase arms from the U.S. government.[8]

Reflecting the shifting emphasis from aid to sales, the number of nations receiving U.S. military assistance declined from

58 in FY 1966 to 46 in FY 1975, while the number of U.S. arms sales recipients increased by a somewhat larger number.[9] In FY 1966, 59 nations received FMS deliveries, with the total reaching 74 in FY 1975.[10] Commercial deliveries reflected a similar growth from 59 countries in FY 1966 to 77 in FY 1974.[11] Not surprisingly, most of the new recipients were relatively small developing countries with rather modest arms imports.

Other more significant markets for U.S. arms could possibly expand in the future. Until recently, Sub-Saharan Africa was an area of relatively low arms imports, in part because the region was assigned a low priority in the strategic calculations of the great powers. But growing competition between the superpowers for influence in the area and the resulting exacerbation of local conflicts have led to increased arms transfers from both the Soviet Union and the United States. Preliminary estimates indicate that U.S. foreign military sales to Africa surged from $35 million in FY 1975 to $129 million in FY 1976.[12] This upward trend is likely to continue with proposed sales of F-5s and other arms to Kenya and Zaire. There is a danger that the superpowers will become committed to the militarization of Sub-Saharan Africa before clearly defining their national security and foreign policy interests in the region.

Rumania, which was added to the list of commercial arms sales recipients in FY 1974, has reportedly expressed interest in acquiring F-5 fighters and other advanced weaponry from the United States.[13] Yugoslavia has long been a small but steady purchaser of U.S. arms and received almost $700 million in military assistance while asserting its independence from Moscow.[14] If tensions rise again after the death of Tito, the United States may increase its arms transfers to Yugoslavia

[199]

considerably. Yet there are obviously major political and national security impediments to developing a sizable U.S. arms market in Eastern Europe.

Only minor quantities of U.S. arms were transferred to South Asia during the past decade, but the volume is bound to increase with the lifting of the U.S. embargo on major arms exports to Pakistan and India.[15] Likewise, the sale of six C-130 transport planes to Egypt may be a harbinger of larger arms transfers in the future.[16] Finally, there has been some speculation that China may become eligible to purchase U.S. armaments in the foreseeable future.[17]

Arms transfers have served as a barometer of U.S. interests in and commitments to particular countries and regions. Military assistance and sales have been widely employed as a signal of growing U.S. interest in areas of the world which formerly had been considered of low priority. This practice has encouraged Third World countries to view arms transfers as a normal, or even necessary, component of friendly relations with the United States. From their perspective, for the United States to deny arms sales or assistance has implied a denial of American interest in improved relations with the particular country. Yet, if arms exports are not carefully controlled, there is a danger that arms transfers in some cases will define the U.S. interest and commitment to certain countries, rather than vice versa. This danger is particularly acute in regions of the world where U.S. foreign policy and national security interests have not been well-defined or are in a state of flux. Unfortunately, this category includes much of the Third World.

Though the new purchasers have thus far accounted for only a small percentage of the recent growth of U.S. arms sales, these transfers may be important as indicators of future trends, both in the arms trade and in foreign policy. Moreover, many of these transactions, while not large on a global scale, may significantly affect military balances in regions of relatively low military preparedness.

Large increases in both the quantity and quality of arms transactions with traditional recipients, especially Iran, Saudi Arabia and Israel, account for most of the expansion of U.S. arms sales orders. Table 2 compares foreign military sales orders for these countries and worldwide, FY 1969-76. During FY 1973-76, these three countries placed almost two-thirds (65 percent) of worldwide FMS orders, compared to only two-fifths (40 percent) for the previous four years. Likewise, Iran and Saudi Arabia alone accounted for slightly more than one-half (51 percent) of the orders during the last four years, more than double their 23 percent figure for the earlier period.

The United States has had security relationships with all three countries for many years; hence, the basic policy issue has not been whether the U.S. would supply them with armaments, but with what kinds of weapons in what quantities. It is widely accepted that these and other major recipient countries are important to U.S. foreign policy, national security, and economic interests, but are these interests best served by the size and scope of the present U.S. arms export program? What qualitative or quantitative limits ought to be placed on the export of weapons to friendly and strategically important nations?

Although executive branch officials have enunciated a number of general guidelines for U.S. arms exports, they have largely failed to address these fundamental questions regarding the overall size and scope of the program. In a prepared statement before the House International Relations Commit-

[201]

TABLE 2

U.S. Foreign Military Sales Orders
(Value in millions of dollars)

Recipient	FY 1969 $ %	FY 1970 $ %	FY 1971 $ %	FY 1972 $ %	FY 1973 $ %	FY 1974 $ %	FY 1975 $ %	FY 1976[1] $ %
Iran	239 (15)	113 (12)	398 (24)	524 (16)	2,115 (48)	3,917 (36)	2,568 (27)	1,289 (15)
Saudi Arabia	4 (0.3)	45 (5)	96 (6)	337 (10)	626 (14)	2,539 (23)	1,374 (14)	2,487 (30)
Sub-total	243 (15)	158 (17)	494 (30)	861 (26)	2,741 (62)	6,456 (59)	3,942 (41)	3,776 (45)
Israel	312 (20)	45 (5)	415 (25)	406 (12)	192 (4)	2,437 (23)	869 (9)	907 (11)
Sub-total	555 (35)	203 (21)	909 (55)	1,267 (39)	2,933 (67)	8,893 (82)	4,811 (51)	4,683 (56)
Worldwide	1,551 (100)	953 (100)	1,657 (100)	3,261 (100)	4,368 (100)	10,809 (100)	9,511 (100)	8,337 (100)

[1] Preliminary DSAA figures for FY 1976.

Source: U.S., Department of Defense, Security Assistance Agency, *Foreign Military Sales and Military Assistance Facts, November 1975*, pp. 14-15.

tee in November 1975, Secretary of State Henry Kissinger listed four factors or criteria which are to be considered on a case-by-case basis for each proposed arms transfer:

> *What is the nature and extent of the threat to the security of the recipient nation?* Do we agree on the nature of the threat? Involved here is the role that country plays in its region and in the world, its capacity to maintain its stability, and its will to defend its own interests.
>
> *What is the United States' interest in helping to preserve that security?* What interests does the recipient have in common with us and where do our interests diverge? What potential influence for restraint or positive conduct is involved?
>
> *What other nations are involved in military transfers to the recipient—now or potentially?* What options has the recipient? Will a refusal lead it to turn to another source of supply, perhaps altering a presently desirable international relationship?
>
> *And what are the consequences for us if we fail to respond?* What are the disadvantages of refusing to sell to a government with which we enjoy good relations? Will regional or even global military balances be affected? What will be the impact on our own readiness? [18]

These are important questions, but they do not provide the basis for a coherent overall arms export policy. In particular, Secretary Kissinger did not emphasize in his list the importance of the determination whether an arms transfer will advance U.S. national security interests. Moreover, there is no reference to economic, human rights and arms control considerations. The first of these is obviously a current factor. The second two have been largely ignored.

The first two of the criteria enumerated by Secretary Kissinger concern whether the United States should provide arms to a particular country, but they present no criteria by which to judge the appropriate quantity or quality of arms transfers. His third and fourth criteria relate primarily to the possible negative consequences if the U.S. turns down an arms request from a particular nation. Implicitly accepting the premise that arms transfers can be an effective means of gaining influence in the recipient countries, Secretary Kissinger exhibits concern about the familiar argument that "if we do not sell arms, others (including the Soviets) will." Indeed, his reference to possible effects on the "global military balance" would suggest that he views U.S. arms transfers as a significant factor in the overall Soviet-American arms competition.

In the same statement, Secretary Kissinger warned: "The United States cannot expect to retain influence with nations whose perceived defense needs we disregard. Defense supply links to these countries can significantly strengthen efforts to achieve cooperation on other issues—whether political, economic or cultural." [19] Many other U.S. officials have also contended that arms transfers are a means for gaining influence over the domestic and foreign policies of the recipient countries.

Yet the U.S. experiences in Vietnam, South Korea, Greece and Turkey and the Soviet debacle in Egypt suggest that the influence obtained through arms transfers may be illusory or temporary. Furthermore, as the United States discovered in Vietnam and the Soviet Union learned in Indonesia, a sudden change of regime can convert an "asset" to a "liability" overnight.[20] This danger appears greatest in volatile Third World countries ruled by autocratic and repressive regimes—a description which fits some of the principal recipients of U.S. arms.

There seems to be no clear linkage between arms transfers and leverage over a variety of important international political and economic issues. Iran is our best arms customer, but persists in urging higher oil prices (which serve in part to pay for the increased arms purchases). The voting records in the United Nations and other multilateral forums of Third World states receiving U.S. arms are frequently unfavorable to the U.S. position. Despite warnings from the United States many major recipients of U.S. arms continue to pursue repressive domestic policies.

Secretary Kissinger's concern about the possibly negative consequences of denying arms requests from particular countries raises the question of who gains more leverage from an arms transfer, the supplier or the recipient. If the United States is reluctant to restrict its arms shipments for fear of losing its influence, then the recipient has gained considerable leverage over U.S. arms export policy. The ultimate threat possessed by the United States—to restrict severely or entirely cut off its supply of arms—is rarely employed, and then only under extreme circumstances. In recent years, this threat has simply not been credible in dealing with a wide range of political and economic issues which the United States would like to influence. The tendency of the United States to become locked-in to particular supplier-recipient relationships has been reinforced by the expectations of many Third World countries that arms transfers are a normal facet of dealing with the United States and not to receive arms is abnormal.

It is interesting to note that the growth of U.S. arms transfers during the past decade has coincided with a period of declining American influence abroad. Arms exports have proved to be neither a necessary nor an effective factor in gaining influence over the policies and actions of foreign countries. Far more important factors are the wisdom of U.S.

foreign policy, the unity of the American people behind that policy, the skill and good sense of our diplomats, the health of our economy, and the strength of our own armed forces. As recent experience has demonstrated, increasing arms sales cannot compensate for weaknesses in these essential foundations of successful foreign relations.

Foreign policy rationales for arms sales, like economic motivations, are open-ended in that they provide no guidance regarding the number or type of weapons which should be transferred.[21] The same foreign policy considerations that lead the United States to begin supplying arms to a particular country may argue against placing well-defined limits on the flow of arms once it has begun. From the perspective of fostering harmonious relations, it unquestionably is difficult to refuse particular arms requests from friendly countries. Accordingly, the ambassadors and Washington officials concerned with particular countries or regions are often advocates for approving their arms requests.

But in the long-term interests of arms control, U.S. national security, and relations with other countries in the region, it may well be important to say "no" more often than we have in the past. Arms sales policy must be consistent with the broad objectives of U.S. foreign policy. In addition, however, arms control and other national security considerations should be taken into account, particularly in determining the size and scope of the arms sales program.

To judge from past patterns of U.S. arms transfers, some general restraints have been observed regarding the kinds of weapons exported. Certain regional distinctions, especially between NATO and non-NATO recipients, have developed. A 1975 statement from the U.S. Arms Control and Disarmament Agency (ACDA) expressed the agency's interest in the arms control implications of arms transfers to all nations except those in NATO.[22]

In 1974 Congressional testimony, John W. Sipes, Director of the State Department's Office of Munitions Control, referred to a "functional" policy "not to proliferate a strategic nuclear delivery capability." [23] Similarly, in 1975 ACDA included "strategic weapons delivery" systems on a list of weapons whose transfer could have arms control implications.[24] The Department of State, in a written response to a question by Senator Case, noted that, "Requests for sales of sophisticated weapons with a specific nuclear capability such as the Lance missile automatically are treated as extremely sensitive and are submitted for decision at the highest level . . . Such highly sophisticated weapons normally are sold only within the NATO sphere." [25]

This general rule appears to have been largely adhered to in transfers to Latin America, Africa, and South Asia. But the definition of "strategic" weapon is difficult to apply in a Third World context, and several recent transfers to the Near East and East Asia seem inconsistent with this principle. For instance, U.S. F-4 Phantoms, multimission aircraft capable of carrying nuclear bombs, have been supplied to several Third World countries, including Iran, Israel, and Korea.[26] Relatively short-range dual-capable surface-to-surface missiles such as the Lance and Pershing, which are considered "tactical" weapons when deployed in Europe, may have greater "strategic" implications when transferred to volatile and confined regions such as the Middle East.[27] The shipment of Lance missiles to Israel has already been approved, but it appears doubtful that the proposed transfer of the longer-range and larger-yield Pershing missiles to Israel will be authorized, despite Secretary Kissinger's promise to give "favorable consideration" to the Israeli request.[28] No strategic nuclear weapons with inter-continental range, such as long-range bombers and land-based ICBMs, have been transferred in recent years to either NATO or non-NATO countries.

The likelihood of direct military involvement by the super-powers in Third World conflicts seems less if the fighting can be confined to the battlefield and populations centers and local industries do not become targets. The resolution of the conflict will be more difficult when there have been large civilian losses, because it will be harder politically for local leaders to compromise their initial objectives. Moreover, the introduction of nuclear-capable aircraft and surface-to-surface missiles into areas of high tension in which at least one recipient appears to have access to nuclear warheads may raise doubts among neighboring countries about that recipient's intentions and capabilities.[29] Today, the Middle East and South Asia fit this description, but tomorrow, with the growing danger of nuclear proliferation, the Persian Gulf, East Asia, Latin America, and even Southern Africa may be included. As the UNA-USA National Policy Panel on Conventional Arms Control has recommended, in the long-term interests of global stability and national security the United States should cease exporting to the Third World aircraft and surface-to-surface missiles with strategic nuclear capabilities and should encourage other suppliers to adopt similar restraints.[30]

The transfer of very sophisticated weaponry, such as F-14 and F-15 aircraft, Cobra helicopters and Spruance destroyers, to the Third World may raise a number of short- and long-term problems, whether or not they possess strategic nuclear capabilities. The importation of very advanced weapons may disturb local military balances and foster uncertainties between potential adversaries, thus fueling a qualitative arms race as each side seeks superior armaments. Besides having possibly destabilizing military consequences, a qualitative competition can be very expensive for the participating states both in terms of capital and trained manpower. Even oil-rich Persian Gulf countries are far from achieving full economic development or more than a modest standard of living for most of their citizens. Countries with very high rates of illiteracy and relatively few skilled workers are simply not able to absorb and utilize effectively significant numbers of the most sophisticated conventional weapons produced in America.

Thousands of U.S. technicians and military personnel are required both to train local forces in the use and maintenance of the new armaments and to service the highly complex weapons systems. These "back-end" problems related to the implementation of arms sales agreements were highlighted in a staff report of the Senate Foreign Relations Committee, which concluded that "it is unlikely that Iran could go to war in the next five to ten years with its current and prospective inventory . . . of sophisticated weapons . . . without U.S. support on a day-to-day basis." [31] Thus, the transfer of very advanced weapons to the Third World may entail greater direct involvement in local affairs and may lead to more far-reaching commitments than originally intended. Finally, there is a risk that some of these weapons could, through battlefield bases, defection, theft, or coup, fall into the possession of unfriendly countries, thus revealing sensitive information concerning recent advances in U.S. weapons technology.

Paradoxically, the danger of unauthorized use or theft of weapons by field commanders or terrorists may often be greatest in those volatile Third World regions that receive the largest arms imports. The new generation of precision-guided anti-tank and anti-aircraft missiles, many of which can be transported and operated effectively by a single person, could be particularly attractive to terrorist groups. The State Department evidently aware of this problem, has stated that, "except in special circumstances we do not sell or otherwise transfer certain sensitive items such as hand transportable surface-to-air missiles and weapons which are primarily designed for use against crowds." [32] Yet the United States has approved the sale of thousands of relatively compact Dragon and TOW precision-guided anti-tank missiles to Iran. In order to reduce the likelihood of the unauthorized use of these and similar weapons, it has been suggested that they be equipped with permissive action links (PALs) which would prevent their detonation without the approval of the recipient government.[33]

A marked increase in the quantity, as well as the quality, of arms shipments to a particular country may spur a regional arms race and foster instability. Iran's military build-up, which began in late 1972 when Iran already had a significant military edge over its Arab neighbors, has been followed by increasing defense expenditures and arms purchases by both Iraq and Saudi Arabia. In 1973, ACDA included this consideration in a list of criteria for arms transfers:

> A transfer should not represent a marked quantitative increase from past patterns of arms acquisitions that might trigger similar requests from other countries, contribute to an arms race, or create a real or perceived threat to neighboring countries with which the U.S. has friendly relations.[34]

However, this criterion has not been included in more recent lists of executive branch guidelines and evidently was not decisive in determining U.S. arms sales policy in the Near East.

In any case, U.S. arms export policy is not simply a com-

[210]

posite of stated guidelines. Rather it is defined by the way those general principles are applied to specific cases. Policy decisions reflect a series of trade-offs among sometimes conflicting considerations and objectives. To judge from recent trends in U.S. arms exports, those factors favoring increased arms transfers have been given a higher priority than those calling for further restraint.

In summary, it appears that the executive branch has placed a few very broad restraints on U.S. arms exports, and even some of these seem to be eroding. Certain unfriendly countries have been declared ineligible to receive U.S. arms shipments, but the number of recipient nations has increased in recent years. To some extent, the distinction between NATO and non-NATO recipients is fading as more and more sophisticated weapons are transferred to the Near East. There has been a general policy not to export certain kinds of weapons, especially strategic nuclear delivery systems, yet the shipment of dual-capable fighter bombers and surface-to-surface missiles to the Third World has stretched even this limit.

Beyond these limits, both the size and scope of U.S. arms exports have shown considerable growth. In determining its arms transfer policy, the executive branch has apparently not yet resolved the difficult issue of "how much is enough?"

TOWARD A NEW POLICY

At present, there seems to be a presumption that arms sales are to be made unless strong objections are raised at the highest levels of the U.S. government against the proposed sale. The predilection for sales puts the burden of proof on critics of a particular transaction and requires them to justify their position more rigorously than those favoring the sale.

[211]

Two widely held perceptions already discussed largely explain the pro-sales predisposition: (1) the assumption that selling arms is the normal course of action, while refusing to sell is abnormal; and (2) greater sensitivity to the possibly negative consequences of denying particular sales than to the adverse effects of approving them. In line with this approach, current guidelines specify certain general conditions and certain weapons systems where sales should not be made, the implicit assumption being that otherwise arms sales should be approved.

It is time to reverse these presumptions and to require that each proposed arms transfer be justified fully before it can be approved. As Anne Hessing Cahn has contended, "America's basic policy should be not to sell weapons as a matter of policy at all." [35] Rather than specifying when arms *cannot* be sold, new guidelines should be formulated which set forth the conditions under which arms *can* be sold.

The basic criterion for arms transfers should be whether they further the national security of the United States. Arms should be sold when (1) a direct threat to the security of the United States can be established and (2) the arms shipments will clearly lessen the threat. Arms control and human rights considerations, as well as the ability of the recipient to absorb and utilize the weapons effectively, should also be given increased attention. Under these general criteria, (1) sales to our NATO partners and Japan would be largely unaffected; [36] (2) Israel and South Korea would continue as recipients, but some qualitative constraints (such as nuclear-capable systems) might be established; and (3) other traditional recipients in the Near East, East Asia, and Latin America would continue to receive some U.S. arms, but both their quality and quantity usually would be reduced.

During recent years, arms transfers frequently have been employed as a tool of foreign policy in seeking influence in countries which have no long history of close ties with the United States. Besides being less than successful, this policy has dangerous long-term implications for arms control and foreign policy and provides no guidance concerning the appropriate size and scope of the arms sales program. In the future, foreign policy rationales should determine only which countries are eligible for U.S. arms transfers, while national security and arms control considerations should decide the quality and quantity of the arms being transferred.

THE POLICY-MAKING PROCESS

U.S. arms transfers are governed by a complex structure of statutes and procedures. The Foreign Assistance Act of 1961 authorizes the President to provide military assistance to friendly nations, while his authority to make government-to-government (FMS) sales and to license commercial sales derives from the Foreign Military Sales Act of 1968 and the Mutual Security Act of 1954, respectively.[37]

Under the Foreign Assistance and Foreign Military Sales Acts, the Secretary of State is responsible for determining not only which countries are eligible for military assistance or sales, but also the overall size and content of arms transfer programs. The Secretary is also responsible for licensing commercial sales, which is carried out by the Office of Munitions Control under the Bureau of Politico-Military Affairs. FMS sales are handled by the Office of Security Assistance and Sales, also part of the Bureau of Politico-Military Affairs. The Foreign Assistance Act of 1971 established the Under Secretary of State for Security Assistance as the prime policymaker and coordinator for military assistance, including both grants and credit sales, under the Secretary of State.

The administration and implementation of the U.S. arms export program is primarily the responsibility of the Secretary of Defense. This task has been delegated to the Defense Security Assistance Agency, which operates in part through a worldwide network of military assistance advisory groups (MAAGs) and military missions. These groups provide technical information and advice to recipient countries and sometimes serve as middlemen between potential buyers and U.S. companies. Congressional critics have charged that these groups tend to promote U.S. arms sales, and the International Security Assistance and Arms Export Control Act of 1976 requires the phasing-out of MAAGs and military missions in foreign countries by September 30, 1977, unless subsequently authorized by Congress. The Department of Defense plays a major role in determining which kinds of weapons should be transferred in each case, but the State Department retains the formal authority for approving all arms transfers.

The Under Secretary of State for Security Assistance is chairman of the Security Assistance Program Review Committee (SAPRC), which includes representatives from the State, Defense and Treasury Departments, the Office of Management and Budget, the National Security Council, the Agency for International Development (AID), and the Arms Control and Disarmament Agency. This group conducts an annual review of the military assistance and credit sales programs, which are informally coordinated by the committee members throughout the year. However, neither this nor any other formal interagency committee has been authorized to oversee FMS cash sales and commercial sales, which together comprise the vast majority of recent U.S. arms transfers.

Military assistance programs are determined in much the same manner as other government appropriations—the administration annually presents its proposed military assistance budget to Congress for approval or modification, subject to Presidential signature or veto. Thus military aid, like other major national security programs, is subject to Congressional debate and some measure of public scrutiny. On the other hand, military sales, whether through government or commercial channels, have largely been beyond effective Congressional control. The shift from aid to sales has not only decreased Congressional influence over U.S. arms transfers, but has also permitted executive policy to become relatively independent of public control. This may in part explain the tendency of U.S. arms sales policy to become divorced from public opinion, which, according to recent polls, is inclined to disapprove of large arms sales to the Third World.

Congressional critics of U.S. arms export policy, frustrated by their decreasing role in the policy-making process, have initiated two pieces of legislation in recent years to increase Congressional control over arms sales. In December 1974, the Foreign Military Sales Act was amended to require the President (1) to report the total amount of FMS sales each quarter and (2) to submit all proposed FMS sales of more than $25 million to Congress, which could prevent the sale if both houses pass resolutions within 20 days.[38] The International Security Assistance and Arms Export Control Act of 1976 expands Congressional oversight (1) by requiring all non-NATO military sales of $25 million or more to be handled through government-to-government (FMS) rather than commercial channels (thus subjecting them to possible veto by Congress), (2) by calling on the President to submit to Congress an annual country-by-country justification, including an arms control impact statement, of the government-to-government arms sales program, and (3) by expanding reporting procedures on both commercial and governmental military exports, requiring data on agents' fees and political contributions.

Though the administration has felt compelled to reach compromises with Congressional opponents on several occasions, chiefly concerning arms transfers which might affect Israeli or Greek interests, Congress has yet to veto any proposed sale.[39] Despite the expansion of the potential influence of Congress over arms sales, the policy-making process is still largely dominated by the executive branch.

The formal decision-making process for government-to-government (FMS) sales is initiated when a foreign government makes an official request through either diplomatic or military channels.[40] However, a formal request is often preceded by s series of informal discussions among officials of the foreign government, U.S. military and civilian officials, and representatives of the arms manufacturer. At this point, American officials have an opportunity either to encourage or to discourage the potential sale. According to some critics of U.S. arms sales, the MAAG groups and local State Department officers typically tend to be sympathetic to arms requests from the local government. In any case, once a formal request has been submitted, it may become more difficult to say "no."

A formal request to purchase U.S. arms is normally referred to the Bureau of Politico-Military Affairs and the appropriate regional bureau within the State Department.[41] The Defense Security Assistance Agency reviews all proposed transfers, and other agencies, such as ACDA, AID, Treasury and NASA, are frequently consulted. Routine sales are handled at relatively low levels of the bureaucracy, while more sensitive requests are submitted to higher officials and major policy decisions are sometimes made by the President. Policy differences between agencies may be resolved through the National Security Council mechanism. Upon executive branch approval of a given FMS sale, a Letter of Offer (DD Form 1513) outlining the terms of the sale is prepared. If the transaction exceeds $25 million, it must be submitted for Congressional review. Once this hurdle is passed, the Letter of Offer is presented to the foreign government, and, if accepted, the appropriate branch of the U.S. armed services carries out the request.

Commercial sales requests may be initiated through the promotional efforts of a private arms manufacturer, but must undergo a similar governmental review process. In practice, the State Department applies the same kind of policy consid-erations to commercial sales as to FMS transactions, even though the controlling statutes are not identical.[42] At present, commercial sales are not subject to Congressional veto.[43] Commercial arms purchases are of course procured through private rather than Department of Defense channels.

Besides these official procedures, private firms and some recipient governments hire agents who serve as middlemen, arranging and facilitating the transactions. The press has re-ported a number of cases in which foreign agents or govern-ment officials have received unusually large commissions from U.S. firms, presumably to encourage the recipient government to approve the proposed sale.[44] Though these cases do not appear to involve U.S. officials directly, these promotional efforts may be one factor behind the increasing demand for U.S. armaments, especially in developing countries. In any case, the precise role of these middlemen, particularly in FMS sales, needs further explication.

The formal procedures for considering U.S. arms sales, as outlined above, are often bypassed in the most important and controversial cases. For instance, during his May 1972 visit to

Teheran, President Nixon promised the Shah either F-14 or F-15 fighters, even though there had been no thorough inter-agency study of the implications of transferring such advanced aircraft to the Persian Gulf. Upon the President's return to Washington, a memorandum was issued to the relevant government agencies giving blanket approval to future Iranian requests for any conventional weapon.[45] These actions excluded the responsible U.S. government bureaucracies from the decision-making process on future sales to Iran, our largest customer, and effectively shifted the locus of policy-making from Washington to Teheran.

Secretary Kissinger's 1975 promise to study the possibility of sending Pershing missiles and other advanced weapons to Israel "with the view of giving a positive response" was also evidently undertaken without the benefit of an interagency discussion.[46] Sale of either the F-14 and the Pershing transactions would represent a significant escalation in the sophistication of military equipment supplied by the United States to the Near East.

Not all relevant U.S. government agencies have had an equal voice in past arms sales decisions, and the Arms Control and Disarmament Agency, in particular, has had relatively little influence. ACDA was not consulted about the sale of either F-14s or Spruance class destroyers to Iran, even though both transactions clearly have significant arms control implications.[47] More recently there has been a effort to expand ACDA's role and the agency is now reportedly consulted on major proposed arms sales.

Perhaps because it is made on a case-by-case basis, U.S. arms sales policy lacks coherence and overall limits. Several government agencies with quite different perspectives and interests are involved in the policy-making process, and it is

[218]

therefore difficult to attribute the policy outcomes to any single agency. Lacking a central focus, the decision-making process appears to vary considerably from case to case. General policy guidelines cannot be effective without an overall policy-making body to apply them consistently both to individual transactions and to the total arms export program. Indeed, in practice it is unclear which individual official or agency is really responsible for U.S. arms sales policy.

The largely middle-level U.S. government officials who decide most routine arms transfer cases have little incentive to refuse any remotely reasonable arms request from a friendly country. As Thomas Stern, Deputy Director of the Bureau of Politico-Military Affairs, has phrased it, the "refusal to sell any military articles and services would be in some cases interpreted as a signal by the United States that we do not support the security concerns of the countries involved, or do not consider them mature enough to be trusted with some types of military equipment." [48] The immediate repercussions of turning down a proposed arms sale may seem to outweigh the less obvious long-run dangers of increasing arms shipments to conflict-prone regions. The lack of a central decision-making body with full responsibility for the program exacerbates the tendency to concentrate on short-term rather than long-term consequences.

As U.S. arms sales have gained momentum during recent years, it may well have become more difficult to refuse specific arms sales requests on a case-by-base basis, particularly when the President and the Secretary of State have employed arms transfers as an important element in their Near Eastern diplomacy. Their decision to sell massive amounts of sophisticated weapons to Iran set the precedent which has been followed since. Thus, though the decision-making process has obvious faults, the basic impetus for the recent growth of U.S. arms sales has stemmed from the perceptions and priorities of the President and Secretary of State.

CONCLUSIONS AND RECOMMENDATIONS

1. The administration should issue a "white paper" on arms sales to clarify U.S. policy and to provide guidance both for the relevant U.S. government agencies and for potential recipients.
2. The administration should publicly enunciate a much stricter and more specific set of policy guidelines for arms sales. These should delineate the special circumstances under which arms transfers will be authorized.
3. The quantity and quality of U.S. arms exports should be determined on the basis of national security and arms control considerations, rather than as a means to increase U.S. influence abroad. Foreign policy rationales should primarily determine which nations are eligible to receive U.S. arms.
4. The administration should establish an interagency committee, chaired by the Secretary of State, to analyze all proposed sales of major defense articles exceeding $25 million from a variety of perspectives and to recommend whether each sale should be approved.
   a. The committee could consider sales of less than $25 million at the request of any of the participating agencies.
   b. The committee should supervise the preparation of the annual estimate and justification for the arms sales program, which are required under the International Security Assistance and Arms Export Control Act of 1976.

   c. The committee should meet much more frequently than has SAPRC.
5. All arms sales proposed by the President or memebers of his cabinet, even if already discussed with foreign leaders, should be submitted to the interagency committee for review, though the committee's decision would not be binding on the President.
6. Congress should pass legislation requiring the executive branch to set an annual ceiling on U.S. arms sales which would provide an overall limit to the sales program. This ceiling and its justification should be transmitted to Congress, but Congressional approval would only be required for proposed increases in the ceiling. (The establishment of a ceiling would supersede the currently required annual sales estimate.)
7. Congress should pass legislation to phase out commercial sales in order to streamline the decision-making process and to reduce the use of private agents as middlemen. As an important factor in U.S. foreign and national security policies, arms sales should be conducted solely on a government-to-government basis

NOTES

1. From 1965 to 1974, U.S. arms transfers totaled $31.6 billion or 49 percent of the world total of $64.4 billion. U.S., Arms Control and Disarmament Agency, *World Military Expenditures and Arms Transfers, 1965-1974* (Washington, D.C.: Government Printing Office, 1976), Table V, p. 73. The term "arms transfers" generally includes not only combat equipment, but also supporting equipment, spare parts, and supporting services such as construction and training. In fact, only about 45 percent of U.S. arms transfers in recent

years has been made up of weapons and ammunition. For a more detailed breakdown provided by the State Department, see U.S., Congress, House, Committee on International Relations, *International Security Assistance Act of 1976,* 94th Cong., 2d. Sess., 1976, p. 213.

2. U.S., Arms Control and Disarmament Agency, *World Military Expenditures,* Table IV, p. 71. The annual volume of arms deliveries may not equal the amount of orders placed during any given year, since many arms are not delivered for several years after their order is placed. Since some of the recent arms orders have been for weapons which have not yet reached the production line, annual deliveries have been much lower than orders during the past few years. The term "arms transfers" refers to deliveries not orders.

3. U.S., Department of Defense, Security Assistance Agency, *Foreign Military Sales and Military Assistance Facts, November 1975,* pp. 16, 17, 22, 23, 24, and 25.

4. *Ibid.* This is based on the Military Assistance Program (MAP), and includes neither Military Assistance–Service Funded (MASF), which was included in the Defense Department budget and primarily used for Vietnam from FY 1966 to 1975, nor the $2.2 billion Emergency Security Assistance for Israel in FY 1974.

5. After peak years in FY 1974 and 1975, preliminary estimates suggest that sales in FY 1976 may show a small decrease. The sales totaled about $8.3 billion in FY 1976. The government does not make preliminary estimates of commercial sales, which have been averaging about $500 to $600 million in recent years.

6. International Security Assistance and Arms Export Control Act of 1976, P.L. 94-329, signed June 30, 1976.

7. U.S., Congress, Senate, Subcommittee on Foreign Assistance of

the Committee on Foreign Relations, *Foreign Assistance Authorization: Arms Sales Issues,* 94th Cong., 1st Sess., 1975, pp. 38-39.

8. *Ibid.,* pp. 41-42. Human rights considerations evidently were not taken into account in compiling this list, but Congress has placed restrictions on the shipment of arms to Chile.

9. U.S., Department of Defense, Security Assistance Agency, *Foreign Military Sales and Military Assistance Facts, November 1975,* pp. 24-25.

10. *Ibid.,* pp. 16-17.

11. *Ibid.,* pp. 22-23.

12. Preliminary Defense Department estimate released by Congressman Les Aspin, July 26, 1976.

13. *Time* magazine, March 3, 1975.

14. U.S., Department of Defense, Security Assistance Agency, *Foreign Military Sales and Military Assistance Facts, November 1975,* pp. 15, 23 and 25.

15. Bernard Gwertzman, "10-Year U.S. Ban on Pakistan Arms Will Halt Today," *New York Times,* February 24, 1975.

16. Bernard Gwertzman, "Kissinger and 3 Senators Meet on Egypt Arms Issue," *New York Times,* March 26, 1976.

17. Michael Pillsbury, "U.S.-Chinese Military Ties?," *Foreign Policy,* No. 20 (Fall 1975), pp. 50-64, and editorial, "Arms Sales to China," *New York Times,* December 18, 1975.

18. U.S., Congress, House, Committee on International Relations,

International Security Assistance Act of 1976, 94th Cong., 1976, p. 7 (emphasis in the original).

19. *Ibid.*

20. UNA-USA National Policy Panel on Conventional Arms Control, interim report on "Controlling the International Arms Trade," April 1976, p. 2.

21. For a more complete, but still very general, State Department list of arms transfer considerations, see U.S., Congress, House, Committee on International Relations, *International Security Assistance Act of 1976,* p. 212.

22. U.S., Congress, Senate, Subcommittee on Foreign Assistance of the Committee on Foreign Relations, *Foreign Assistance Authorization: Arms Sales Issues,* p. 216.

23. U.S., Congress, House, Subcommittee on the Near East and South Asia of the Committee on Foreign Affairs, *The Persian Gulf 1974: Money, Politics, Arms and Power,* 93rd Cong., 2d sess., 1974, p. 4.

24. U.S., Congress, Senate, Subcommittee on Foreign Assistance of the Committee on Foreign Relations, *Foreign Assistance Authorization: Arms Sales Issues,* p. 217.

25. *Ibid.,* p. 218.

26. International Institute for Strategic Studies, *The Military Balance, 1975-1976* (London: IISS, 1976), pp. 33, 34, 56 and 72. Though it is claimed that only non-nuclear-capable models of these weapon systems have been exported to the Third World, there evidently is not a significant technical difference between the nuclear and non-nuclear models. The crucial factor appears to be the warhead design rather than the delivery system.

27.   The Pershing, with a range of 450 miles, was initially designed solely to carry nuclear warheads, but a conventional model is under development. The Lance has a range of 70 miles and is dual-capable in its present form. *Ibid.,* p. 71.

28.   Richard J. Levine, "U.S. Appears Unlikely to Supply Israel With Nuclear-Capable Pershing Missile," *The Wall Street Journal,* September 22, 1975.

29.   For a fuller exposition of these points, see Edward C. Luck, "Does the U.S. Have A Conventional Arms Sales Policy?" *Arms Control Today,* Vol. 6, No. 5 (May 1976), pp. 1-2.

30.   Interim report on "Controlling the International Arms Trade," April 1976, pp. 13-14.

31.   U.S., Congress, Senate, Subcommittee on Foreign Assistance of the Committee on Foreign Relations, *U.S. Military Sales to Iran,* 94th Cong., 2nd Sess., July 1976, p. x.

32.   U.S., Congress, House, Committee on International Relations, *International Security Assistance Act of 1976,* p. 212.

33.   UNA-USA National Policy Panel on Conventional Arms Control, *Controlling the Conventional Arms Race.*

34.   U.S., Congress, House, Committee on Foreign Affairs, *The International Transfer of Conventional Arms,* Report to the Congress from the U.S. Arms Control and Disarmament Agency, 93rd, Cong., 2d Sess., 1974, p. 31.

35.   "America the Arsenal," *Harvard Magazine,* June 1976, p. 26.

36.   U.S. sales to NATO, however, should be consistent with the objectives of arms standardization and a "two-way street" in NATO procurement.

[225]

37.   A fuller discussion of these laws can be found in the U.S. Arms Control and Disarmament Agency, *The International Transfer of Conventional Arms,* pp. 29-30.

38.   The time period has been expanded to 30 calendar days by the International Security Assistance and Arms Export Control Act of 1976.

39.   The International Security Assistance and Arms Export Control Act of 1976 also prohibits military aid or sales to Chile because of human rights violations.

40.   For further descriptions of the policy-making process, see U.S., Congress, House, Committee on International Relations, *International Security Assistance Act of 1976,* pp. 7-8 and 211-212; U.S., Congress, Senate, Subcommittee on Foreign Assistance of the Committee on Foreign Relations, *Foreign Assistance Authorization: Arms Sales Issues,* pp. 115-116; and U.S., Congress, House, Subcommittee on the Near East and South Asia of the Committee on Foreign Affairs, *The Persian Gulf, 1974: Money, Politics, Arms, and Power,* pp. 3 and 18-19: U.S. Congress, Senate, Subcommittee on Foreign Assistance of the Committee on Foreign Relations, *U.S. Military Sales to Iran,* pp. 38-41.

41.   However, the Defense Department is not required to refer sales to Category A countries, which include most of NATO, Japan and Australia, to the State Department for policy guidance. Sales to other nations (Category B) require approval by the State Department. U.S., Congress, Senate, Subcommittee on Foreign Assistance of the Committee on Foreign Relations, *U.S. Military Sales to Iran,* p. 39.

42.   U.S., Congress, Senate, Subcommittee on Foreign Assistance of the Committee on Foreign Relations, *Foreign Assistance Authorization: Arms Sales Issues,* p. 154.

[226]

43. However, the International Security Assistance and Arms Export Control Act of 1976 does not permit non-NATO commercial sales to exceed $25 million.

44. Also see U.S., Congress, Senate, Subcommittee on Multinational Corporations of the Committee on Foreign Relations, *Multinational Corporations and United States Foreign Policy*, pt. 13, 94th Cong., 1st. Sess., 1975, pp. 107-238 and 341-1172.

45. Letter from Representative Clarence D. Long to President Ford, December 20, 1974, and U.S., Congress, Senate, Subcommittee on Foreign Assistance of the Committee on Foreign Relations, *U.S. Military Sales to Iran,* p. 41.

46. Richard J. Levine, "U.S. Appears Unlikely to Supply Israel With Nuclear-Capable Pershing Missile," *The Wall Street Journal,* September 22, 1975; and Robert Keatley, "New Doubts About the Mideast Pact," *The Wall Street Journal,* October 3, 1975.

47. U.S., Congress, Senate, Subcommittee on Foreign Assistance of the Committee on Foreign Relations, *Foreign Assistance Authorization: Arms Sales Issues,* p. 218.

48. *Ibid.,* p. 125.

FIVE

Congress and Arms Transfers

Richard M. Moose
with Daniel L. Spiegel

A combination of many factors—the end of the Vietnam war, the personal style of a Secretary of State, the oil price hike of 1973, and the recession—contributed to growing Congressional involvement in the issue of conventional arms transfers during the 94th Congress. Not since the 1930s had a Congress so immersed itself in the arms sales issue. However, unlike earlier efforts designed to highlight and expose the activities of private arms manufacturers, Congressional activities in 1975-76 had very different objectives.

The main intention was directed at achieving restraint in the sale of U.S. arms abroad. Those in Congress concerned about arms transfers sought to realize this objective by writing into legislation new policy statements advocating restraint, opening the arms sales process to public and Congressional scrutiny, bringing significant sales under more centralized executive branch control and, finally, giving the Congress a right to block certain sales.

By the time the Congress had adjourned in early October 1976, it was clear that proponents of new American arms sales policies had been only partially successful in achieving their objectives. A totally new statutory framework regulating government and commercial arms sales had been signed into law on June 30, 1976, after an initial veto and nine months of intense and often bitter negotiations between the Foreign Relations Committee and the Ford Administration. Both the Congress and the executive branch seemed to be more sensitive to the need for greater public explanation and justification of multibillion dollar arms deals involving the most sophisticated aircraft and weaponry.

But, as the Congress gave tacit approval to $5.9 billion worth of arms sales to eleven countries in the final weeks of the 94th Congress, it was obvious that the new mechanisms in the International Security Assistance and Arms Export Control Act had not achieved the desired results. They had not led to the formulation of an overall policy framework for arms sales in the executive branch. They had failed to restrain the Administration even slightly in the magnitude of the sales or to make it more discriminating. And it was discovered that the design of the new law did not enable the Congress to evaluate seriously or to reject individual arms sales without being accused of disrupting America's bilateral relations with the recipient government. Worst of all, in the closing days of the session, the Congress had been forced to acquiesce in sales about which it had serious misgivings.

II

It is significant to note that one of the first serious efforts by the Congress to deal with the arms transfer issue occurred five months before the Yom Kippur war and the subsequent oil price rise at the end of 1973. At that time, the Senate Foreign

Relations Committee had developed controversial legislation with the strong personal backing of its chairman, J.W. Fulbright of Arkansas. The principal focus of this legislation was a four-year phase-out of the military grant aid program and the military assistance groups. The measure also called for a new credit sales system of loan guarantees through commercial banks and allowing the Export-Import Bank to finance sales of arms to developing nations.

The Fulbright bill of the early summer of 1973 was more than an effort to restructure the Nixon Administration's military assistance programs. It was part of a general attack on the bilateral foreign aid concept which had been becoming increasingly unpopular with Congressional liberals as they struggled to terminate the Vietnam war through the appropriations process. For many years military aid legislation had been appended to the economic aid bill and had sustained it as it wound its way through the numerous stages of Congressional consideration. Senator Fulbright had at last collected the necessary votes in the Senate to separate the two bills and restructure the military program, thus leaving the bilateral economic aid program without its protective armor.

The Fulbright concern of 1973 had roots which antedated the Indochina war. In January 1967 Fulbright had endorsed a Foreign Relations Committee staff study on the subject of arms sales and foreign policy, stating that "the problems and responsibilities that the United States has acquired with its ever-increasing arms exports are of prime concern to the Congress." The study written in 1967 by Committee consultant William B. Bader precisely defined a problem which was not to be seriously addressed by the Congress until 1976:

It is the general conclusion of this study that it is incumbent on the United States to reappraise the adequacy of the present machinery of policy control and legislative oversight governing the sale of arms. On the basis of the available evidence, there is sufficient justification for tentatively concluding that the adjustments in policy and administrative procedure necessitated by the change in the composition of military aid have been marred by a lack of information, by weaknesses in interdepartmental coordination at the highest levels, and, finally, by a lack of serious attention to the problem of reconciling an active arms control policy with an arms sales program.

The rationale underlying the Foreign Relations Committee's 1973 military legislation was significant. The cold war was over. Foreign aid was unpopular and was under strong Congressional criticism in a period of heavy deficit spending. Military grant assistance was viewed as a relic of the past which had supported military dictatorships, as in South Vietnam, Cambodia, Thailand and Korea. The Committee believed it desirable to lower the profile of American involvement abroad. However, one of the most important goals of the legislation was stated very clearly in the Committee's report: "The ultimate objective of the bill is to get the State and Defense Departments out of the arms sales business and get these transactions back to a free enterprise, commercial basis, where they belong."

While those who supported the bill did not necessarily believe that arms sales were bad *per se,* many of them seemed to believe that the arms business was tainted. The way to solve this problem was to prohibit government involvement in the arms trade. The unsavory traffic in arms was the business of business—not of government.

The Fulbright bill never became law in its original form. But it was an important precursor of the legislation subse-

[231]

quently signed into law. In a number of ways, it provided a foundation for later efforts.

One of the critical assumptions of this legislation was the fundamental desirability of Congressional involvement in foreign policy decision-making. Although it had the power to control the authorizing and appropriating power in a wide range of foreign policy programs, the Congress moved only reluctantly to exercise that power. To be sure, in 1973 Congress was locked in a profound struggle with the President over the war in Vietnam. But introduction of the Fulbright bill advanced the principle that the Congress should have a crucial role in shaping overall security policy as well as influencing a host of bilateral relationships outside of the context of an emergency or war situation. Moreover, it was assumed that if the Congress could play a role, its influence could be effectively directed to force qualitative policy changes on a reluctant executive branch.

What the President wanted in the security assistance area was not what growing numbers of senators and representatives were ready to give. The principle of greater Congressional involvement in the foreign policy decision-making process was, of course, not born in this legislation sponsored by Senator Fulbright. But, like all events which help to erode fixed patterns of behavior, its influence was important in breaking down inhibitions which had for years allowed a President almost total control of the options in the foreign grant aid and sales programs.

By the fall of 1975, changes in Congress, in the Presidency, and in the international system had created a situation where consideration of new legislation dealing with the issue of conventional arms sales seemed possible. Earlier that year, the Senate Foreign Relations Committee had created a new Foreign Assistance Subcommittee, chaired by Senator Hubert H.

Humphrey, who had been one of the chief supporters of bilateral aid during the latter Fulbright days. Humphrey was committed to the survival, reform and expansion of development assistance legislation, as well as exerting greater Congressional control over the arms sales and grant programs. The two goals were mutually reinforcing.

In the other body, a restructured House International Relations Committee was now willing to separate foreign aid legislation into its component parts despite opposition to this approach from the Ford Administration. This was a practical necessity because the military aid legislation had become so unpopular among liberals and some conservatives in the Senate as to make questionable passage of a combined economic and military aid package.

After the Senate had passed a House-sponsored economic aid initiative which was built on the reforms of the previous year, the Humphrey Subcommittee staff and the foreign policy staffs of Subcommittee members began work on a new approach to the military aid legislation. The decision by the Foreign Assistance Subcommittee to proceed with the development of new legislation was not a difficult one to make. The majority of Foreign Relations Committee members and a significant number of individual senators were not anxious to support another traditional military aid bill sent forward by the White House for a variety of reasons.

The fall of Vietnam and Cambodia in the spring of 1975 precipitated in the Congress a widespread reassessment of what type of aid policies were genuinely in the U.S. interest. There seemed to be a heightened sensitivity in Congress to the ultimate effect security-related aid decisions had on bilateral relations between the United States and the recipient countries. The Administration did not share, nor did it seem to understand, this Congressional concern.

The anti-Communist rationale of previous years for large arms grant programs had been undermined by the Vietnam experience as well as by the Nixon and Ford Administrations' own détente policies. It was extremely difficult for the executive branch to predicate the traditional range of security programs on a cold war threat at a time when the public and the Congress were inclined to view the cold war as dead.

Moreover, the need and rationale for large military grant assistance programs no longer existed. Under executive pressure to use all available military aid money for Indochina and increasing Congressional opposition to grant military aid to other parts of the world, the non-Indochina grant military programs had steadily decreased. Concurrently, a vast new area of arms transfer activity was taking shape, largely outside the Congress' notice. This involved the sale of weapons with the government acting as a formal intermediary. Although referred to as government-to-government sales, they were generally commercial in origin. Ironically, Fulbright's push to get the government out of the arms sales business came just as the bulk of sales was shifting from the government-guaranteed credit sale category to the new government-to-government cash sale basis.

The increase in oil prices and the sudden shift in economic power to the Persian Gulf resulted in an incredible escalation in arms sales through Foreign Military Sales and commercial channels. In the fiscal year immediately preceding the drafting of the International Security Assistance and Arms Export Control Act, arms sales had reached the $9.5 billion level.

We were selling highly sophisticated weapons to Iran, Saudi Arabia, and Kuwait in exchange for petrodollars. The Congress had been notified of some of these sales pursuant to a new provision of law sponsored by Senator Gaylord Nelson and Representative Jonathan Bingham, which also provided that any government-to-government sale over $25 million could be blocked by the passage of a concurrent resolution of disapproval. Despite this procedure, enacted in December, 1974, the policy rationale underlying the sales was not shared with the Congress. Many Foreign Relations Committee members were suspicious that Persian Gulf arms sales were not governed by any careful or deliberate policy. As members of Congress realized what was happening in the Persian Gulf, they found themselves without adequate information and controls and were uncertain as to how to proceed.

Another cause of mounting concern had to do with the identity of the new arms purchasers. Whereas the grant military aid recipients of the 1950s and 1960s had been European and other cold war allies, the new recipients were Moslem countries. Many members were concerned over the possible uses to which large new deliveries of arms might be put in a future Middle East war.

In the post-Indochina period, the spirit of opposition within Congress to U.S. involvement in the security affairs of other countries was strong. The emergence of the U.S. government as the active intermediary in long-term arms supply relationships raised the possibility of a new form of high-profile U.S. involvement.

Moreover, many members of Congress and significant sectors of the informed public did not like the notion of the United States being the world's leading arms merchant. Moral currents, a disbelief in the utility of force, and a preference that resources be directed toward meeting domestic needs or human needs abroad all contributed to this view.

Finally, another critical factor propelling a small group of senators on the Foreign Relations Committee to design new legislation to deal with the sale and grant of arms was their reaction to a style of diplomacy pursued by Secretary Kiss-

[235]

inger, which relied on arms transfers as one of the major incentives in negotiations or as an important element in bilateral relations. Committee members were aware of large arms deals negotiated by the Secretary or his associates with Persian Gulf and Middle Eastern nations that were potential adversaries of Israel. But knowledge of these transactions came after they were concluded. With a few possible exceptions the Committee was never consulted in advance of major weapons sales.

A corollary to the frustration with the Secretary of State's use of arms sales in his diplomacy was the suspicion that the Defense Department and the large arms manufacturers, particularly those in the aerospace industries, were the main driving force behind many of the sales. The Congress had little evidence to corroborate this theory, but interested members knew that, although the State Department supposedly had the final word in arms transfer decisions, the Defense Department and the armed services were more knowledgeable than the State Department. And, in any event, the Defense Department has been in complete charge of all aspects of negotiations until the very last moment when State is brought in.

It was clear to the Humphrey Subcommittee members that, at a minimum, the Congress must have more informaton in a timely fashion if it were to reverse its near total exclusion from the arms transfer process.

III

All of these factors helped the Foreign Assistance Subcommittee come to a decision concerning the desirability of new legislation in the arms transfer field; they created institutional relationships and a political climate that was favorable to the consideration of legislative restraints on arms sales. On the one side was an executive branch attempting to perpetuate a program based on outmoded concepts, the most salient feature of which was the provision of arms to often unpopular or questionable allies. On the other side was the Congress responding to public concern that "something be done about this business." Congress was the reformer. Congress was going to become involved as a counterweight to the unbridled proclivity of an executive branch absorbed in maintaining existing relationships and forgetful of the long-range policy implications of its actions.

The Subcommittee did not expect an institutional struggle as it began preparing the legislation. In fact, Senator Humphrey obtained a commitment from Secretary Kissinger that, once the legislation was initially drafted, his staff would work with the Senate staff to iron out differences, minimize conflicts, and develop a document acceptable to all. But, underlying the spirit of accommodation were widely differing perceptions of arms sales, which soon exacerbated existing institutional tensions and led to an eventual clash.

IV

Certain key decisions were made in the drafting of the International Security Assistance and Arms Export Control Act which shed light on how the Congress perceived its own role and that of the executive branch as it related to the arms transfer issue.

One of the first critical decisions faced by Senator Humphrey, as the chief sponsor of the legislation, and his colleagues was how deeply the U.S. government should be involved in the arms sales business. One of the early drafts proposed a ceiling on Foreign Military Sales (FMS) credits and government-to-government sales designed to drive large amounts of arms purchases into commercial channels. The rationale for this approach was grounded in the original Fulbright bill discussed above. If arms sales and grant programs led to unwanted foreign involvements and perhaps to foreign conflict, should the government participate in the sale of weapons? Should it not disentangle itself from the danger of foreign entrapment by letting private companies handle the traffic in arms while the government supervised their activities?

Senator Humphrey personally rejected this approach to the problem. He came to this decision after conferring with a number of former executive branch officials and academic experts who doubted that forcing a shift of sales from government to commercial channels would result in either tighter control or a lessening of ultimate government involvement in relationships between the United States and recipient countries. This seemed particularly undesirable at a time when overall arms sales were mounting. Clearly, this was not the time to relinquish controls altogether, and no one believed that commercial sales could be drastically curtailed.

Furthermore, Humphrey was skeptical of the earlier approach as a result of his involvement at that time in efforts to prevent abuses in grain inspection. It seemed to him that there should be greater, not less, government control and supervision of trade in certain critical arms transactions which could greatly affect our foreign policy. If private corporations are allowed to set standards, supervise sales and make other important determinations, the government loses control over the consequences of the acts of companies, which may place their own interests before those of the U.S. government.

The draft legislation was revised to reflect this decision. During the extensive consultation process on the legislation

[238]

which began in November 1975, the Department of Defense suggested strengthening this approach by prohibiting commercial sales of major combat equipment in amounts over $25 million. This was intended to force all major sales into FMS channels, thereby expanding substantially the opportunity for government control of the sales programs and, in particular, ensuring that the more sensitive sales would be subject to government management.

In making this decision concerning the extent of governmental supervision of sales, Senator Humphrey was convinced that the Congress should participate in the control system. To establish wider controls while permitting the executive branch to continue its total domination of policy formulation and implementation was viewed as unacceptable. The question was how to establish a system of greater Congressional participation in the policy process.

Two significant options were considered and rejected in the search for a means by which the Congress could establish an appropriate role for itself.

The first possibility considered was the establishment of an overall ceiling on total U.S. arms sales by whatever means. This concept was strongly backed by some members of the House International Relations Committee, as well as by some major academics working on arms sales and by many editorial writers who saw in it a way to begin the process of limiting sales.

The Subcommittee members and staff debated this provision at considerable length. It had political appeal and would easily be understood by the public and the press. It would be an expression of unmistakable clarity to the Administration that the Congress wanted to achieve a policy of restraint as well as Congressional influence.

But there were major problems with the ceiling. The Subcommittee was told that the level of arms sales to the Persian Gulf would be declining, not increasing. Various procedural questions were raised: Where was the level to be set? How could unanticipated contingencies be dealt with? How would the ceiling be apportioned among prospective purchasers? How could all possible sales be known at the time the ceiling was set and country allocations made? Finally, there was the distinct danger that the ceiling would become a target as sales declined, instead of a restraining force. In sum, the yearly enactment of a ceiling was thought to be entirely too cumbersome a procedure.

Furthermore, to establish a ceiling in the Senate bill that would reduce sales was virtually certain to earn the total opposition of the executive branch to the entire legislative effort. It would also surely arouse the arms manufacturers from their relative indifference to the legislation at that time.

It was decided not to include a ceiling but to wait for its possible inclusion in a House bill that would be considered at the end of the process in the Conference Committee. It should be noted that when the Senate did accept the House ceiling in the Conference, this mechanism was structured to be more a statement of principle than an absolute restraint.

Two observations are needed at this point. First, it was clear that the Foreign Relations Committee was reluctant to force a gross reduction in arms sales by "legislative fiat." Its members preferred to encourage restraint by means of policy statements, the termination of the rather small grant program, and the elimination of the Military Advisory Assistance Groups, whom they viewed as sales agents. The legislation was supposedly designed to require both branches to evaluate arms sales policies based on new procedures and better management controls. It was through this process that the Committee hoped a reduction in sales would be considered and evaluated.

Second, it should be recognized that except at the margin—in connection with freeing small commercial sales from government controls—arms manufacturers had no influence on the drafting and initial consultations between the legislative and executive branches. The Subcommittee was, of course, aware that a substantial reduction in sales would have an impact on various industries and on an already depressed economy. But lobbyists for the arms industry did not become interested in the legislation until the final hours of its consideration in the Foreign Relations Committee prior to legislation being reported to the full Senate in January 1976. To those who were involved in the process, the absence of industry interest and pressure was surprising. There are only two possible explanations to explain industry's absence from this process. Some Congressional participants believed that industry must have felt its interests were being adequately represented by the State and Defense Departments in the weeks of working sessions held with the Congressional staffs. Others believed that industry representatives did not take seriously efforts by Congress to restructure the sales system and stayed away from Capitol Hill.

The second option initially rejected by the Subcommittee would have required prior Congressional authorization of sales program levels on a country or regional basis. Senators Humphrey, Javits and Case, as the principal drafters of the legislation, immediately saw considerable difficulties with the prior approval option.

These Senators were frankly reluctant to design a system which would have placed the Congress in a role of primary decision-making on such a detailed basis. It was argued that although the Congress was to participate in decisions relating to sales, the prior approval method came too close to having the Congress actually run the program. The Senators did not want this to happen, being strongly opposed to the idea that the Congress could or should run foreign policy. Moreover, they believed that the information and judgments needed for this approach to work might be beyond the level of Congressional competence or interest.

They understood that despite the significance and public awareness of the arms sales issue, there were other interests competing vigorously for Congressional attention. The fact that the original Nelson amendment device had never been utilized was an important signal of the general lack of interest beyond the Foreign Relations Committee. The Subcommittee members could not envision how the entire Congress could fairly and competently judge the needs of an individual country or entire region for arms at the beginning of a calendar or fiscal year. Acutely aware of their limitations in this respect, they were reluctant to substitute their judgment for that of the executive branch on such a detailed basis. Nevertheless, they feared that if they went along with the executive's proposals and gave them affirmative endorsement, they might be giving blanket approval to transactions they did not fully understand, which, when consummated at some future date, might prove to be highly undesirable.

The Foreign Assistance Subcommittee finally decided that the major vehicle for Congressional participation in the arms transfer process should be a significant expansion of the earlier Nelson amendment mechanism. Adoption of an expanded Nelson amendment approach avoided placing the Congress in the position of fixing a ceiling on sales or of having to enact prior country-by-country authorizations. Either of these would have been a substantial enlargement of the Congressional role in regulating commercial exports or a denial of executive discretionary authority. The Nelson approach, however, was not a neutral course of action. It left existing executive branch discretionary authority intact but made the executive's use of this authority subject to case-by-case Congressional review. The essential operative feature of this review was the use of a concurrent resolution veto, a device which came to be strenuously opposed by President Ford.

After weighing the problem carefully, the Committee decided that its primary concern centered on the possible problems which could arise from specific sales of sophisticated weapons systems in sensitive regional situations. It also realized that under certain circumstances even relatively small sales of certain types of weapons could have a destabilizing effect. On the basis of this analysis, the Committee first came up with the idea of extending the Nelson amendment concurrent resolution (a resolution requiring both Houses' concurrence but not requiring Presidential signature) veto to all sales of *major* weapons systems in addition to the original Nelson application to sales of over $25 million, whether commercial or government-to-government. As a means of ensuring an additional measure of control it was later decided to prohibit the commercial export of major weapons items in amounts over $25 million, requiring instead that such sales go through government-to-government channels.

As later modified in the process of discussion and compromise with the executive branch and the House, these provisions were modified so that the concurrent resolution veto would apply only to government-to-government sales of over $25 million and of major defense equipment over $7 million. A further compromise allowed a NATO exemption to the requirement specifying sales which would have to be made government-to-government. And it was eventually decided to permit commercial sales or ordinary defense equipment without regard to the size of the contract, including major defense equipment valued up to $25 million—provided that applications for export licenses of commercial sales of ordinary equipment over $25 million and for the export of major items between $7 million and $25 million would have to be reported to the Congress thirty days before the licenses were issued.

The basic notion behind the Committee's approach was that, once supplied with sufficient information, the Congress could evaluate the policy consequences of individual government sales and commercial exports before they were consummated. This evaluation process was to be made meaningful by virtue of the power which the Congress was to have either to block questionable sales if they were to be made by the government or, in the case of significant commercial sales, to provide a waiting period in which the Congress could express its disapproval, albeit in a non-binding form. This checking process, it was assumed, would compel a prudent executive to evaluate sales proposals more carefully before commiting itself at the risk of Congressional rejection or protest. No one expected many sales to be blocked or even seriously threatened, but the power to do so would represent a club kept in the closet ready for use if the executive did not exercise restraint and discretion.

In addition to the expanded Nelson provision, there were numerous reports, justifications and projections required of the executive branch so that it and the Congress would have more and better information on which to analyze the sales programs and review the overall policy.

The Committee decided that it wanted to centralize the coordination of arms transfer decisions in the Department of State. One of the assumptions of this move was the belief that the Department of Defense had historically been a pusher of arms sales and that the State Department was more likely to be responsive to Congressional pressures for restraint. While this view is not wholly wrong, it was probably over-simplified.

There are interesting cross-currents in both institutions. Quite clearly the Defense Security Assistance Agency (DSAA) has been under orders to facilitate, if not actually to promote, U.S. arms sales abroad. Moreover, the various service branches have on various occasions been interested in pushing foreign sales of given weapons systems in order to lower the per unit cost of its own acquisition of the same weapon. But, at the same time, other parts in the defense establishment, including elements of the services and the JCS itself, have been concerned over the impact of sales on the readiness of U.S. forces and on our own production and logistics. By the same token, while some officers at State share Congressional concern over the apparently ad hoc and short-sighted nature of certain sales decisions, many others adhere to the traditional view that arms sales are effective in balancing regional power relationships and useful sweeteners in the maintenance of bilateral relations.

In any event, the State Department did not welcome the Committee's efforts to accord it primary coordinating and policy authority in the arms sales area. Defense openly fought the concept in discussions with the Committee staff; and when State demurred at the attempt to give it an enhanced role, the Defense Department won out.

Although the Committee's effort to place State in the driver's seat with regard to reporting requirements failed, the new legislation did provide for a greatly expanded flow of information to the Congress. There was extensive discussion as to how much of the information provided Congress could be made public. The Subcommittee at first favored a total sunshine approach to permit maximum public scrutiny. It was felt that classification for the convenience of the recipient nation could not be justified except in very exceptional circumstances. However, as a result of relentless Administration pressure,

[245]

which received a sympathetic hearing in the House, the Senate altered its position and allowed the President to classify some of the information sent to Congress with a rather broad "national security" justification.

The theory of the sunshine approach again was that if the executive knew that transfers had to face public review, they might be more carefully considered. It was hoped that the threat of public and Congressional criticism would strengthen the hand of those within the executive branch who might question certain sales but whose views would otherwise be smothered or overridden so long as decisions were made in secret.

The secrecy issue is another example of how the authors of the legislation tried through compromise to avoid an outright confrontation with the Ford Administration. Some in Congress later regretted the extent to which the Senate relented on this issue when the executive promptly submitted an advance notification which it would only allow to be described as a sale of classified items in an unspecified amount to an unidentified country! In response to embarrassed complaints from the sponsor, the Defense Department blamed the State Department, which in turn claimed that its primary concern was to protect the competitive position of U.S. firms. Other State officials acknowledged privately that admittedly excessive classification was usually undertaken at the request of purchasing governments, which frequently wished to conceal their actions from their own neighbors, legislatures, or public.

Compromise with the White House, which was often damned by outside observers of this process, was a necessity for survival of the legislation.

Despite the "reform" nature of the arms sales provisions, the legislative vehicle of which they were a part would inevitably be regarded as a "foreign aid" bill by many members of the Congress. As such it was unpopular, and especially so in an election year. The Senators who backed the legislation knew that it would need White House support if it were to pass the Congress. The general distaste with foreign aid of any variety was so profound that some members apparently felt that even constructive involvement with the program would not mitigate the potential political harm which could result from any association with a "foreign aid" bill. Thus, limited compromise and careful maneuver were required on several occasions so that strong bipartisan backing of the legislation could be maintained.

In the context of general political support of the legislation, its sponsors endeavored to accommodate the specialized concerns of as many of the members of the Senate as possible. In this connection, the Subcommittee was more than willing to include provisions in the legislation on human rights and anti-discrimination. The Subcommittee sponsors were of the belief that these issues should be linked to arms transfers in an unequivocal manner. Eventually, the concurrent resolutions enforcement features of these two provisions were partly responsible for the Presidential veto of the legislation on May 7, 1976.

The veto of the legislation by President Ford, after nearly seven months of intensive cooperation and negotiation between the Congress and the executive branch, was more than a disappointment to those who had participated in the effort. From the Congressional vantage point, the veto was a classic example of a Presidential reaction to a move by the Congress which appeared to limit his accustomed flexibility in foreign policy. Despite the fact that the legislation had been supported by the Secretary of State, who had not recommended a veto, and by other high-ranking executive branch officials who had participated in the molding of the measure, the veto was predicated squarely on the dangers it posed to ". . . the President's constitutional responsibilities for the conduct of foreign affairs." Despite the fact that the Foreign Assistance Subcommittee had chosen policy mechanisms which would keep it out of the day-to-day operations of the arms sales program, the President depicted the many provisions of the legislation as allowing the Congress to become "virtual co-administrator in operational decisions . . ."

This theme was relevant to more than the traditional Presidential perception of power abridged. Many Congressional observers felt that the President and his advisers were influenced by the then very real challenge to the President by Governor Reagan in hotly contested Presidential primaries. Commentators both in the Congress and the press charged that the President and his associates were searching for ways to emphasize strong Presidential leadership.

Suspicions that the veto was politically motivated were strengthened when White House staff members acknowledged privately that the reasons for the veto were primarily the ceiling on arms sales, the removal of trade restrictions on North Vietnam, the strong human rights and nondiscrimination provisions, and the termination of the MAP program and the MAAG missions. The Administration was fully knowledgeable as to exactly how these specific provisions would function and what minimal impact they would have on the President's overall foreign policy program. Certainly the various concurrent veto provisions were nothing new since some 46 similar provisions were to be found elsewhere in the federal statutes, including the original Nelson amendment which became law as part of a bill signed by President Ford himself.

V

After almost thirteen months of intense legislative activity on the subject of arms transfers, some tentative conclusions can be drawn about the process established by the 94th Congress.

In the Arms Export Control Act of 1976 the Congress had written, and a President had signed into law, an unmistakable declaration of policy:

> It shall be the policy of the United States to exert leadership in the world community to bring about arrangements for reducing the international trade in implements of war and to lessen the danger of outbreak of regional conflict and the burdens of armaments. United States programs for or procedures governing the export, sale, and grant of defense articles and defense services to foreign countries and international organizations shall be administered in a manner which will carry out this policy.

This mandate for restraint in the sale of arms has not been followed since its adoption by either the Congress or the executive branch.

In the year since the Arms Export Control Act was signed into law, the Congress has been notified of proposed government-to-government sales totaling almost $6 billion. Clearly, the executive branch has exercised neither leadership nor restraint.

It is clear that an important element of this problem arises from the Administration's unwillingness—except on very rare occasions—to bring the Congress into the picture at an early stage while possible sales are still being formulated. Under current procedures, the Congress is not informed of possible sales until all details of a letter of offer have been decided. During months and even years of negotiation on individual sales, the Congress is left in the dark. (Interestingly enough, high State Department officials have now testified that State usually is not informed of many sales discussions until they are almost final.) Given the complicated and obscure nature of sales discussions, it is very difficult for the Congress, without executive branch cooperation, to find out about such transactions on its own initiative.

One consequence of this situation is that it prevents Congressmen, either as individuals or groups, from having any role in sales issues prior to the submission of formal notices to the Congress. The executive branch gains maximum flexibility with this approach. But the potential for conflict between the branches of government is increased, and the possibility of harm being done to U.S. foreign policy is present as well.

The record of the debate which took place in the Committee on Foreign Relations over sales to the Persian Gulf area during the closing days of the 94th Congress is particularly instructive in this regard. Members of the Committee were shocked when, barely thirty days before the Congress adjourned, the executive branch gave notice of its intention to make sales offers totaling $5.9 billion.

Among the proposed transactions, two were seriously questioned: the sale of Maverick and Sidewinder missiles to Saudi Arabia, and the sale of $3.8 billion of F-16 aircraft to Iran. While the first sale was rather small, Saudi Arabia is one of the so-called confrontation states, and the strength of the opposition reflected an acute concern over the possible misuse of these weapons in the event of another Middle East war. Opposition to the Iranian sale was attributable to its size, to allegations of bribery by agents of U.S. firms in connection with other aircraft sales, to the disclosure of a sweeping Presidential directive allowing virtually unlimited arms sales to Iran, and to the publication of the Foreign Assistance Subcommittee staff report documenting the chaos in the handling of $10 billion of sales which followed a Presidential decision in 1972.

As a result of these and other concerns, several hearings were held on the Saudi and Iranian sales. Committee members devoted dozens of hours in the busy closing days of the session to examining the proposed transactions. Extensive testimony was received from executive branch and outside experts.

From these hearings a number of new facts emerged. Some of them were viewed by members of the Committee as seriously undermining the Administration's justifications for the proposed sales. It appeared, for example, that the Saudis had previously ordered substantial quantities of the two missiles under investigation. Delivery of the new orders would give them inventories which seemed to many to be far in excess of Saudi Arabia's legitimate self-defense requirements. In the case of the proposed Iranian F-16 sale, it was learned that Iran was very probably planning to place another equally large order for the same aircraft. Moreover, industry sources also disclosed that Iran was seeking large numbers of yet another super-sophisticated U.S. jet fighter.

Countering these disclosures was the persistent argument, advanced by Administration witnesses, that disapproval of the sales to Iran and Saudi Arabia would result in extremely serious consequences to our bilateral relations with those nations. The goodwill of both governments was described as crucial to the maintenance of tolerable OPEC oil prices. Saudi Arabia, it was argued, had been and was expected to continue to be a moderating force among the Arab nations on the question of the Middle East cease-fire agreement. Moreover, it was pointed out that Saudi Arabia and particularly Iran had long been staunch anti-Communist allies. Finally, and inevitably, Administration witnesses argued that if we did not sell, one of our Western European allies would grab the business.

In the final analysis, the Administration's arguments prevailed. Members of the Committee deplored the proposed sales and expressed deep misgivings. Much was said on both sides about the need to develop an agreed long-term policy to guide future sales. Committee members reported that the Secretary of State had acknowledged that long-term sales policies did not exist, that the existing interagency sales review procedures were inadequate, and that he, personally, often did not learn about many sales until the last minute.

No one was particularly happy at the end of the hearings. Certainly not the Secretary of State, who had been compelled to acknowledge the disarray in his own house and the inadequacy of policy—which he blamed on "the State Department's" procedures. In the course of three extraordinary sessions with the Committee, he disclosed plans to form a high-level interagency Arms Export Review Board to coordinate policy and implementation. One of the purposes of this bureaucratic device, the Committee was told, was to strengthen the State Department's role in implementing arms policy, which had been one of the Committee's objectives six weeks earlier. Finally, mindful of mounting Congressional concern, the Secretary promised that no further major sales commitments would be made until the Congress returned in January 1977.

The Committee, for its part, was unhappy at having been compelled to give its tacit approval to sales about which it had serious reservations. In its frustration it adopted two resolutions urging the executive branch to put its policy house in order and demanding the early delivery of a worldwide arms study mandated in the 1976 legislation. With particular regard to the Persian Gulf, the Committee indicated quite strongly that it did not wish to see further sales until the results of a long-pending National Security Council study of Persian Gulf arms sales policy were known.

Notwithstanding these acts, the reality was that in the cases under question, discussions between the United States and the buyers had proceeded to a point of no return long before the Congress could make itself heard. The threat of serious adverse reactions on the part of the potential buyers seemed very real to the Foreign Relations Committee members. Weighed against these consequences, and in view of precedents already set, the danger of the additional sales did not seem immediately tangible.

In the aftermath of the Saudi and Iranian sales confrontation, attention in the Congress and the press tended to focus on the procedural deficiencies of the new law, particularly as it related to the expanded Nelson concurrent resolution veto provision. Although the Committee had succeeded in generating an unprecedented amount of attention to the arms issue, no sale had been blocked.

The experience with the Saudi and Iranian sales revealed that the nature of the expanded Nelson amendment device, which is at the core of the new legislation, actually has the effect of inhibiting Congressional action. To reject a sale once a letter of offer has been signed injects the Congress into the process at a point so late that Congressional action could cause a disruption in overall relations between the United States and the recipient country. Members of Congress are understandably uneasy about the foreign policy consequences of such action and therefore are responsive to Administration pressure not to reject individual sales. This is true despite their recogni-

[253]

tion that even if a rejection would not harm relations with the purchaser, the Administration is likely to avail itself of the argument that harm will come about if Congress takes action or even considers a rejection publicly.

Committee members fully recognized the inadequacies of the Nelson amendment approach. It seems likely, therefore, that in the future a move will be made to amend the law with a new mechanism which will enable the Congress to become involved in arms transfer decisions before the letter of offer stage.

One possibility under discussion would be reconsideration of the approach rejected in 1975 of requiring the Congress to participate in the setting of general sales levels on a country or regional basis each year. Another approach would involve redesigning sales procedures so that the Congress could have an opportunity to reject a sale at a point earlier than the letter of offer stage and at a time when the purchaser understands the very tentative nature of the negotiation.

But while many would agree on the difficulties inherent in implementing the Nelson provision and on the need to strengthen it, others doubt that the individual sales veto or even worldwide and regional ceilings with all their mechanical difficulties can ever be, by themselves, adequate means whereby the Congress can force a more rational arms transfer policy. Those who hold this view argue that change can only come from within the executive branch.

Others who discount the importance or practicality of Congressional review procedures argue that sales are not bad per se and that the general notion of continuously mounting sales is unjustified since the increases came only in the Persian Gulf area where sales in 1976 accounted for about two-thirds of the worldwide total. They point out that there is a valid rationale for most other sales, for example, to NATO allies, Israel, Japan, Australia and Korea and to countries such as Spain, Greece, Turkey and the Philippines, where the United States is seeking to maintain its base rights.

This latter line of argument seems to point again to the need for clearly understood policies appropriate to the differing circumstances of potential purchasers. They suggest that rather than concentrate on procedural means of blocking sales, the Congress needs to take a closer look at arms transfer policy in its broader contexts, at regional security balances, and at the arms transfer decision-making and implementing processes.

Members of Congress who have thought most about this problem recognize the need to differentiate between purchasers. They acknowledge that no one worldwide policy will fit all situations. And they recognize the strong free enterprise and economic rationale for avoiding gross restraints on sales. As long as individual sales do not seem to carry with them obvious dangers and sales go to nations whose present policies and interests are compatible with our own, many members may see no need to be concerned about the overall magnitude of sales.

Another very real influence which mitigates against Congressionally led efforts to limit or restrict sales comes from the arms industry and the trade union movement. Such pressure was barely in evidence during consideration of the new legislation. But it is highly unlikely that these forces would possibly accept substantial limitations on sales. The labor unions and the industry have a strong commonality of interest in "preserving jobs in aerospace." It has been claimed by the arms industry that every $30,000 in sales represents one job. Labor and industry, in combination, have been extremely effective in working against reductions in domestic arms procurement; nor is there any reason to doubt their effectiveness in the field of foreign military sales as long as nations want to buy arms, especially in times of recession and high unemployment.

Linked to the possible pressure from combined industry and labor is the strong belief prevailing in Congress that if the United States does not sell arms, the business will go to a European seller or even a Communist supplier. To lose a sales advantage is considered by many to be highly undesirable. However, little research has been done anywhere in the executive branch as to the capability of foreign arms manufacturers to meet demand, whether prospective purchasers would readily deny themselves the unique advantages which a supply relationship with the United States offers, or the willingness of purchasers to use Communist sources. This is one area of research where the Arms Control and Disarmament Agency could be especially helpful.

While citing factors both pro and con on Congressional concerns about arms, it is important to note that many members of Congress share with the executive branch one important philosophical concept: that the United States can constructively manage situations of potential conflict through the supply of arms. Secretary Kissinger made the following point in testimony before the Senate Foreign Relations Committee: "Conflicts must be contained through upholding stable balances of power in volatile regions through the carefully considered transfer of defense equipment."

Perhaps this concept has such appeal because it is the basis for American policy in the Middle East, and perhaps because other areas seem of marginal importance. The dependence on arms transfers as a method of conflict control has become so pervasive in American foreign policy that other alternatives to achieve the same goal are often regarded as frivolous or unworkable. But the risks of balance-of-power diplomacy based on American conventional arms seem so great as to necessitate a reconsideration of the theory. At least this is what many members of Congress are saying, despite partially successful examples of the balance-of-power model in areas of potential conflict.

Despite all that can be said about the tendency of Congress to follow the executive and the valid reasons for doing so, there remains a strong uneasiness in the Congress and the public about our sales activities. Although adequate rationales may be found for many sales, there is a deep-seated suspicion that sales decisions are still made on an ad hoc basis to meet the immediate exigencies of bilateral relationships. In this connection, many believe that some of the sales which seem innocuous in the context of present relationships carry with them the seeds of serious future difficulties. Because these fears of future trouble are so much more difficult to substantiate than the immediate consequences of refusals to sell—particularly in the context of Congressional debate—they seldom receive adequate attention. In addition, there is a considerable body of opinion which holds that the United States could, if only the executive branch had the will and shared a belief in the desirability of even incremental restraint, take a much stronger stand in discouraging sales.

Finally, some members of Congress are beginning to develop a concern, which until now has only been understood and discussed within the defense establishment, over the impact of sales, future deliveries and long-term replacement, parts and maintenance obligations, and our own production and logistics system. At several points in the discussion of the 1977 legislation, members of the Senate Armed Services Committee conferred and spoke with members of the Humphrey

Subcommittee about these all-too-little-understood problems. Such concerns may well become more acute in coming sessions.

But the Congress as an institution is probably not capable of mandating a change in our present style of arms sales diplomacy. The most important lesson of the past months is that Congress is almost incapable of unilaterally legislating restraint or substantial limitations on an unwilling executive branch. If the principal executive officers are not anxious to limit arms sales, if they won't assess long-range risks and instead base policy only on short-range benefits, the Congress cannot quickly compel a change in behavior. At best, Congress can pose a political threat to executive action or may force it to justify sales decisions more fully. But the new law will yield little unless the tools it provides are creatively and aggressively applied.

The Congress' broad ranging efforts over the past decade have demonstrated the limits of its ability to reach into the executive branch policy process in order to effect decisions before they are made, or to prescribe the processes by which decisions should be made. The Congress can deny funds, and grant or take away statutory authority. But this is usually a reactive process. As such, it is not well-suited for efforts to fine-tune policy or to participate in the day-to-day implementation of policy.

Yet it has become apparent that the sale or grant of arms is too important a matter to have government deeply divided on the precise role that arms transfers should play in the foreign policy of our nation. The present divisions between the executive and legislative branches are not tenable over an extended period of time. It would be naive to expect a unanimity of views on this issue. But the two branches of government need not be so far apart as to prevent effective cooperation between them on devising a policy which both could support over the long term.

At present, no one should pretend that the Congress is unified in its views on the arms sales issue. Many of those who have been most critical in general terms do not oppose the great majority of sales. But they are beset by misgivings over future consequences and by doubts that future contingencies are being adequately explored. In short, there is a lack of confidence in the executive's methods.

The record of recent years seems to bear out these misgivings. In May 1975 the National Security Council ordered a comprehensive review of arms sales policy. Known as NSSM 223, this study has never been completed. Similarly, another NSC study on the Persian Gulf, NSSM 238, has been pending since February 1976. Since these studies were begun, billions of dollars of sales have been made to Iran and Saudi Arabia, among others. The Congress is aware of these uncompleted studies and is concerned that sales are proceeding as usual without the benefit of completed policy reviews.

Secretary of State Kissinger publicly committed the United States, in the presence of the Shah of Iran, to sell Iran another $10 billion of arms over the next five years. Not only was the Congress not consulted on this, but neither were those elements of the executive branch which are responsible for sales activities. Yet the Kissinger commitment of 1976, like the Nixon decision of 1972, may be a major determining factor in U.S. policy toward Iran for the next decade.

Secretary Kissinger has charged that the Congress is trying to make tactical decisions on arms sales. The charge is ironic since one of the things which most worries some members of Congress is that the Secretary may have dealt excessively in arms sales commitments as tactical ploys.

The adoption of a comprehensive set of clearly defined and

[259]

well-examined arms transfer policies with however large or small a scope would do much to restore the confidence of Congress. Unless this occurs, the internecine warfare is likely to continue.

Of course, the main argument for such a course is not simply to quiet Congressional critics. The President himself would benefit from advice of the sort which more thoughtful procedures would yield.

By opening this process to Congressional participation, the President could further strengthen it. He would be assured that if all points of view were not adequately represented in the executive branch staff work which he received, they would likely be raised in the Congress. This in turn would improve the quality of discussion within the executive branch by giving courage and credibility to individuals or agencies whose point of view may not have been effectively presented or adequately considered.

In the long term, by providing an official forum for public discussion and a hearing for alternative views, the Congress may be making its most important contribution to the evolution of a government policy restraining the sale of arms. As we have seen, laws by themselves are not the final answer. Active oversight by the Congress and informed public debate are, in our view, the key to the evolution of a more reasonable policy for arms transfers.

[SIX]

An Economic Assessment of the Arms Transfer Problem

Edward R. Fried *

There seems to be general agreement that arms transfers should be judged principally on the basis of political and security consequences, not on presumed economic or commercial advantages. The Foreign Military Sales Act of 1976, in outlining the considerations to be taken into account in deciding on arms sales, pointedly omits any reference to possible economic benefits.

Nonetheless, economic considerations have a habit of intruding, and this is not a recent phenomenon. During the 1960s, a suspicion arose abroad that the United States was sending arms salesmen around the world principally to cope with the latter-day problems of the dollar under the Bretton Woods system of fixed exchange rates. In the United States,

* This chapter was prepared with the assistance of Amy F. Belasco, who shared in the research and contributed to the analysis.

[261]

arms sales were seen as the principal means of offsetting the special charges on the balance of payments resulting from the stationing of U.S. forces abroad in fulfillment of collective defense arrangements. At times, the controversy over this issue within NATO and with Japan overshadowed security questions. After the onset of the oil crisis and the quadrupling of oil prices, arms sales were portrayed as a useful if not necessary means of whittling down OPEC financial surpluses, and even of helping a bit in getting through the 1974-75 recession.

This chapter seeks to explore some of the economic consequences of the post-1973 surge in arms sales so as to provide perspective on its possible economic importance. The analysis centers on the United States; data on U.S. arms sales are extensive and their economic significance has been systematically assessed in a number of recent studies. Are sales of military goods and services becoming a newly important factor in maintaining employment in the United States, or in supporting the exchange value of the dollar, or in reducing unit costs of U.S. defense procurement? Following upon this analysis, data on worldwide arms sales are examined to see what might be said about the economic benefits to other suppliers in the new situation in arms sales, and to determine whether the economic burden of arms purchases for the non-OPEC developing countries is threatening to get out of hand.

The United States

Concepts

Arms transfers in the most inclusive sense consist of military goods and services that are given away, sold on credit (either at market or at concessional rates), or sold for cash. Their economic consequences, by including one or more of the following sources of economic gains or losses, could:

—generate savings by reducing unit procurement costs of military equipment supplied to U.S. defense forces;
—generate employment by adding to aggregate demand;
—generate exports and thereby strengthen the U.S. international payments position and the exchange rate;
—generate savings for the U.S. defense budget to the extent that (a) they meet requirements which otherwise would have had to be met in whole or in part by U.S. defense forces; or (b) enable U.S. forces to operate more effectively, or at lower cost;
—incur losses, insofar as military goods and services are given away, or are sold at prices that do not cover costs.

For present purposes we consider only arms *sales:* both those under the Foreign Military Sales program (FMS) and commercial sales. Military Assistance Program (MAP) grants and credits to Israel, on which payment is waived, are excluded on the grounds that they involve economic costs, not benefits. They obviously do not improve the balance of payments since they are given away. Since they are government grants, they are not, by themselves, a stimulus to aggregate demand; that is, the United States could achieve much the same employment effect by spending the money on some other government program or by cutting taxes. Military production for MAP would contribute to reducing unit procurement costs, but such savings would be much smaller than the cost of producing the equipment. (In theory, MAP grants to other countries could reduce the need for U.S. forces; and if thereby the U.S. force structure is reduced or existing forces used more effectively, a net economic benefit might follow.

The chain of reasoning is usually complicated and the net effect difficult to prove, but in any event this area of inquiry is outside the scope of our analysis.)

Whether arms sales bring economic benefits, and how much, depends not only on the terms under which they are made (grant or sales) but on prevailing economic circumstances. For example, if productive facilities are fully employed, additional arms sales would add principally to inflationary pressures rather than to employment. In a recession, the opposite would more likely be true.

Finally, it is important to recognize that an economic assessment of the arms sales program, to be useful, requires that sales to countries where the United States seeks an expanded collective defense effort, as in NATO, be distinguished from sales to countries where the political or security consequences might turn out to be adverse. Only in the latter case might it be useful to know what economic benefits would be lost if sales were reduced or cut off entirely. For this reason, we have focused our analysis on a breakdown of the arms sales program into country categories that are designed to bring out these fundamental differences.

Patterns and Projections

Economic effects have to be measured principally on the basis of deliveries rather than sales.[1] Future deliveries, in turn, depend on present contracts (sales), which are assumed to take four years on average to fulfill. For present purposes we project annual deliveries over the period FY 1978-FY 1981 to average $11 billion (in constant FY 1976 dollars). This projection, broken down by country or region, is shown in Table 1, along with roughly comparable data for FY 1974 and the preceding decade.

Taking average deliveries during the period 1965-74 as the baseline, or "normal," level,[2] several points stand out:

- —Projected deliveries are almost three and one-half times the baseline volume.
- —Roughly four-fifths of the increase is accounted for by deliveries to the Middle East, mostly to Iran and Saudi Arabia, where the quantum jump in oil revenues provided the necessary financing for a quantum jump in arms purchases.
- —Most of the remaining increase in projected deliveries will go to U.S. allies among the industrial countries.
- —Deliveries to developing countries with which we have base rights or other special security arrangements will be at about the baseline level. Transfers in the past, however, were mostly grants; those in the future will consist mostly of sales, reflecting the greatly improved economic position of these countries,
- —Deliveries to developing countries other than those mentioned above will be about double the baseline volume but will still be comparatively small.

Aggregate Economic Effects

How much does $11 billion in arms sales abroad mean to the economy?

Budgetary Savings: We consider first the possible savings for the defense budget. Such savings could occur because export sales absorb part of the R & D investment in specific weapons systems procured for U.S. forces or because they reduce unit production costs. R & D cost savings necessarily are restricted to systems that contain sophisticated and fairly recent technol-

TABLE 1

U.S. Arms Deliveries, FMS and Commercial:
1965-74 Average, 1974, and Projected 1978-81
(In millions of FY 1976 dollars) [a]

Country or Region	1965-74 Annual Average [b]	FY 1974	Projected FY 1978-81 Annual Average [e]
Industrial Countries			
Europe [c]	760	960	1,510
Canada	60	160	190
Japan	80	100	120
Aus/NZ	110	130	220
Sub-total	1,010	1,350	2,040
"Base Rights"			
Developing Countries			
Greece	150	120	280
Turkey	280	20	90
Spain	70	70	160
Korea	340	10	430
Taiwan	220	130	170
Philippines	30	—	40
Sub-total	1,090	350	1,170
Middle East			
Israel	450	1,260	900 [d]
Iran	240	730	3,720
Saudi Arabia	60	310	2,020
Jordan	40	10	170
Morocco	10	—	120
Other	10	—	280
Sub-total	810	2,310	7,210
Other Developing			
Africa	40	20	120
Asia	100	70	200
Latin America	120	130	200
Sub-total	260	220	520
TOTAL	3,170	4,230	10,940

ogy. Reductions in unit production costs could be realized if export sales: (a) absorb overhead; (b) make possible more efficiently sized production units and bring about learning curve effects; (c) avoid gaps in production lines; and (d) absorb non-recurring costs. Two Congressional Budget Office (CBO) studies[3] describe these possible effects of the arms sales program and estimate how large the savings might be, using cost savings data for specific weapon systems supplied by the Department of Defense. We use this analysis in the estimates shown below.

To start with, only about one-half the arms sales program (based on FY 1975 FMS orders) consists of items that could produce significant cost savings. The balance consists of services (20 percent), where there there are no cost savings to the United States, and ships and ammunition where potential savings are very small. A breakdown is shown in Table 2.

Using the CBO-calculated ratio of savings to the size of the program, $11 billion in arms sales (assuming the FY 1975 sales

---

[a] Data converted to FY 1976 dollars on basis of GNP deflator.

[b] This column is not strictly comparable to the columns showing deliveries for 1974 and projected deliveries for 1978-81. It is based on ACDA, *World Military Expenditures and Arms Transfers, 1965-74,* and includes all arms *transfers* (grants and credits) but excludes services and consumables. The figures have been adjusted to exclude transfers to Vietnam, Laos and Cambodia, which averaged approximately $1 billion a year during this period.

[c] Excludes Greece, Turkey, and Spain, which are shown separately as "base rights" countries.

[d] Sales figures for Israel were reduced by an average of $670 million a year, or by the amount of credits for which payment is waived. This is taken to be equal to half of recorded FMS sales agreements for each of the years 1974-77, converted into FY 1976 dollars.

[e] Projection equals average of actual sales figures for FY 1974-77, as shown in *Foreign Military Sales and Military Assistance Facts,* December 1976, and the 36(4) Quarterly Reports to the Congress for 1977. (The fourth quarter is estimated.) Commercial deliveries are taken to be equal to estimated deliveries for the FY 1977 (presentation to Congress), which are assumed to be constant for the period.

TABLE 2

Composition of Foreign Military Sales, FY 1975: by
Potentiality for Realizing Savings in U.S. Defense Budget

	Percent of Total Sales
Items Where Potential Cost Savings	
to the U.S. Are Significant	
Aircraft	29
Vehicles and weapons	8
Missiles	15
Communications equipment	2
Sub-total	54
Items Where Potential Cost Savings	
to the U.S. Are Small or Nonexistent	
Ships	16
Ammunition	10
Services:	
Construction	2
Repair and Rehabilitation	2
Supply Operations	4
Training	3
Other	9
Sub-total	46
Total	100

Source: Based on Breakdown of FMS sales for FY 1975 in *Foreign Military Sales and Military Assistance Facts, November 1975*, p. 8. Figures for "Other Equipment" and for "Undefinitized Adjustments" are allocated pro rata to other listed categories.

Categorization of items is based on information and analysis in the Congressional Budget Office studies cited in Note 3 to text.

mix) would produce defense budget savings of approximately $770 million a year, or about one-half of 1 percent (0.5%) of current defense outlays.[4] Of this amount, $220 million would result from shared R & D and $550 million from lower unit production costs of weapon systems procured for U.S. defense forces. Another way of looking at these estimates is to note that projected sales of military equipment (as distinct from services) would amount to approximately 40 percent of U.S. defense procurement of major weapon systems and would reduce unit procurement costs by 3 percent. The savings from arms sales through absorption of R & D costs would amount to about 2 percent of current annual U.S. defense expenditures on R & D.

Employment: Arms sales deliveries of $11 billion a year would require approximately 570,000 jobs, or roughly one-half of one percent of total employment. This estimate is based on Bureau of Labor Statistics input-output calculations of direct and supporting labor needs for arms sales deliveries in FY 1975.[5] (It does not allow for the substantial additional employment, or multiplier effects, that would be generated by an increase in expenditures on arms sales when the nation's productive facilities are less than fully employed.) As a matter of general interest, arms sales (good and services) embody somewhat more labor than exports generally and somewhat less labor than the average mix of personal consumption expenditures or of private investment.

Balance of Payments: Projected arms deliveries would be equal to almost 7 percent of nonmilitary merchandise exports and about 5 percent of exports of both goods and services. By convention in balance-of-payment accounting, arms sales are treated as an offset to U.S. military expenditures abroad, principally, expenditures for contractual services, payments to foreign employees, and personal expenditures by defense personnel stationed abroad. These defense expenditures abroad derive mostly from the stationing of U.S. forces in NATO Europe and to a lesser degree from forces stationed in Japan and Korea. They amounted to approximately $5 billion in

1975 and, barring either a drastic policy change or a military conflict, are likely to remain at about that level (in constant dollars) for the rest of the decade. Thus instead of the usual U.S. net deficit on military transactions of $2 billion to $3 billion, the likely prospect for the next few years is a net surplus on this so-called military account of approximately $6 billion a year.

A more useful measure of the input of recent trends in arms sales is to focus on the *change* in their size rather than on the total amount. We have noted above that deliveries in 1978-81 would be approximately twice the 1974-75 level, which gives a better measure of their *incremental* economic impact than is shown by the budgetary and employment consequences of *total* deliveries. Even more significant, however, is the question of what economic costs would be incurred by a policy decision to reduce the total volume of arms sales. To address this question, it is necessary to distinguish among the different categories of purchasing countries, since they would not be equally affected by such a change in policy.

A Disaggregated View

As shown in Table 1, projected U.S. deliveries of military goods and services during the period 1978-81 can be broken down among four categories of purchasing countries: the industrial allies, the "Base Rights" developing countries, Middle-East countries, and other developing countries.

The Industrial Allies: Sales to this group would account for almost one-fifth of projected deliveries. The recipients are countries that share common security objectives with the United States and with which the United States has its strong-

[270]

est military ties. U.S. security interests call for these countries to increase their spending on defense and to get the maximum defense capabilities out of what they spend. The interests of the recipient countries are to make sure that defense arrangements with the United States will be collective, effective, and based on the premise that security requirements are indivisible.

In these circumstances, the economic (and security) objectives of arms trade within this group of countries can best be met by the efficiency test: military production should take place where costs are lowest. The governing principle should be free trade in military goods, as in other products. Unfortunately, because of domestic political factors, the more apt parallel is to protectionism (for example, as in trade in agricultural products), with liberalization in the exchange of military products slow and grudging. Strong pressures exist to maintain national defense industries, no matter how high the cost, and no matter how anachronistic they may be in a security system that rests on collective rather than national defense. As a result, substantial economic or welfare losses are incurred all around.

The United States should have strong comparative advantages over other industrial countries in military production. U.S. defense expenditures are roughly twice those of the European NATO countries combined, and Japan's military expenditures are exceptionally small. Hence, military unit production costs in the United States for most of the reasonably sophisticated weapon systems are low because of economies of scale; and U.S. weapon capabilities tend to be technologically the most advanced because of the enormously large U.S. expenditures on R & D, compared with those of its industrial allies.

In this light, U.S. arms sales to these countries are not large. Projected deliveries of $2 billion a year would amount to

[271]

perhaps 20 percent of what these countries will spend on major items of military equipment. Moreover, these projected figures are heavily influenced by the F-16 contract, which is unusually large. Normally, the proportion would be closer to 10 percent. Furthermore, U.S. arms sales would be only half the amount of U.S. military expenditures in the industrial allies, so that the employment and balance-of-payments effects of U.S. military transactions with this group of countries would continue to be negative.

In sum, the United States would have no policy reasons to reduce arms sales to this group of countries. To the contrary, it would make economic sense for the United States, as a low-cost producer, to be exporting even larger quantities of aircraft and other sophisticated weapon systems to this group of countries and, symbolically speaking, receiving European and Japanese automobiles in exchange. This would bring economic and welfare gains to all the countries concerned. It would also produce greater defense capabilities for any given level of military outlays. Unfortunately, the strong tendency everywhere to protect domestic military production severely limits the extension of this process so that second-best choices have to be pursued. These include co-production arangements and provisions to achieve greater interoperability (rather than standardization) of weapon systems among alliance countries. Nonetheless, U.S. arms sales policies toward this group of countries should continue to be directed not toward constraints but toward measures to maximize liberalization of trade in military products, standardization of weapons, and specialization in military production. This trade in military products, in short, should be viewed no differently from trade in nonmilitary products.[6]

"Base Rights" Developing Countries: All the countries in this group, as shown in Table 1, have been long-term recipients of

U.S. arms either in payment for base rights or because the United States has security treaties with them, or a combination of both reasons. Political problems exist in making decisions on arms sales to this group of countries, as for example in the effects of such sales on the military balance between Greece and Turkey; or, in the case of sales to Taiwan, on U.S. policy toward China; or, in sales to South Korea, on the stability of the military balance on the Korean peninsula. The main point is that these issues follow well-trodden paths. They are not likely to be influenced by consideration of any commercial or economic advantages arising from such sales.

In fact, the projected flow of arms to this group of countries seems to contain little that is new or unusual, since in real terms the projected volume of deliveries is remarkably similar to what it was over the decade 1965-74. As noted earlier, the major new factor will be a shift from grants to sales. Thus in incremental terms, the economic effects of projected arms deliveries to this group of countries will be negligible for U.S. military procurement costs and for employment, while showing a modest improvement in the U.S. international payments position and in U.S. budgetary resources available for some other use.

The Middle East: The incremental economic effects of the jump in arms sales are concentrated in sales to this group—so much so, that arms policy toward these countries is the heart of the arms sales issue as a whole. As shown in Table 1, the increase (over "normal" levels) in arms sales to three countries—Iran, Saudi Arabia, and Israel—amounts to $6.4 billion. On the basis of the data discussed earlier, these additional sales would: (a) create about 330,000 U.S. jobs (and in current conditions of underutilized capacity generate additional employment of perhaps the same amount); (b) reduce U.S. defense costs by perhaps $450 million a year; and (c) increase foreign exchange receipts by an amount equal to about one-fourth of that received from all U.S. agricultural exports.

Adjustments over the longer term would substantially reduce the size of these initial economic effects. The projected increase in U.S. arms sales would bring about an appreciation of the exchange rate (or cause it to depreciate less). Eventually this would cause exports of nonmilitary goods to increase less than otherwise and imports to increase more than otherwise. Thus the counterpart of higher employment in the arms industries would be somewhat lower employment in other industries. In other words, in a fully employed economy, U.S. total employment would be approximately the same with or without the increase in arms sales, but the position of the military and nonmilitary industries would be different, to say nothing of the fortunes of specific firms or the difficult adjustment problems faced by different regions. With full adjustment, the net economic benefit from increased sales would derive from the efficiency gains realized because of U.S. cost advantages in the production of military goods.

Other Developing Countries: Arms sales to this group are comparatively small. While they are expected to double over the four years 1978-81 compared to the 1965-74 average, their incremental economic effect on the United States will continue to be trivial.

Impact of a Reduction in Arms Sales

This disaggregation of the arms sales program makes it easier to speculate on the possible effect of additional policy restraints. How much would deliveries be reduced and what economic costs would be incurred?

[274]

On the reasoning outlined earlier, the effect on volume of a restraint policy would be predominantly a function of the size of the decline in deliveries to the Middle East. There would be no change in sales to industrial allies and at most a marginal change in sales to "base rights" developing countries. Sales to other developing countries could be expected to fall, although the absolute size of such a reduction would be small.

Suppose for these purposes that a policy of restraint is defined to call at a maximum for a reduction to the 1974 level in deliveries to the Middle East and to the category of "other developing countries." Based on the figures in Table 1, this policy change would result in a decline of $5.2 billion, or almost 50 percent in projected deliveries over the period 1978-81.

The President's 1977 report to the Congress on arms transfers contains an estimate by the Treasury Department on the economic losses that would be incurred by a restraint program that would reduce deliveries by $3.6 billion.[7] We use this analysis to calculate the impact of the somewhat larger cuts assumed here. If exchange rates are assumed to remain the same (because additional inflows of liquid funds are assumed to match the reduction in military exports of goods and services), a reduction of about $5.2 billion in military sales in FY 1979 would cause a drop of $4 billion (1976 dollars) in GNP by FY 1983 from the level that would have existed with constant military sales. Employment would fall by almost 0.2 percent.[8]

On the other hand, if exchange rates are assumed to depreciate (by an estimated 3 percent on a trade-weighted basis), increases in exports of nonmilitary goods by FY 1983 would cancel out the demand-depressing effect of the reduction in military sales, so that the level of GNP would be unaffected.

These estimates, which were obtained through the use of large models of the U.S. economy, should be viewed as no-tional orders of magnitude rather than precise forecasts. They serve to indicate that the economic cost of even a sudden, drastic, change in arms sales policy, while significant in absolute size, would be comparatively quite small in an economy the size of the United States. Nonetheless, the short-run adjustment problems would be sizable, particularly in a situation where economic capacity in general was underutilized. If the restraint in arms sales was implemented more gradually, or if offsetting policy changes were introduced, these adjustment problems would be mitigated and the medium- and longer-term costs would be reduced or eliminated.[9]

So far as economic costs and benefits are concerned, the overriding significance of sales to Iran and Saudi Arabia is worth stressing again. These two countries alone account for 90% of what might be called the discretionary portion of the surge in U.S. arms sales since 1973. In large measure, therefore, the economic consequences of any new U.S. action to restrain sales comes down to U.S. policy toward these two countries.

Other Arms-Exporting Countries

The United States accounts for about half of total world arms exports, with the remainder divided among a handful of other industrial countries, both Communist and non-Communist. How significant is this commerce to these other supplying countries?

A picture of the sources of world arms exports and indications of their comparative economic importance to the supplying countries is shown in Table 3. The underlying data are from the U.S. Arms Control and Disarmament Agency (ACDA) publication, *World Military Expenditures and Arms*

TABLE 3

World Arms Exports:

Sources and Economic Importance to Supplying Countries

Supplying Country	Percent of World Total[a] 1965-74	1974	Exports as a Percent of Domestic Military Procurement 1974[b]	Percent to "Alliance" Countries[c] 1965-74	Percent to Middle East 1965-74	Percent to All Others 1965-74	Arms Exports as a Percent of Total Exports 1974	Arms Exports as a Percent of GNP 1974
West								
U.S.	49	46	27	61	18	21	4.2	0.3
France	4	6	33	27	16	56	1.2	0.2
U.K.	3	5	26	24	29	47	1.2	0.2
Germany	2	2	13	59	15	26	0.3	0.1
Other	5	4	n.a.	n.a.	n.a.	n.a.	n.a.	n.a.
East								
USSR	29	31	13	58	31	12	12.5	0.4
China	3	4	6	76	—	24	6.7	0.1
Czechoslovakia	2	1	19	58	24	17	n.a.	0.1
Other	2	Neg.	n.a.	n.a.	n.a.	n.a.	n.a.	n.a.
Total	100	100						

[a] Source: Based on data in ACDA: *World Military Expenditures and Arms Transfers, 1965-74.*

[b] For NATO—NATO Press Release M-DCP-2(75) Dec. 18, 1975. For USSR, China, and Czechoslovakia—rough estimates.

[c] "Alliance" is defined as follows: For US: NATO, Japan, S. Korea, S. Vietnam; for France, U.K. and Germany: NATO; for USSR: Warsaw Pact, N. Vietnam, N. Korea and India; for China: Cambodia, N. Korea, N. Vietnam; and for Czechoslovakia: Warsaw Pact; figures from ACDA, *World Military Expenditures and Arms Transfers, 1965-74.*

Transfers, 1965-1974. They include equipment but exclude services and consumables, and they include grants as well as sales. Hence they are not strictly comparable to the data for actual deliveries in 1974 and for projected deliveries for 1978-81 presented above for the United States. Also, we do not have data on *orders* received by suppliers other than the United States, which means that these data give little indication of how higher oil revenues have affected OPEC purchases from these suppliers.

With these qualifications in mind, several points emerge from the data in Table 3:

—The United States and the U.S.S.R. dominate arms exports, together accounting for over three-fourths of the total.

—Among Western countries, France and Britain are the only significant suppliers other than the United States. For each, arms sales represent a substantial share of their total military procurement—about the same proportion as for the United States. For this reason, their budgetary savings from arms sales might be proportionately comparable to those obtained by the United States.

—Before the jump in sales to Iran and Saudi Arabia, most U.S. arms transfers went to countries where the United States had a strong security involvement (NATO, Japan, Indochina and Korea). Outside of its shipments to the industrial countries, most U.S. arms transfers were grants. For France and Britain, on the other hand, most arms transfers went to essentially commercial markets.

—Arms trade for both France and Britain has been comparatively less significant in broad economic terms (in

[278]

relation to GNP or to total exports) than it was for the
United States, but in all three cases the proportionate
significance is small.

Soviet arms transfers followed more closely the U.S. pattern, going mostly to countries with which the U.S.S.R. has a
close security involvement, by treaty or otherwise. These
arms transfers represent a comparatively small proportion of
Soviet military procurement and thus may be less important in
reducing Soviet unit production costs for military equipment
than is true for the United States, France or the United
Kingdom. On the other hand, the contribution of arms sales to
relieving the chronic Soviet shortage of convertible currency
suggests they have a higher value to the Soviet economy than
the nominal figures suggest. According to a recent CIA study,
current Soviet hard currency receipts from arms sales amount
to $1.5 billion to $2 billion, or perhaps 10-15 percent of Soviet
hard currency receipts from nonmilitary merchandise exports.[10]

What might be said about the economic importance of arms
sales to France and the United Kingdom—the major non-
Communist suppliers other than the United States? In recent
years (1972-75), average exports of military goods and services are estimated (in 1976 dollars) at $850 million for France
and $600 million for the United Kingdom.[11] Suppose as an
outsized example that in the wake of the oil revenue bonanza,
each country tripled its sales of military goods and services to
the Middle East, as was the case in the United States. In that
event, total deliveries of military goods and services over the
next five years might average about $1.1 billion for France and
$950 million for the United Kingdom.[12] These total deliveries
of military goods and services would be equal to about one-
third of 1 percent of the GNP of each country and, based on

[279]

the calculations for the United States, would account for about 60,000 jobs in France and 50,000 jobs in the United Kingdom. As for the balance of payments, this level of deliveries of military goods and services might account for about 2 percent of the total exports of goods and services of each country.

Savings for the French and British defense budgets would also be comparatively small. Again, using the savings to sales ratios derived for the United States, foreign arms sales, by sharing in the R & D overhead and by increasing the opportunities for economies of scale, might provide budgetary savings of perhaps $80 million for France and $70 million for the United Kingdom.

These figures, it should be stressed, show the aggregate economic impact of all arms sales rather than the losses that might be attributed to a policy of restraint. Under a restraint policy, sales within NATO would not be affected and for other countries sales would be only partly curtailed. Suppose at the outside that a restraint policy consisted of holding sales to the Middle East to the 1972-75 level and reducing sales to other developing countries by 25 percent. In that event, total arms deliveries would be reduced by 40 percent from the levels hypothesized earlier and the economic losses considerably reduced from the figures shown above for the income, employment, and exports estimated to be associated with the total arms deliveries of each country.

The point is frequently made that despite their comparatively small aggregate economic impact, arms sales are critical to the viability of the defense industries of France and Britain. Most often cited are two examples in the Stockholm International Peace Research Institute's 1971 study of the world arms trade, namely: (a) "One-half the output of the French aircraft industry must be exported or the industry will cease to exist"; and (b) "Over one-half the output of British naval ship production must be exported or the industry may not survive." We do not have the data for a careful assessment of these claims, but in some respects at least they seem to exaggerate the extent to which the arms industries are dependent on sales to countries where policy issues exist.

For example, a recent study by the European Commission indicates that production of military aircraft in the Community accounts for 72 percent of total EEC aerospace sales. The study also suggests that exports of military aircraft to non-EEC countries is equal to 28 percent of total production of military aircraft.[13] About one-third of these exports, moreover, are to non-EEC *industrial* countries, including the United States,[14] which suggests that the dependence of the European military aircaft industry *on arms sales to developing countries* is only about 17 percent.

Two points are worth stressing in this connection. The first is that in circumstances where collective defense arrangements are the principal determinant of national security, there is little justification for maintaining high-cost defense industries, certainly not national industries that seek to develop military production capabilities across the board. Second, while increased specialization and trade among industrial countries might mean a smaller military arms industry for countries such as France and the United Kingdom, it would almost certainly offer much greater potentialities for efficient military production and economic gains than would the indiscriminate pursuit of greater sales to developing countries.

BURDEN ON DEVELOPING COUNTRY ARMS IMPORTERS

Most of the concern about the economic effect of arms sales on recipient countries understandably centers on the developing countries. Two questions are important: (a) Do arms imports represent a growing burden on the foreign exchange availability of these countries and therefore a growing impediment to their development program? (b) Do arms imports affect the total military spending of these countries?

Here again disaggregation of the data is necessary to gain a useful appreciation of trends and their significance. The disaggregation shown in Table 4 compares estimates of deliveries of military goods and services in 1966-67 and 1974-75 and indicates the relationships of recent deliveries to GNP.

TABLE 4

Developing Country Imports of Military Goods and Services,
1966-67 Average and 1974-75 Average
(In millions of 1976 dollars)

Country Categories	1966-67 Average	1974-75 Average	1974-75 Arms Imports as a Percentage of GNP
OPEC Countries	655	3,175	1.4
Non-OPEC Middle East	510	1,790	5.4
Other Developing Countries:			
Africa	140	420	0.6
East Asia	1,045	795	0.9
South Asia	655	390	0.3
Latin America	330	600	0.1
Sub-Total	2,170	2,205	0.4

Source: ACDA, *World Military Expenditures and Arms Transfers, 1966-1975.* Figures on imports were increased by 25 percent to allow for services. U.S. GNP deflator was used to convert data into 1976 dollars. Figures do not include arms imports of Indochina, which were $3.2 billion in 1966-67 and $1.9 billion in 1974-75, but are no longer significant.

The OPEC countries are in a separate category for these purposes because of the extraordinary financial support they now receive from oil revenues. These revenues have greatly reduced the normal financial restraints on arms spending and have been the major cause of the sudden, quantum jump in the arms purchases of these countries.

The non-OPEC countries in the Middle East consists essentially of the confrontation states in the region. These countries are burdened both by their large arms purchases from abroad and by their large military budgets in general.

For the large number of other developing countries a rather different picture emerges. Total deliveries to these countries from all sources in recent years have been running at $2.2 billion a year—virtually the same as the volume of a decade previously. These expenditures amount to less than one-half of one percent of their GNP and perhaps 10-15 percent of their military budgets.

Expenditures at this level clearly are not on a scale that would put development programs in jeopardy, nor have these countries in the aggregate been devoting a rising proportion of their GNP to military spending. Nonetheless, the growing arms imports of particular countries (for example, Ethiopia, Somalia, Angola, Kenya, Uganda, and Peru) is clearly disturbing. It is possible furthermore that the projection of a rise in U.S. deliveries to developing countries in Africa, Asia, and Latin America (Table 1) may indicate that their arms purchases from all countries are expanding. If so, this might carry with it a rise in their total military budgets and point to a heavier military burden on their economies in the future.

In any event, whether they rise or not, these arms purchases siphon off scarce foreign exchange, equal to about 10 percent of the net capital imports of these countries. If they could be reduced, military budgets might also decline, thus saving a large volume of both foreign exchange and domestic resources that potentially at least would be available for investment and social development.[15]

Conclusions

A survey such as this should serve to emphasize how misleading it is to view the sharp rise in arms sales and its economic and military consequences in undifferentiated terms.[16]

As far as U.S. economic stakes in this traffic are concerned, the issues ride almost entirely on U.S. policy toward Iran and Saudi Arabia. For all practical purposes, these two countries account for the sharp rise in "discretionary" sales and projected deliveries. If the United States in the extreme case chose to curtail sales to these two countries suddenly and sharply, it would have to absorb some moderately unpleasant economic shocks. These would be concentrated in the form of short-run adjustment problems in the aerospace industries but there would be associated job and income losses elsewhere in the economy as well. Over the medium and longer term, these shocks could be fully absorbed, with no lasting adverse economic consequences.

Arms sales have helped the United States and other industrial countries to pay OPEC countries higher prices for their oil. Arms sales, however, are small in comparison to the increase in sales of nonmilitary goods to these countries as a consequence of their larger oil revenues. This is most dramatically exemplified by the fact that the most rapid balance-of-payments adjustment to higher oil prices has been made by Germany and Japan, countries whose sales of arms are insignificant.

Finally, it is worth stressing that sales of arms to the non-OPEC developing countries outside the Middle East are too small to be of economic significance to the major supplying countries—the United States, the U.S.S.R., France and the

United Kingdom. The arms sale issues in this part of the developing world are clearly political. If the major supplying countries could act together to dampen down the importation of arms that are tied to ongoing conflicts or threats of conflict, their economic losses from curtailing sales would be trivial. In contrast, the risks and dangers that would be averted could have very substantial economic benefits.

NOTES

1. An increase in sales could stimulate investment in additional capacity and thus have an immediate economic impact, but this effect is disregarded for present purposes.

2. The sharp increase in sales which began in 1973 has only gradually been reflected in deliveries during subsequent years.

3. Congressional Budget Office, *Budgetary Cost Savings to the Department of Defense Resulting from Foreign Military Sales,* by James R. Capra, Robert E. Schafer, and Patrick L. Renehan, May 24, 1976; and Congressional Budget Office, *Foreign Military Sales and U.S. Weapons Costs,* by Sheila Kean Fifer, May 5, 1976.

4. A Treasury Department study shows considerably higher savings (the ratios in this study would indicate savings of approximately $1 billion from an $11 billion program), although the estimates are based on the CBO study cited above. See *Report to Congress on Arms Transfer Policy Pursuant to Sections 202(B) and 218 of the International Security Assistance and Arms Export Control Act of 1976,* Annex 2, pp. 15-16.

5. See Bureau of Labor Statistics, *Foreign Defense Sales and Grants, Fiscal Years 1973-1975: Labor and Material Requirements,* July 1977, p. 20.

[285]

6. This seems to be official policy. In his statement of May 19, 1977, on arms transfer policy, President Carter specifically excluded these countries from any new actions of restraint.

7. *Report to Congress, op.cit.,* Annex 2.

8. The macroeconomic effects of a *total* ban on arm sales are estimated in a CBO study: James Copra and Stephen H. Brooks, *"The Effect of Foreign Military Sales on the U.S. Economy,"* July 23, 1976. The authors calculate that a total ban would reduce 1981 GNP by $12 billion and employment by 0.3 percent. However, they assume fixed exchange rates in addition to making no allowance for offsetting policy changes.

9. The Treasury study indicates that if the reduction in sales were to be spread over four years, the decline in employment would be cut almost in half, as would the depreciation in exchange rate necessary to bring about offsetting increases in nonmilitary exports.

10. CIA, *USSR: Hard Currency Trade and Payments, 1977-78,* March 1977, Table 2, p.7.

11. These estimates are derived by taking average exports of military goods for 1972-75, as shown in ACDA, *World Military Expenditures and Arms Transfers, 1966-1975,* and adding an allowance of 25 percent for services, this being the ratio of services to goods shown for the United States (see Table 2).

12. U.K. exports would increase more than those of France, on this assumption, because the U.K. normally sells proportionately more to the Middle East than does France (see Table 3).

13. Commission of the European Communities, *The European Aerospace Industry, Trading Position and Figures,* Brussels August 2, 1977. See Table 44, p. 30.

14. *Ibid.*, p. 18.

15. For an elaboration of such possibilities see Barry M. Blechman and Edward R. Fried, *Disarmament and Development: An Analytical Survey and Pointers for Action,* UN Document E/AC.54/L.90, January 26, 1977.

16. The *New York Times* in a number of its editorials has been guilty of this error. See, for example, an editorial of March 3, 1976, entitled "United States, Pusher." The editorial argues that the military expenditures of the developing countries have been rising faster than the economic base to support them and that "the international arms traffic that made this possible is as much the responsibility of the pushers as the addicts. The chief pusher is the United States." It goes on to say that "The time has clearly come for the United States to pull back from this increasing militarization of the developing world." Iran and Saudi Arabia are hardly typical of the developing world.

[SEVEN]

Multilateral Restraints on Arms Transfers

Andrew J. Pierre

A new American approach to the sale of conventional arms, designed to produce greater restraints than have existed in past years, can only be one part of the attempt to deal with this vexing problem. The other approach—complementary in nature—must seek to develop some multilateral restraints on the transfer and the purchase of arms. At the heart of the question of how to moderate the international arms trade is the widely perceived view that unilaterally imposed restraints are likely to be self-defeating—this for the basic reason that if *we* do not sell arms to a country that wants them, *some other* nation will be only too pleased to oblige. Accordingly there is inherent logic in seeking to develop a multilateral framework for regulating the flow of arms transfers.

Surprisingly little serious attention has, however, been given to date to this critical dimension of the arms transfer problem. Most analyses have focused on American policy and policy-making; almost as an afterthought, they have mentioned the need to encourage other supplier countries to moderate their arms sales. But this has usually been suggested in a perfunctory manner, with not much sustained thought as to how it might be achieved and the problems entailed. Little analysis is to be found regarding the perspectives on arms sales held within the other supplier countries, the attitudes of the recipient nations purchasing arms, or the forms of mutually agreed upon restraints which might be developed either among suppliers or between suppliers and recipients.

The reason for these intellectual and policy lacunae can be traced to the existence of three assumptions which have, thus far, created the parameters for the public and intra-governmental debate. More to the point, these assertions have functioned in such a way as to restrain serious thought about the opportunities which may exist for an arms control approach to the arms trade. Although these assertions do have some validity, it will be argued here that none of them need present insurmountable obstacles to an initiative which seeks to construct multilateral *cooperative restraints* on arms transfers.

THREE ASSUMPTIONS

The first assumption is that supplier states will be unwilling to regulate internationally the sale of arms because these exports are essential to their economic well-being and to the viability of their defense industries. Arms exports are said to be so essential to the balance of payments, to levels of employment, and to the unit costs of manufacturer weapons that any thought of regulating them will be totally and effectively resisted.

Such reasoning fails to acknowledge that, as discussed in

Fried's Chapter 6 and in this one, weapons exports are in fact a relatively small proportion of total exports for each of the major suppliers, and their total economic impact is not as great as many believe it to be. It also assumes that the cooperative regulation of arms exports would necessarily lead to drastically reduced arms sales. Yet an attempt to regulate the arms trade so as to avoid the transfer of particularly destabilizing technologies might only lead to a relatively insignificant amount of reductions. Indeed, sophisticated weapons might be replaced with a larger number of less destabilizing weapons, thereby actually *increasing* the level of exports (and jobs, foreign exchange earnings, etc.). All depends, therefore, on the particular types of qualitative and quantitative restraints which are agreed upon.

A second assumption involves the attitude of the recipient countries. It is frequently asserted that purchasing countries in the developing world will see all attempts to restrain arms transfers as discriminatory or as evidence of an unwarranted paternalism on the part of the suppliers. Such attempts are therefore assumed to be completely unacceptable.

Obviously there is a risk that supplier-initiated restraints will be perceived in this manner. The nations of the "South" are suspicious of attempts of the "North" to manipulate the transfer of technology. Yet the dangers of uncontrolled arms transfers are by no means unperceived among the developing countries. Just as the great majority of Third World countries have ratified the Non-Proliferation Treaty because of their own national interests in retarding the spread of nuclear weapons, so there may be common interests in avoiding the introduction of certain types of weapons into a particular region. Agreements on restraints might be worked out between suppliers and groups of recipients. Surely it is wrong to presume that recipient countries in the developing world will resist all

[290]

efforts to ease regional tensions and prevent local arms races through restraints on arms transfers.

The third assumption brings us back to the cliché that "if we do not sell, others will." This automatically assumes that other countries will not share one nation's evaluation that selling a particular weapon is against the national or international interest. But this need not be the case and is in fact belied by past experience: all suppliers have at one time or another refused to sell. Nations provide arms with varying degrees of caution with respect to the long-term impact of the transfer, but surely considerations of regional stability, against whom the arms might be used, and the effect on the receiving country are never totally disregarded. Thus the implication that unilateral restraint by country X will never be matched by country Y or Z is misleading. There is nothing unavoidable about competitive arms sales. Moreover, the purchasing country may have a strong preference, politically based, for buying arms from a particular supplier and be willing to relinquish a prospective weapon rather than enter into an arms relationship with another supplier.

Perspectives of Suppliers

In order better to understand what may be within the range of possibility for a multilateral regulation of arms transfers it is necessary to examine carefully the perspectives on arms sales held in the major supplier countries. However briefly done in this chapter, we may then be able to judge, in a more sophisticated way, the validity of the assumptions listed above. We should also be in a better position to evaluate the opportunities and pitfalls in an international initiative seeking cooperative regulation.

[291]

It is important to bear in mind the critical connection between multilateral restraints and the reform of American policy on arms transfers, as discussed in the previous chapters.
The United States cannot embark on an international initiative
with any realistic hope of success without getting its own
house in order, or at least being seen in a credible manner by
other countries as having seriously begun the process. But
conversely, it makes little sense to reform American policy
and practice without attempting to create a multinational
framework for the regulation of arms transfers. Without an
international approach to the problem, even the most judicious
and far-sighted American policy on arms transfers can only be
of limited effectiveness in dealing with the rising global diffusion of conventional arms.

The number of countries exporting arms to the developing
world is surprisingly small. Although more countries are currently entering the arms business, and some Third World
countries are developing indigenous armament industries, the
export of major arms such as aircraft, missiles, naval vessels and
armored fighting vehicles is still essentially in the hands of four
countries. The identity of these countries and of their allies, all
present participants in other arms control negotiations, suggests that an agreement on multinational restraints may be
worth pursuing.

The United States (53%), the Soviet Union (21%), France
(8%), and Britain (8%) exported 90% of the major weapons
transferred to the developing world in 1976.[1] When one adds
a few members of the NATO alliance (West Germany,
Canada, Italy, the Netherlands) as well as the Soviet Union's
Warsaw Pact ally, Czechoslovakia, the figure is raised to 95%.
(NATO accounts for 74% and the Warsaw Pact for 21%.)
The largest supplier not included in either alliance is the
Peoples Republic of China, but it only accounts for slightly

less than 1% of arms transfers to developing countries. Other industrialized countries exporting arms, such as Sweden, Switzerland and Belgium, or new arms manufacturers such as Israel or Brazil, must be considered as still relatively minor suppliers. The significance of the domination of the "Big Four" among the countries which transfer arms to the developing world not only lies in the fact that they are few in number, thereby facilitating the task of regulating the flow of arms, but is heightened by their past involvement in the pursuit of common objectives either through East-West arms control negotiations or West-West alliance diplomacy.

The perspective of supplier countries toward possible multilateral restraints will be influenced by a wide range of economic, domestic, political, bureaucratic, strategic, and general international considerations.

Economic considerations will include the role of overseas exports in the armaments industry of the country; their contribution to lowered unit costs of production; the place of the arms industry in the national economy, including the degree to which it is government-owned or -controlled; the relationship between levels of employment and overseas arms sales; and the contribution of arms exports to the balance of payments. Another type of economic, as well as political, motivation relates to the availability of critical resources (such as oil) in exchange for arms.

Domestic political considerations cannot, of course, be separated from the economic ones listed above. In addition, they will include the extent to which an autonomous or independent arms industry is perceived as essential to the national interest. The nature of the national debate within the political parties, the parliament, among business and intellectual elites, in the press and in public opinion regarding the government's arms transfer policy is also an essential determinant.

[293]

Bureaucratic considerations will be of two sorts. Some will relate to the inherent interests of the military in making possible the acquisition of arms for their own services through an export program which assures their production. Quite another type of bureaucratic consideration influencing attitudes on arms transfers involves the nature of the governmental decision-making process on sales.

Strategic and general international considerations have been discussed elsewhere in this volume, especially in Chapter 1, and need not be rehearsed here. Suffice it to say that despite the importance of the other factors, national security and foreign policy considerations will in the last analysis be the most consequential and ought to be the primary ones in shaping attitudes toward arms transfer decisions.

Quite obviously each country will be influenced by a particular cluster of considerations. It is therefore useful to examine what these are in the potential partners of the United States prior to making some judgments about possible forms of multilateral restraints and the attendant problems.

France

Arms sales by France expanded dramatically in the first half of the 1970s, with most computations estimating an increase of approximately 300%. This has led to the claim—usually made with some pride in Paris—that French arms sales have now surpassed those of Britain, making France the third-ranking exporter of arms. Available data suggest that this may just be a temporary lead, and that France and Britain are in essentially equal positions. Approximately 37% of arms produced in 1976 in France were made for export, compared to 17% in 1971. This does not, however, signify as heavy a dependence on arms exports for balance-of-payments purposes as is often assumed. Of total French foreign trade, arms sales accounted for only 4.6% in 1976. Only 20% of the trade with the oil-producing countries was accounted for by the sale of arms. Similarly, care must be taken not to exaggerate the importance, at least in statistical terms, of arms exports to the nation's employment levels. Of a total work force of 22 million citizens, official figures indicate 270,000 are in arms-producing industries and only 70,000 or 0.003% of the work force is estimated to be manufacturing arms intended for export.

Nevertheless, arms sales are viewed in France as having important significance in the nation's economy and in its international trade and monetary position. A special government organization, the "Délégation Générale pour l'Armement" (DGA), is charged with overseeing the production of French arms and maximizing their export. The DGA owns and runs arsenals producing 20% of arms, another 30% comes from "nationalized" industries, and 50% of the arms are made in the "private" sector. The latter includes companies such as the aircraft manufacturers Dassault and Aerospatiale, which are so intimately linked with the state that they are in reality quasi-governmental. Indeed, it is more accurate to speak of the existence of a "military-industrial" complex in France than in the United States. In recent years the DGA has organized elaborate fairs for prospective overseas buyers, mainly from the Third World, at which the advantages of French arms are touted. The promotional activity of the DGA is well-financed, goes on year-round, and has allegedly involved practices of questionable ethics.

The political rationale for the arms industry is given even more importance in France than its economic benefits. France has traditionally accorded the highest priority to the independence of its foreign policy and the national autonomy of its defense capabilities, which are perceived as making possible France's influence in Europe and the world. A national armaments industry is viewed as essential to the maintenance of automony in defense. The first task of the industry is the supplying of France's own armed forces. It is increasingly the case, however, that only the existence of exports permits national production to remain relatively cost-efficient. Beyond this, furnishing the military establishments of other nations is thought to enhance French influence and prestige. Not unrelated is the factor of the nation's pride in its advanced technology, especially in the aeronautical industry. The maintenance of France's technological base is a high priority for the French "establishment."

Political and economic factors, therefore, help account for the relative lack of public debate about French arms sales policy. Although concern about France having become a "merchant of death" has been expressed, it has remained relatively muted. The most vocal opposition has come from religious groups, in particular the "Pax Christi" movement within the Catholic Church. Early in 1976, the Archbishop of Paris, François Cardinal Marty, attracted wide attention when he condemned France's export of arms, but even he was forced to acknowledge that they were of considerable importance to the national economy. Labor unions, including the Communist C.G.T., have spoken of the long-term desirability of the conversion of the arms industry to civil products, but the unions also are quick to note that for the present the exports of arms account for a significant number of jobs. The "programme commun" of the left (Communists and Socialists) took a moral position, especially with regard to supplying weapons to South Africa and Chile, but did not advocate a halt to arms sales; this issue received little attention in the March 1978 elections. The government discourages public debate of the question, issuing little in the way of economic data. In 1974, Minister of the Army Robert Galley ordered government officials to keep their public discussions of arms sales to a bare minimum. Thus there is little opposition to arms sales; what does exist is more attuned to questions of morality than to concern about the foreign policy or regional stability consequences of the export of arms.

France is often criticized as having the most permissive arms transfer policy of any of the supplier states, allegedly being willing to sell almost any weapon to anyone. This is denied by French policy-makers. They point to a number of regulations which establish strict controls regarding the transfer of arms. Conventional weapons are not to be transferred to belligerent states in open conflict; great caution is to be exercised in sending arms to areas of tension; a distinction is to be made between arms which can be legitimately used to protect the external security of a state and arms which can be used internally for police action and repression; recently it has been said that particular care is to be exercised with respect to the sale of sophisticated arms.

Such laudable criteria must, of course, be judged against the reality of their application. Critics have pointed to French willingness to sell helicopters, usable for internal repression, to South Africa, the retransfer of Mirage fighters sold to Libya to Egypt during the 1973 war, and other questionable arms transfer decisions or uses of French arms. They note, moreover, that the purchasers often find French arms attractive because of the French government's stated principle of selling arms without making judgments about the internal politics of the recipients, and of not attaching to sales contracts clauses which can be seen as imposing any restrictions on the recipient's national sovereignty.

Whatever may be the degree of permissiveness with which

[297]

arms are sold and to whom, the actual process of case-by-case arms sales decisions is highly centralized and controlled. An intra-governmental commission (Commission Interministeri-elle pour l'Etude des Exportations de Matériels de Guerre), on which all relevant government departments are represented, meets frequently and must pass on all arms transfers, including those made nominally through commercial channels. The Commission, a reasonably high-level one, is responsible to the Prime Minister. Industrial interests do not normally try to circumvent it. The Quai d'Orsay is well represented. Accordingly, whatever may be the French practice in selling arms, it does not come about because of a lack of direction on policy.

The French attitude toward the possibility of multilateral restraints, suggested by President Carter, has been one of skepticism and caution. The generally nationalistic approach toward arms sales and the prevalance of the economic factors and political climate cited above do not provide much ground for optimism. There are, on the other hand, some emerging conditions which could lead toward a more positive response.

It is doubtful that the export of French arms will continue at their present level; quite possibly the sales books have reached their peak in orders, with prospects for the future of dwindling sales. New orders in 1977 maintained the pattern of rising sales that has existed since 1974. But this has been accompanied by an increasing concern about a saturation of markets, especially in the Persian Gulf and the Middle East. French confidence was substantially shaken by the failure to win the Mirage F-1 *versus* F-16 competition for the "sale of the century." The future of the next-generation Mirage 2000, and especially its export version, the Mirage 4000, is now in doubt. Thus there is an increasing awareness of the uncertainty of an arms industry which has become highly export-dependent. Almost 70% of French military aircraft are now sold abroad.

As exports are not likely to remain at this magnitude the arms industry may face serious difficulties, for the domestic market is not of sufficient size to support it. This is the major reason for whatever continuing interest there is in Paris in cooperative weapons production in Western Europe. With dim prospects for maintaining as autonomous a defense industry as has existed in the past, the possibility of coordinated arms sales based on an international specialization of labor may in time appear attractive—especially if it could be linked to greater Western European cooperation in arms production.

There are, moreover, signs of increasing sensitivity in Paris to the potentially dangerous consequences of selling very advanced technologies to unstable areas. In a speech before the Institut des Hautes Etudes de Défense Nationale in March 1976, the chief of French military forces, General Mery, cited the need for a better-defined French arms sales policy that takes into account all relevant factors. Mery noted in particular that the transfer of sophisticated arms or of long-range weapons should be examined in political and military as well as economic terms. Acknowledgment of the risk of selling "sensitive" nuclear technology with its prospect for nuclear proliferation eventually resulted in an important tightening of policy on the export of nuclear technology.

Giscard d'Estaing has expressed concern about the worldwide proliferation of conventional arms. During his 1974 campaign for the Presidency he spoke of his intention to curb French arms sales, but as with many of his other project for reform, this idea was quietly dropped in the following years as he led the country without a governing majority. The realignment following the 1978 legislative elections has given him new political strength, and this has been accompanied by a reawakened French interest in problems of arms control and disarmament. In early 1978 Giscard d'Estaing spoke of the

[299]

possibility of restraints on arms sales to the Middle East by the great powers.

French participation in multilateral restraints would be enhanced if it were part of a "concertation" on foreign policy among the four principal suppliers. To seek French cooperation within the NATO Council or the NATO disarmament experts is unlikely to be productive, nor would the French take seriously an initiative by the United Nations or within the Geneva Disarmament Conference. The attractiveness of a multilateral approach for the French would depend upon the extent to which it could be seen as a return to a "directoire" concept among the small group of nations which "count" in this area. The foreign policy consultation among the big four concerning developments in the Third World, which would accompany multilateral regulation, would be seen as a great benefit. Soviet participation would have to be assured. Hence there are likely to be some difficult political requirements which would have to be met; but if these could be satisfied, the government of Giscard d'Estaing might be persuaded to participate in multilateral restraints.

Britain

The increase in British arms sales in the 1970s has more or less kept pace with those of France and the United States. Exports, measured as arms delivered rather than sold, have almost tripled from £257 million in 1971-72 to a level of £700 million for 1976-77. This represents approximately 30% of Britain's arms production.

The British weapons systems most exported are tanks, aircraft, missiles and naval vessels. In recent years some weapons have been designed for export, somewhat to the detriment of the requirements set by the British armed forces which also acquire them. A particularly successful item has been the Chieftain tank. Indeed, there are more Chieftain tanks in Iran than in the British army!

British governments do not stress openly, as do the French, the need for the maintenance of an autonomous defense industry as an underpinning of national sovereignty. Rather, the importance of arms exports to the balance of payments is given prominence. Arms sales to the developing world are still seen by many as somewhat distasteful. Accordingly, neither of the two major parties when in power has released much data or drawn attention to arms exports. When attention is nevertheless given to arms sales, it is usually pointed out that they are a source of employment. Deputy Minister of Defence William Rodgers stated in the House of Commons that approximately 70,000-80,000 jobs could be attributed to exports. About 25% of these jobs are in the thirteen government-owned Royal Ordnance factories. The proportion of the arms industries that is controlled by Whitehall has increased with the nationalization of the aircraft and shipbuilding industries. As is to be expected, there is a keen awareness of the benefits of lower unit costs for arms for the British forces through lengthened production runs made possible by exports. The successive reductions in the British defense budget in the mid-1970s has served to increase the pressure for exports.

Since 1966, Britain has had a special unit within the Ministry of Defence, known as the Defence Sales Organization, whose mission it is to promote the sale of British arms. The impetus for the unit came when the British saw the success of the arms sales program under Henry Kuss, which Secretary of Defense Robert McNamara created in the early 1960s. The Defence Sales Organization has had two directors, both of whom came from the business world, and has a staff of 350, including personnel stationed in some of the key embassies abroad. In 1976, a special arms trade fair was organized at Aldershot. The recent head of the organization, Sir Lester Suffield, traveled widely and for several years paid special attention to Iran, going there on almost a monthly basis.

Decisions on arms sales are not, however, made by the Defence Sales Organization, which works within the mandate established by the foreign affairs bureaucracy and ultimately the cabinet. An Arms Working Party representing various ministers, but chaired by the Foreign and Commonwealth Office (FCO) makes most decisions. When there are differences of views between the Ministry of Defence and the FCO, the latter's appraisal of the political consequences of a sale is usually given priority. Occasionally, difficult cases are sent to a Cabinet committee for approval.

Arms sales decisions in Britain tend to be made in a pragmatic, case-by-case manner, rather than following comprehensive policy guidelines. The most notable refusals to sell arms have been the result of emotive and politically charged questions. Hence arms sales to South Africa (on which there is at present a ban) have had a particular sensitivity, in part stemming from the historically close relationship between the two countries. The same type of moral or human rights considerations have been involved in decisions regarding Nigeria and Chile. Prospective sales to these countries have been the subject of vehement debates in the House of Commons. To some extent, therefore, the Parliament acts as an implicit form of constraint on truly egregious sales. But except for special cases, little attention is paid to this question and general arms sales policy is rarely debated. Concerns about arms stability or the political effect of sales in regions such as the Persian Gulf or Latin America are not often heard. When Julian Critchley, a Tory backbencher well versed in foreign affairs, suggested in the Commons in July 1975 that there should be greater concern about the impact of cumulative arms transfers to the Persian Gulf, he found very little interest among his colleagues.

The Labour Party is not unaware of the dilemma that arms sales present. Members of the left-wing Tribune group maintain an ideological opposition to arms sales—which in fact is part of a broader opposition to defense expenditures. Yet this has little influence upon a Labour government which is necessarily concerned about economic considerations. As a way out of the dilemma the Labour Party's program, agreed upon at the 1976 annual conference, called for greater study of forms of alternative employment which might be created through the conversion of the arms industry to other products. Except for the left wing of the Labour Party, however, there is little public attention to, or criticism of, arms transfers.

A comprehensive American proposal for multilateral restraints on arms transfers would be better received in London than in Paris. True, the same impediments to reductions in the amount of the transfers would be cited in the United Kingdom—balance of payments, employment, and lowered unit costs. Although these have real validity, they would not likely be of sufficient force, however, to block a full consideration of some forms of multilateral regulation of exports.

There are a number of reasons for this. First, an American proposal that is seriously prepared and undertaken, and presented at the senior level of the governments, is likely to be accorded careful consideration. The British instinct in dealing with Americans—unlike that of some others—is to maximize common interests and objectives. Moreover, the British tend to share American conceptions of world politics and international security. Thus a Washington initiative that was perceived both as serious and in the general global interest, rather than motivated by American economic competition, would be understood and accepted as such.

Second, private British companies manufacturing weapons have increasingly diversified their products beyond defense equipment in recent years in the expectation of reduced U.K. expenditures for arms. Accordingly, it is quite possible that they could weather, without great hardships, a reduction in their weapons exports. Recent reductions in British defense budgets have increased the movement away from dependence upon the production of military equipment.

Third, the nationalization of the aircraft and shipbuilding industries has increased government control of them, making them publicly owned and more amenable to political leadership.

Fourth, and most significant, the British are prepared to deepen their involvement in, and dependence upon, joint European weapons production. Indeed, most British politicians and analysts who have examined the future of the U.K. defense industry see no future for it except in a European context. The increase in the export of arms in recent years has only served to postpone a greater involvement in weapons cooperation across the channel. With the prognosis for the British defense industry less than favorable, an approach toward multilateral regulation of arms exports that included other supplier countries would be welcomed if it was seen as leading toward some type of a future market-sharing arrangement.

The Soviet Union

As the second largest supplier of arms the Soviet Union would have to participate in any truly effective multilateral regulation of arms transfers. Gaining Soviet adherence and cooperation would be no easy task, for arms transfers are, and will remain, one of their few relatively successful instruments in the continuing competition with the West. This question can best be broached with Moscow, therefore, within the wider context of détente and discussions on international arms control. What is noteworthy is that the economic difficulties which such an initiative would raise may be comparatively less of a problem for the Soviet Union than in Western Europe. Politics, rather than economics, has been the driving force behind Soviet arms transfers.

For the past quarter-century the Soviets have carefully calibrated their arms transfers to serve political purposes. Arms transfers have been used to give support to movements of national liberation, to "progressive" countries and left-leaning, radical regimes, as well as to other nations whose favor Moscow has wanted to court. Until recent years, arms have either been granted at no cost, or have been sold on extraordinarily generous terms. Quite commonly, long-term credits have been available for repayment at 2.5% interest over the course of six to ten years; these repayments have been made in soft, local currency, which is then used for the purchase of domestic goods. Since the early 1970s there has been a shift toward repayment in hard currency, especially from oil-rich clients such as Iraq and Libya. Yet balance-of-payments considerations are not as important in arms sales decisions as in the West. A country that is politically "interesting," such as Ethiopia or Angola, will receive arms without the necessity of cash repayment. Nor do the lowered unit costs made available through exports, or the employment factor, appear to play a large role. The number of weapons sent to the developing world, in comparison to those used by Soviet and Warsaw Pact forces, remains comparatively small. The Soviet military-industrial complex does not seem subject to as strong domestic economic pressures as in the West.

On the other hand, the Soviet Union has often used arms supplies as a means of enhancing its influence. The largest recipients of Soviet arms, other than the Warsaw Pact countries, have been states whose allegiance Moscow has sought in areas of regional competition—North Korea, North Vietnam, Iraq, Syria, Libya, Egypt, Algeria, Somalia, India, Cuba, and Peru. Arms are used to establish a local presence. They are often accompanied by large cadres of technical advisers, too numerous for their avowed advisory capacity. Support for ideological positions appears to weigh heavily in Soviet arms decisions. There is every reason to believe that weapons transfers are perceived as a perfectly legitimate and desirable instrument in the continuing struggle with democratic or "imperialist" societies.

The Soviet Union will not take the initiative in seeking a multilateral regulation, despite its rhetorical support for disarmament at the United Nations. Yet one should not presume at the same time that it would necessarily reject American or Western proposals. Success in bringing arms transfers to the negotiating table would depend upon the way the Soviets perceive their self-interests and the seriousness of purpose behind a Western initiative. A general linkage of any effort to restrain conventional arms transfers with other arms control negotiations, such as SALT or MBFR, might improve the atmosphere for such an initiative and should be considered. Where there is a mutual Soviet and Western interest in restraints on transfers it should be exploited. There is considerable evidence that in the Middle East the desire to avoid a superpower confrontation has led to self-imposed restraints by the Soviet Union at various times over the past two decades. Although these restraints were partially eroded at periods of high tension (such as in 1973), they have never been totally jettisoned, thus suggesting that between the Soviet Union and the United States there has already been a tacit form of restraints on arms transfers to the Middle East.[2]

The Other Suppliers

As discussed above, the "big four" export 90% of the major weapons transferred to the developing world; and when their NATO or Warsaw Pact allies are added, the total is raised to over 95%. The fifth largest exporter is the Federal Republic of Germany, but its transfers to the Third World are still one-fourth of those of France or Britain. Moreover, Bonn's arms sales are still relatively unimportant, representing only three-tenths of 1 percent of the total exports.

Much attention has been paid in recent times to the growth of indigenous arms industries in such countries as Israel, South Africa, Brazil, India, Taiwan and Spain. Some of them are new additions to the ranks of exporters. Israel has succeeded in increasing its exports fivefold since the 1973 war, with the Kfir fighter plane becoming a highly desirable item in international markets. Co-production or licensing arrangements with advanced industrialized countries can facilitate the development of arms industries in the Third World, making them less dependent upon outside suppliers and raising expectations of their becoming suppliers themselves. This is, no doubt, the case of the Arab Military Industrial Organization (consisting of Egypt, Saudi Arabia, Qatar, and the United Arab Emirates) which has entered into an agreement with France for the creation of its own weapons industry and which will want to sell to other Arab countries.

Nevertheless, it is most unlikely that these new producers

will have a major impact on the international arms trade. Manufacturing sophisticated weapons requires skilled labor, a commodity that is in short supply in the developing world. Moreover, such weapons require engineering and technical knowledge which is also not readily available. Therefore, while weapons of low sophistication may be increasingly manufactured by indigenous industries, Third World countries will continue to import the more sophisticated items. These advanced and complex weapons will still come mainly from the "big four" and a few of their allies, since countries like Sweden and Switzerland will not have sufficiently large markets at home to make possible the manufacture of most of the sophisticated weapons systems. The present "big four" are relatively confident that they will retain the lion's share of the international market for at least the next decade. This cartel-like situation creates conditions which make agreements by suppliers on the export of arms possible, provided that the political will exists.

Forms of Multilateral Regulation

The cooperative regulation of arms sales could take many forms. The general aim would be to establish multilateral restraints on the flow of arms, which would be jointly agreed upon by the suppliers—and, it is to be hoped, deemed "acceptable" by the recipients.

1. Mutual Example

Policies of restraint which were adopted unilaterally, but which were undertaken with the expectation that other countries would reciprocate, would be the easiest to adopt. Unilateral restraints could be intentionally signaled to the other suppliers, along with an indication of what is expected or desired from them. The drawbacks in such an approach are, however, fairly evident. Countries such as Sweden or Switzerland may announce that they will not export to "areas of conflict or tension," but greater differentiation is required on the part of the main suppliers, all of which have direct political interests in most, if not all, areas of actual or potential conflict. An additional complication, if qualitative limitations on transfers were sought, would be the difficulty in identifying comparable weapons systems, or arms below a certain technological threshold; this would entail direct contacts among suppliers which would go beyond an approach based upon expectations of reciprocal restraints. Finally, the approach by mutual example lends itself too readily to misunderstandings and misperceptions. Exposed to the pressure of competitive arms sales, it could prove vulnerable and in time collapse.

2. Formal Agreement

Theoretically, it should be possible to set specific limits, or prohibitions, on transfers of certain weapons or on sales to identified regions. However, this also is unlikely to commend itself as an approach. The first question that would have to be addressed is whether verification was necessary, and if so, how verification was to be achieved. But even if verification were not to be required, negotiations leading to a formal agreement would face immense difficulties in dealing with continuously changing conditions of two sorts. Weapons technology is in a constant state of evolution; reaching set agreements on such technologies would not only be difficult, but possibly self-defeating, since perceptions of the transfer of certain technologies are likely to shift over a period of time. Second, except in cases where one might want a worldwide prohibition, restraints are likely to have a geographical focus. Political balances and conditions in a region also shift over a period of time. Nations will not want to lock themselves into prohibitions through formal agreements when the regional political conditions are subject to change. Finally, the mind boggles at the thought of a truly comprehensive agreement on arms transfers given the variety of arms that could be involved. Negotiating such an agreement would make SALT look like child's play.

3. Informal Negotiations

Such an approach might be the most suitable in that it would permit the close, continuing contact which would not exist under "mutual example" and would also provide the flexibility which would be lacking in the legalism of "formal agreements."

A possibility worth consideration would be a forum for informal negotiations on Conventional Arms Transfer Restraints (CATR) at which the principal suppliers would discuss qualitative, quantitative, and regional limitations to which they might agree on an informal basis. At first limited to the "big four" suppliers, CATR might in time be expanded to include secondary suppliers. CATR would seek to establish *criteria* by which to *regulate* transfers. In doing this it might create guidelines which lead toward a certain specialization of sales. Some guidelines might be geographical, while others might be qualitative. For example, country *A* might be given the dominant role in transfers to country *Y*, or perhaps more broadly to the region in which it is located; or country *A* might be given a free rein in selling a certain type of weapons system, leaving other arms to other suppliers. Accordingly, we have here the makings of a market-sharing approach, which might not only restrain a competitive arms sales race, but have a direct benefit in ordering a more rational international arms production pattern based upon a specialization of labor.

CATR would be most useful, and successful, not as a one-time international conference but as a continuing forum, meeting as required, for purposes of discussion and the reaching of informal agreements on the regulation of arms transfers. It would be analogous, in some ways, to the London suppliers' conference which deals with the export of nuclear technology.

In developing criteria for the transfer of arms, CATR would seek to regulate exports so as to avoid sales which would have a destabilizing influence within a region. Among sales which would be subject to restraints are those which could:

—create an imbalance which upsets an existing balance,
—feed a local arms race,
—foster instability because of the sudden acquisition of new arms,
—provide incentives for a surprise attack,
—provide incentives for a pre-emptive action,
—quicken the pace and scale of escalation,
—introduce starkly inhuman weapons into a region,
—provide weapons which might be used internally in civil war, police action, or violation of human rights.

A more difficult and delicate task would be to regulate the flow of arms according to the judgment of the CATR nations as to whether the recipient needs the arms for its national

[311]

security, or whether such arms are the most optimal way to use financial resources which might be better employed otherwise. Most nations are reluctant to form judgments, at least openly, which impinge upon the decisions of other states. Yet there is no obligation to sell arms. Accordingly, the CATR countries might decide not to sell certain arms for reasons relating to the domestic politics or economy of the recipient. This is, in fact, already widely done on an individual basis.

Restraints might be qualitative, quantitative, or geographical. In practice they would be combined. Although some qualitative restraints might be worldwide, many of the qualitative and perhaps all the quantitative restraints might be regional or national.

Qualitative restraints might include:

—surface-to-surface missiles over a certain range,
—dual purpose weapons that could deliver nuclear as well as non-nuclear warheads,
—arms that can be used by terrorists, such as the shoulder-fired Redeye
—inhuman weapons such as concussion bombs,
—highly destructive weapons designed essentially for offensive purposes,
—weapons that could inflict large-scale damage on population centers,
—certain arms such as aircraft carriers, attack submarines, etc.

Quantitative restraints might include:

—overall arms ceilings within a region,
—the maintenance of a prescribed ratio of arms among states within a region,

—limits on the arms possessed by a country,
—permissible rates of replacement.

Transfers would be made with greater selectivity than in the past, according to the criteria agreed upon by the CATR members. An important consideration would be to avoid the rapid infusion of arms into an area, involving a major leap in inventories, in such a manner as to create instability either in military terms or through drastically altered political perceptions. The criteria might favor arms of a defensive, non-provocative nature. The CATR states might also agree to discuss among themselves all sales over a certain amount. Finally, the member states might agree on a fundamental principle: all transfers to which one of the nations participating in CATR has grounds for objection, or regarding which it seeks consultations, will be discussed multilaterally in the CATR forum before they are approved.

In order to control arms transfers effectively it would also be necessary for the CATR participants to deal with co-production programs. Agreements might be reached among the supplier governments on the types of assistance extended to countries that want to achieve indigenous weapons-manufacturing capabilities. Licensing arrangements could be limited to assistance within certain categories of arms.

Finally, the CATR participants might agree on controls over the end-use of arms and their retransfer. Such controls would be intended to forestall the unwanted retransfer of arms to third areas. They might apply to relatively new arms provided by a recipient nation to its allies during a time of war or increased tensions, or to the transfer of used and surplus equipment. The applicability of such controls to the Middle East, where unauthorized retransfers have taken place, is evident. The CATR states could, for example, agree among themselves that none will provide additional weapons to any government that has violated an agreement on retransfer or end-use.

Recipient Restraints

Restraints observed by the supplier countries may be the most promising approach to develop some workable international control over the arms trade. This proposition is contrary to the often-stated views of the suppliers, expressed in such contexts as the Geneva disarmament talks, that control must begin with restraints by recipients on the purchase of arms. Nevertheless, the recipients can make an important contribution in helping to shape supplier restraint.

When developed *regionally,* supplier restraints should, to the maximum extent feasible, be worked out in a coordinated manner with the recipient states in the region. In some cases the forbearance of the recipients may be needed to assure the effectiveness of supplier restraints. Ideally, restraints on arms flows should be agreed upon by both the purchasers and the producers. An agreement of this type on arms transfers to the Middle East could become a key component of an overall political settlement in the area.

Another important approach, however, would be the initiation of restraints on arms imports by the recipient states themselves. Regional arms control arrangements or zones of limited armaments could be negotiated by states within an area. This has already been attempted with somewhat limited, but not insignificant, success in Latin America among the Andean states in the Declaration of Ayacucho. The relatively small volume of arms transfers to sub-Saharan Africa provides another opportunity for genuine, regionally inspired restraint. Recipient states within a geographical zone might set quantitative limitations with ceilings on the purchase of certain types of arms. Such limitations would recognize legitimate defense needs but, within a regional plan, seek to avoid an excess transfer of arms. They might restrict the importation of certain types of military technology; this might be especially feasible if such weaponry has not previously been introduced into the area. Recipient initiatives of this kind could be an extremely important complement to attempts by the suppliers to regulate their arms sales.

It is often assumed that recipient states do not want to accept any self-restraint on their arms imports. The common corollary to this is that any restraints set by the suppliers on their exports would be perceived by the recipients as inherently discriminatory actions, or an arrogant manifestation of paternalistic attitudes.

Certainly, every state has the right to make its own determination of its national security requirements. But this does not mean that all supplier restraints will be viewed by the potential recipients as undesirable encroachments upon their sovereign right of self-defense. Nor does it prove that states within a region may not see value in limited restraints on transfers into their area, thereby avoiding, perhaps, a local arms race.

The assumption that recipient states will automatically oppose supplier restraints, and be uninterested in initiatives designed to impose on themselves restraints on imports, has been accepted far too uncritically. The negotiation of the Declaration of Ayacucho is evidence to the contrary. More recently, a new and significant different perspective on arms transfers has emerged at the United Nations. In a widely discussed speech before the General Assembly in the fall of 1976, S. Rajaratnam, the Foreign Minister of Singapore, criticized the transfer of arms in these terms:

[315]

The massive flow of arms to the Third World confronts it with a new danger. It is first of all a drain on their economies. But even more important, is the fact that it creates a new form of dependence on the Great Powers who can exploit the Third World's dependence on them for arms, to manipulate them, to engineer conflicts between them, and to use them as proxies in their competition for influence and dominance.[3]

Whether or not such a radical perspective on arms transfers gains currency within the developing world, there are a number of incentives for Third World countries to reduce the inflow of conventional arms. The purchase of weapons may divert scarce economic resources from pressing social and developmental needs. The availability of arms in massive quantities, or of a sophisticated nature, may encourage the undue growth of the influence of the military within a society. Further, the transfer of arms may create political tensions within an area through the military build-up of a state, or a competitive arms environment within a region. Thus there may be a mutuality of interests in preventing the adverse effect of arms transfers upon the existing political and military balance within a region. Such consensus will certainly not apply to all recipient states, and will only be relevant to certain countries in given circumstances. It is quite possible, however, that there exists a structure of disincentives, as well as of incentives, for receiving arms. The international regulation of arms sales, one may conclude, is potentially attractive to recipient as well as supplier states.

The Task Ahead: Opportunities and Pitfalls

A number of proposals have been made in past years for ways to achieve international restraints on transfers. A world conference of arms suppliers and recipients was endorsed by over 100 members of Congress in 1975; this would be too unwieldy a forum and would be unlikely to be productive. In the context of the Geneva Disarmament Conference, countries such as Britain and the United States have traditionally called upon purchasing states within a Third World region to undertake on their own initiatives a regimen of self-restraint; this may be asking for too much. The Carter Administration has sought discussions with the principal suppliers of arms; this is a step in the right direction, but it has been a very low key approach and does not appear to have achieved much thus far.

Any major effort to seek multilateral restraint among suppliers—perhaps along the lines of the CATR discussions outlined here—must be based on an American initiative. Some would argue on moral grounds that as the world's leading "arms merchant" it is the United States which should seek to reduce the international trade in arms. There is, however, a more practical consideration. If the American government does not take the lead, no other country is likely to, for an adequately strong motivation to attempt to deal with the proliferation of conventional weapons can only come from the two superpowers which have a clear, direct interest in international security and stability as a way to avoid being drawn into a major nuclear confrontation. Moreover, together the United States and the Soviet Union supply 70% of the arms transferred to the Third World. For complex reasons of bureaucratic inertia, a lack of creativity in initiating arms control proposals, and the absence of strong interest or motivation in restraining conventional arms transfer, it is highly unlikely that the U.S.S.R. will do more than respond to any American initiative.

Progress in the international domain will depend, however, upon the credibility of America's own efforts to restrain unilaterally its arms transfers. Thus it is of the utmost importance that the Carter Administration be seen as implementing its avowed aims. Unless the United States appears to be serious about moderating its own transfers, it is unlikely to persuade the other main suppliers—and competitors—to participate in an arrangement for joint moderation. It should be borne in mind that in years past the United States has probably followed the least rigorous policy-making process, among the principal suppliers, for assuring that arms sales decisions are considered in the context of long-term foreign policy and arms stability, and has probably been the most permissive in transferring large quantities of sophisticated weapons.

Soviet participation in multilateral restraints would be essential, and they may well be unwilling to cooperate. Arms transfers will, in all probability, remain a key element of the continuing East-West competition in the Third World. Yet some interests of the U.S.S.R. in joining a forum such as CATR can be identified. Avoidance of an unbridled conventional arms transfer competition with the West may be desirable in areas of high tension such as the Middle East, in areas of incipient rivalry such as southern Africa, or in areas of confrontation such as the two Koreas, where a regional arms race could have a destabilizing impact. Arms transfers for the Soviet government are more costly than they are for Western governments since they are still more in the form of military assistance or long-term, soft currency loans. As suggested above, Soviet willingness to take part in CATR is likely to be increased if it is presented as being within the overall context of détente and East-West arms control.

The greatest difficulties and pitfalls in achieving a cooperative regulation of arms transfers may lie, however, not on the West-East axis, but the West-West one. There is an undercurrent of suspicion in Western Europe regarding American intentions, fostered by the intense competition among the Atlantic countries for both exports to the developing countries and sales within NATO. Here there is considerable potential for disagreement. Some Europeans fear that the U.S. government will seek a suppliers' agreement not to sell certain arms, and that once such an agreement is achieved, it will be circumvented by American industry. This has occurred, some Europeans are persuaded, in the COCOM system for regulating trade with the Communist countries, where, after a prohibition has been agreed upon, it has been circumvented through some technical considerations or a questionable interpretation of the regulations.

Considerable diplomatic skill would therefore be required in dealing with allies. The initial goals should be modest, involving limited and relatively easy first steps such as regulating the flow of new, sophisticated weapons into a particular region. This would minimize the challenge to vested economic and technological interests. The United States should avoid the appearance of moral superiority or of economic and technological heavy-handedness. We should take care not to confront the Europeans, at a time of disagreement over nuclear exports and economic issues, but rather seek their involvement in a joint venture in which all supplier nations share common interests.

There is an important linkage between the aim of arms standardization within the Atlantic alliance and the cooperative regulation of arms sales to the Third World. Arms exports, for the West Europeans especially, permit economies of scale and thereby help maintain national production runs which would not be otherwise viable. Accordingly, competition for exports has an adverse effect on the goal of NATO standardization. It permits the continuation—by giving a new lease on life—of national weapons programs which otherwise would have to be subjugated to the discipline of either a specialization of tasks within the alliance or multilateral European weapons cooperation. The potential for exports has led both France and Britain to develop advanced weapons systems which they would otherwise not have developed for their own armed forces, thus encouraging trends which run counter to standardization. Conversely, restraints on exports would create valuable new incentives for standardization in the alliance.

Cooperative restraints on arms transfers should create a political climate conducive to a greater specialization of labor on defense production in the West. If each major weapons-producing country could be assured of a fair share of the total world export market, each country could concentrate on manufacturing certain items, thereby permitting it to maintain a viable defense industry. A "market-sharing" approach would provide economies through the avoidance of duplication at a time when all Western defense budgets are under great economic stress. As weapons systems become more sophisticated, and therefore more costly, they run the risk of being priced so high as to not be affordable.

The United States, as the largest exporter of arms and the dominant weapons producer in the West, might have to accept a smaller share of the market in a fair division of world markets. Although this might create hardships for particular American corporations, the major components of the defense industry itself are not so export-dependent as to suffer seriously. This contrasts with the European nations, where because of their smaller size, entire industries are threatened. An Atlantic common market on armaments requires the creation of a "two-way street" through the opening of the American home market to European defense industries. This, in turn, would reduce the European need to export to the Third World.

A multilateral attempt to moderate arms transfers to the developing countries should therefore be coupled with intensified efforts toward a greater European-American arms cooperation, as well as augmented intra-West European collaboration. An American proposal of something like CATR, if wisely and carefully formulated, need not be negatively perceived by the Europeans. The maintenance of viable defense industries in Western Europe is in the political interest of the United States. Once it is understood that cooperative restraints would not undermine the European or American defense industries, the Atlantic nations will be well on the road toward a common arms transfer policy. Then if *we* (United States) do not sell, the French and British may not either . . .

The proliferation of conventional arms has become a major component of the global diffusion of military power. In some respects it presents risks which are more immediate than the proliferation of nuclear arms. A war in such tinderbox areas as the Middle East or in southern Africa will start, and may well be completely fought, with non-nuclear arms. All the suppliers, including the Soviet Union, have vital interests in preventing such conflicts. Moreover, arms transfers have become a common coin in contemporary diplomacy. The maintenance of peace is increasingly perceived as dependent upon a balance of conventional forces. The achievement of future political

[321]

settlements, as in the Middle East, may well be linked to guarantees and restraints involving the availability of arms. The need for a cooperative, multilateral regulation of arms transfers is clear.

NOTES

1. Stockholm International Peace Research Institute, *World Armaments and Disarmament, SIPRI Yearbook 1977* (Cambridge, Mass., and London: The MIT Press; Stockholm: Almqvist & Wiksell, 1977), p. 309.

2. See Jon D. Glassman, *Arms for the Arabs: The Soviet Union and War in the Middle East* (Baltimore: Johns Hopkins University Press, 1975).

3. Statement of Mr. S. Rajaratnam, Minister for Foreign Affairs of Singapore and Chairman of the Delegation before the Thirty-first Session of the United Nations General Assembly, Permanent Mission of Singapore to the U.N., September 29, 1976.

Index